DATE DUE			

HEIDEGGER
and the
LANGUAGE OF POETRY

HEIDEGGER
and the
LANGUAGE OF POETRY

David A. White

UNIVERSITY OF NEBRASKA PRESS
LINCOLN AND LONDON

The publication of this book was assisted by a grant from the Ludwig Vogelstein Foundation.

Publishers on the Plains

UNP

Library of Congress Cataloging in Publication Data
White, David A   1942–
  Heidegger and the language of poetry.

  Based on the author's thesis, University of
Toronto.
  Bibliography: p. 233
  Includes index.
  1. Heidegger, Martin, 1889–1976. 2. Languages—
Philosophy. 3. Poetry. 4. Thought and thinking.
I. Title.
P85.H37W5   149'.94   78–5610
ISBN 0–8032–4703–6

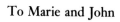
To Marie and John

Contents

Preface   ix

Abbreviations   2

Introduction   3

PART 1 LANGUAGE AS AN ONTOLOGICAL
PHENOMENON

1. Word, Name, and Thing   19
2. Saying and Speaking   35
3. The Appropriation of Language   53

PART 2 THE ILLUMINATIONS
OF POETIC LANGUAGE

4. Poetizing and Man   75
5. Earth and Heavens   93
6. The Divine and the Holy   115

PART 3 THE CONFRONTATION BETWEEN
POETIZING AND THINKING

7. Poetizing and Thinking   143
8. Thinking and Releasement *(Gelassenheit)*   168
9. Three Perspectives on Being and Time: A Critique   190

Notes   219

Bibliography   233

Index   239

Preface

For the early Greeks, philosophy and poetry were intimately connected. There was no sharp distinction for a Heraclitus or a Parmenides between reason providing the ultimate standards of philosophy and imagination guiding the endeavors of poetry. This tradition underwent a slow, struggling death. As late as the fourth century, Plato's Socrates often quotes the poets, especially Homer, when he requires some ready-made wisdom direct from a revered source. It is true Socrates' attitude toward the veracity of these utterances is frequently tinged with something approaching profane disbelief. But we should not miss the relevant point. That Plato should be so well read in the history of poetry and that he should feel relatively at ease citing it to advance indirectly his "rational" ends reveals the hold poetry still had on the originator of Western philosophical thought.

Times have changed. In the contemporary philosophical community, the activity of poetry is generally banished to the darker regions of aesthetics, its problems debated only by the few who deem them worthy of consideration. Ordinary language and the discourse of science provide more respectable fields for philosophical discussion. The distinction between philosophy and poetry is now so rigidly drawn that a philosopher may absorb all the poetry he wants, but need not (perhaps ought not) integrate any of it into his work—and still be considered a philosopher. To the Greek mind, this state of affairs would have been naive, perhaps even unthinkable. To the modern mind, such discrimination is a symbol of progress in rigorous thinking.

For Martin Heidegger, this progress is of questionable value. In seeking to join again these now sundered human activities, Heidegger is Greek in the classical mold. His published work from the 1930s to the present has as one constant refrain—sometimes explicit, sometimes hidden in dark corners—the interrelation between *thinking (Denken)* and *poetizing (Dichten)*. Heidegger has also devoted book-length studies to each activity, but never without maintaining the most vigilant concern for the demands of the other. Heidegger is aware that the cohesive unity of a culture such as that of Greece, which advanced language about man and the cosmos without explicit regard for divergent canons of meaning and evaluation, can more than likely never be reclaimed. But there is a strong moral tug in Heidegger compelling him to resurrect some sense of this unity for our contemporary world. The reasons for this resurrection are many and difficult, and their enumeration takes the student of Heidegger straight into the core of his most abstruse teaching.

Heidegger's philosophy is in all respects speculative in the grand manner, and books purporting to unravel an aspect or aspects of this speculation have and are being produced at a fairly continuous rate. As far as I know, however, there is no book-length study of Heidegger's development of poetic language. The reason for this lack may be based on a view held by Joseph Kockelmans, editor of a recent volume entitled *On Heidegger and Language*. Kockelmans is explaining the general purpose and scope of the book:

All of the papers combined do not give an adequate idea of Heidegger's conception of language, for it is not possible at this point in time to do so. Heidegger's view is still in the process of development, and many of his publications on the subject are not yet available. In view of this situation, it seems that this book points to many basic problems for which Heidegger has tried to find an acceptable solution.

Now, if a systematic study of Heidegger and language was and is lacking because of incomplete experience with Heidegger's principles on that topic, then a work on Heidegger and poetic language could hardly be expected. But, after we make due allowance for scholarly reserve, Kockelmans's observations concerning the feasibility of the volume he himself edited appear in a somewhat unfavorable light. For if the authors of the various articles in that volume have contributed significantly to our understanding of Heidegger, then their grasp of Heidegger's principles is basically sound. The only reason why each of the articles could not be expanded into book-length form (some, indeed, are excerpts from books, but not on this particular theme) would be because of personal considerations pertaining to those authors such as a lack of time or energy. But if these hypothetical book-length expansions are not feasible because of lack of comprehensive insight, then we must wonder about the value of brief essays which purport to be even approximate presentations of "problematic" aspects of Heidegger's thinking on language. It seems, in this case, that some knowledge of the whole must precede any knowledge of the part, if the part is to be at all reliable.

Nevertheless, Professor Kockelmans's cautionary proviso is worthy of note and must be addressed by anyone daring enough to offer such a systematic study. The following remarks detail the scope of this interpretation and the sense in which it is intended as a contribution to Heideggerian exegesis. Incompleteness, and probably mediocrity, may be all that can be achieved in interpreting this phase of Heidegger's thought. If so, then perhaps Kockelmans's reservations compel silence on the part of prospective commentators, at least until one sufficiently gifted can shed light where all previous students, in mind if not in print, have discerned only shadows. But it does not seem to me that Heidegger's teaching on language in general and poetic language in particular is so oracular that it necessarily confounds all attempts at reconstruction and evaluation. And even if that teaching is generally impervious to more prosaic commentary, attempts at such commentary must be initiated at some time. After the large-scale work of such scholars as William J. Richardson and Otto Pöggeler, students of Heidegger must now begin the task of assessing more restricted areas of his work. If Heidegger's thinking is truly seminal, it must fructify other minds, and this eventuality certainly implies some understanding of his principles. If his teaching is not truly seminal but merely idiosyncratic, then an inadequate commentary is only a harmless hermeneutic exercise affixed to still another minor ripple in the flow of philosophical ideas.

The claim that poetic language is something more than a musing pastime is, of course, no novelty. In a well-known passage, Plato spoke of an ancient quarrel between poetry and philosophy. Heidegger takes this quarrel very seriously, and transcribes the two opposed forces into thinking *(Denken)* and poetizing *(Dichten)*, each interacting with the other, both emerging from a fundamental source—language. Thus, any discussion of Heidegger's interest and development of poetic language, and the sense in which he resolves or extends Plato's ancient quarrel, must deal with the relation between poetizing and thinking, their respective similarities and differences, and their joint emergence from language. My analyses of Heidegger's poetic illuminations are intended to clarify the meaning of these illuminations and also to indicate how these meanings have

xi

been integrated into the very core of Heidegger's own thought. These analyses are in no way numerically exhaustive; the texts dealt with are taken from *Unterwegs zur Sprache* and *Erläuterungen zu Hölderlins Dichtung*, works which I take to contain Heidegger's most complete statement on poetic language. Thus, for example, no attempt has been made to analyze the illumination of Sophocles in *Einführung in die Metaphysik* and the poet-mystic Angelus Silesius in *Der Satz vom Grund*. Similarly, my discussions of the repercussions poetizing has had on thinking are selective; the central analysis deals with Heidegger's opusculum *Gelassenheit* and its connections to the general problems of thinking as envisioned by Heidegger.

The fundamental connection linking poetizing and thinking with language has already been noted, but some additional prefatory remarks are required to situate Heidegger's presuppositions concerning the problem of language. The principles underlying these presuppositions, their structure and significance for both poetizing and thinking, will of course occupy the body of this study, but it is crucial to approach Heidegger on his own ground before the delineation of these principles can begin. Heidegger's basic premise is that it is impossible to isolate and describe accurately any aspect of language unless those concepts and distinctions which are taken to be proper to language *as such* are themselves scrutinized in their relations to a fundamental—and extralinguistic—ontological base. Consequently, Heidegger's reflections on language include what has come to be called ontology, although ontology in the midst of sustained, but still somewhat eccentric discussion employing a number of typically linguistic notions and distinctions. This phase of Heidegger's project will obviously appeal only to those students of language who wish to see language taken to its ultimate ontological roots. And there is little reason to think that such a quest can be anything other than speculative. For those who prefer to remain within the familiar confines of contemporary linguistic philosophy in the Anglo-American style, where ontological considerations of the Heideggerian stripe are minimal or nonexistent, Heidegger's approach to language will appear quixotic and arbitrary at best. But such an attitude is based on the assumption—for assumption it certainly is—that contemporary linguistic philosophy either has no determinate, albeit subterranean, ontological presuppositions (which surely must be false) or that if these presuppositions are exposed and studied they will satisfy requisite ontological criteria (which remains to be seen). For Heidegger, language is especially crucial because there are no paths to being *(Sein)* except those which are grounded in language; therefore, the relations between language and being must be studied in order to realize some comprehension of the similarities and differences between the two. Otto Pöggeler's axiom, that to interpret Heidegger today would mean to interpret him as a classical philosopher in the tradition running from Anaximander to Nietzsche,[1] is perfectly sound and applies with special force as a prerequisite for understanding Heidegger's work on language and its relation to being.

It goes without saying that Heidegger's problem cannot be solved by refusing to consider it philosophically significant. One may well question both Heidegger's own approach to the problem and his (usually tentative) attempts at its resolution; but to ignore the problem simply because it implies speculation seems to be philosophical naiveté on an epic, perhaps tragic, scale. Now, Heidegger's formulation of the problem (insofar as I have grasped its formulation) is of considerable amplitude and complexity. Respect for this amplitude and complexity requires that the following study be given over in its entirety to the exposition and at least partial evaluation of Heidegger's position, without attempting to compare or confront that position with the above mentioned analytic standpoint. This standpoint, as represented by, e.g., the later Wittgenstein, has its own distinctive character and is sufficiently powerful to preclude readily available comparisions with what I take to be the radically different position of a Heidegger. Heidegger and Wittgenstein were contemporaries, and both have written on language. One suspects, therefore, that points of tangency exist. If these points can be broadened, then perhaps the ideological rift separating continental from Anglo-American philosophy can be narrowed. Presumably some attention should be paid by the proper parties to the healing of this rift, but not, it seems to me, at the expense of falsifying or distorting the respective positions for the sake of fragmentary tangencies. A comparative study of, say, Wittgenstein and Heidegger on language would be successful only if each individual position was itself comprehended.[2] Since we have already seen doubts expressed as to whether Heidegger's views alone can be expounded, the prospect of a high-level confrontation between Heidegger and Wittgenstein does not appear imminent. Such a confrontation is desirable, I would think, but it will not be attempted here.

What will be attempted may be outlined as follows. The Introduction is primarily a statement of some important principles of interpretation I have applied to Heidegger's works. Chapters 1 through 3 gradually build the structure on which Heidegger has based his description of language as an ontological phenomenon. Chapters 4 through 6 develop and explain a number of Heidegger's own interpretations, or illuminations, of poetic language. The illuminations were selected in order to illustrate how the structure Heidegger finds in language at its most fundamental guides his experience of the meaning of poetic language and how the results of these illuminations are both directional and constitutive of his own thoughtful works. Chapters 7 and 8 discuss the confrontation between poetizing and thinking; here an appropriate perspective for appreciating their interaction is suggested, along with an examination of the effect poetizing has had on Heidegger's thought, especially in terms of the notion of releasement *(Gelassenheit)*. Chapter 9 concludes the study with a commentary on some of the central problems that emerge from the sequence of themes discussed throughout the work, especially with respect to the relation between being and time.

An earlier draft of this work was accepted as a doctoral dissertation at the University of Toronto. I would like to thank Professor David Savan for a number of suggestions to clarify "Heideggerese" for the sympathic reader. Professor Zygmunt Adamczsewski made several useful suggestions, especially with regard to the difficult notion of saying *(Sagen)*. And Professor Thomas Langan was continuously judicious with his considerable knowledge of Heidegger and also with his sharp wit. This version has been expanded and completely rewritten from the earlier draft, but whatever merits it displays are due in no small measure to the efforts of these men. I am, of course, entirely responsible for the final interpretation. A special debt of gratitude goes to Marie White for her careful typing of the manuscript. And last, I would thank with grateful and full heart Mary Jeanne Larrabee, who read the entire manuscript and did not allow her position as spouse to interfere with her sagacity as critic and editor.

I wish to thank Max Niemeyer Verlag, Tübingen, for permission to quote from the German editions of *Was Heisst Denken?* and *Zur Sache des Denkens*. Vittorio Klostermann Verlag, Frankfurt, has consented to my citing from *Holzwege* and the fourth edition of the *Erläuterungen zu Hölderlins Dichtung*. And Gunther Neske Verlag, Pfullingen, has allowed me to cite from *Unterwegs zur Sprache*, *Gelassenheit*, and *Vorträge und Aufsätze*.

HEIDEGGER
and the
LANGUAGE OF POETRY

Abbreviations of Heidegger's works

AED   *Aus der Erfahrung des Denkens*
EH   *Erläuterungen zu Hölderlin's Dichtung* (4th ed.)
EM   *Einführung in die Metaphysik*
FD   *Die Frage nach dem Ding*
G   *Gelassenheit*
H   *Holzwege*
HH   *Hebel der Hausfreund*
ID   *Identität und Differenz*
K   *Die Technik und die Kehre*
KP   *Kant und das Problem der Metaphysik*
KR   *Die Kunst und der Raum*
MHG   *Martin Heidegger zum 80. Geburtstag*
NI, II   *Nietzsche I, II*
PT   *Phänomenologie und Theologie*
S   *Schellings Abhandlung über das Wesen der Menschlichen Freiheit* (1809)
SD   *Zur Sache des Denkens*
SG   *Der Satz vom Grund*
SH   "Sprache und Heimat"
SZ   *Sein und Zeit*
US   *Unterwegs zur Sprache*
VA   *Vorträge und Aufsätze*
W   *Wegmarken*
WD   *Was Heisst Denken?*
WP   *Was ist Das-Die Philosophie?*

Introduction: Principles of Interpretation

THIS STUDY will deal principally with Heidegger's thought on language and poetry—*Unterwegs zur Sprache, Erläuterungen zu Hölderlins Dichtung*, the essay on Rilke in *Holzwege*—and with some of the implications of that thought. For Heidegger, philosophy means the history of philosophy, and he is most insistent on the distinction between philosophy understood in this sense and thinking, especially his own. Philosophy has certainly been thoughtful—Heidegger never denies this. But the demands of thinking about language, poetry, and anything else transcend the limits which philosophy and its history have set on those who would pursue the delicate art of reflection. All philosophy has been thoughtful, but thinking need not be philosophical, at least according to what Heidegger conceives as philosophy's traditional domain.

This revisionist strain, as it might be called, increases the problems for the interpreter of Heidegger's work. A commentary must be arranged into parts, and the selection of parts must be according to some criterion which must be justifiable. Normally, this criterion will be based on the importance of some fairly traditional series of pivotal concepts or distinctions. However, it then appears that the presence of such orderly procedure constitutes an immediately falsifying imposition on the spirit, if not the letter, of Heidegger's writings. But if, to avoid this apparent hermeneutical pitfall, the order and presentation of themes treated were not extra-Heideggerian but rather derived from the ethereal swing of Heidegger's own thinking, then the commentary may well require another commentary in order to be as intelligible as the texts originally scrutinized. The intended project seems to be in principle either self-destructive or unrealizable.

If this conclusion is sound, then it follows that by the very nature of Heidegger's thought, every attempt to interpret his work must, at best, falsify that work. But recall Otto Pöggeler's conviction that Heidegger is in the mainstream of Western philosophy. Thus, if it is

3

possible to interpret meaningfully the giants of that tradition, then it must be possible to interpret Heidegger (who may or may not be another giant). If Pöggeler is correct, then something is wrong with the above argument. The fallacy derives from the following two sources: first, assuming that Heidegger's position is completely *de novo*; second, inferring that a commentary arranged according to a traditional thematic structure necessarily distorts the content which the commentary is intended to illuminate. As for the first, it is true that when Heidegger confronts the ontological depths of language, he finds it necessary to introduce hypostatizations—e.g., "the four-fold" *(das Geviert)*—and to use terminology which, by reason of its inherent vagueness, has rarely or never figured in the work of his speculative predecessors—e.g. pain *(Schmerz)* and silence *(Schweigen)*. But such novelty is intentional, carefully considered, and amenable to reformulation according to existing guidelines. As for the second, if the representation of that which is distinctive in Heidegger is impossible to achieve in traditional terminology, then his teaching is a closed book until someone finds the correct interpretive vocabulary. But if it is possible to achieve even partial representation of that content, then its idiosyncratic nature has perhaps been overstated. The latter alternative is clearly preferable and is also, I believe, warranted on the basis of the texts themselves.

The direction of the order selected and imposed on Heidegger's work will become evident as the interpretation is developed. But two additional points should be noted here. The first concerns the fact that this order has emerged as the most fertile, given my understanding of the texts considered. Other systematizations may, however, be equally feasible, not to mention superior. The justification for the order selected is that it contributes to results which are generally illuminating and, in light of Heidegger's image as a quasi mystic, strikingly coherent. The second point is that the sequence of topics has been arranged thematically and not according to the chronological succession of Heidegger's writings. Thus, I have discounted Richardson's distinction between a "Heidegger I" and a "Heidegger II" (as, I believe, did Heidegger himself in muted and nonpolemical tones in his introductory letter to the Richardson volume). Also, and I feel more important, my development of Heidegger on language and poetic language is based on the premise that there is a fairly stable body of argument present in many different books, essays, and lectures spread over a considerable period of

4

Heidegger's long creative lifetime, works which frequently concern matters which apparently have little to do with either language or poetic language. Once again, judgments concerning the adequacy of this premise should be made only after studying the results of its implementation. My conviction is that, although Heidegger's way includes many twists, turns, and even dead ends, there remains a continuous line of argument which cuts across both the passage of time and Heidegger's own shifting interests. Such conviction may be misguided, of course, but it seems a prerequisite if one grants the possibility of expounding and critically analyzing Heidegger on a given topic. I would hope that the results will endorse the acceptance of such a premise.

The preceding remarks have been general but necessary, given that Heidegger intends his thought to counterbalance an entire tradition. But there remain more specific hermeneutical matters to consider before we turn to the topic at hand—the language of poetry. Everyone knows that Heidegger's writings are rarely self-evidently clear. However, the problems posed by the density and verbal eccentricities of *Sein und Zeit* are not the problems of apparent arbitrariness and critical laxity inherent in the primarily "poetical" commentaries. The latter works are unarguably idiosyncratic, so much so that their interpretation will profitably be prefigured by a statement charting the procedure of the interpreter.

But poetic language is language before it is poetic. Thus, the interpretation of Heidegger's treatment of poetic language must first be situated within the larger context of his thinking on language itself. Heidegger's interest in language as a vehicle for philosophical activity and insight is of course matched by the extensive contemporary Anglo-American literature on the subject. But there is an important difference between their respective approaches, and this difference must be noted before any critical assessment of Heidegger's position can begin. The following will extend the introductory remarks stated in the Preface, now applied to the explicit business of interpretation. Ideally perhaps, hermeneutical principles should be developed as far as possible in their own terms, but the intimacy between doctrinal content and interpretive form will necessarily result in some overlap. Issues are raised and discussed here which can be adequately dealt with only when the letter of Heidegger's teaching is in full view. But the statement of principles of interpretation as they face these doctrines with some degree of immediacy should prevent some misconceptions concerning Heidegger's intentions before the argument is studied at the required depth.

Heidegger is in agreement with the English tradition in accepting many of the empirical facts having to do with, say, the origin of language. For example, it is not of especial philosophical concern to inquire into the physiological sources of vocal human sounds. Now given the factual occurrence of language, the English format assumes that the philosophical dimension involves a careful systematizing and resolution of conceptual puzzles that emerge from the event of language—for example, the problems from the now classic distinction between the sense of a proposition and what the proposition refers to. Heidegger's interest in language comes from a different direction. Heidegger seeks what might be termed a transcendental ontology of language, that set of conditions which accounts for the way in which language can mean and refer in the first place, or even more abstractly, how language can *be*. Thus, while English linguistic philosophy would typically assume that reference is an evident property of language, with philosophical problems resulting after the fact of this property, Heidegger hopes to discover how and why language can refer at all and before any philosophical issues can be formalized based on the existence of that property. His belief is that such subsequent formalization depends on the (as yet undiscovered) ontological conditions which ground the relation between language and being. A shortsighted apprehension of these ontological conditions may result in shortsighted philosophical problems. It is not unfair to generalize that the English tradition seeks to avoid undue metaphysical confrontation in their pursuit of linguistic philosophy. Heidegger, on the other hand, finds it essential to develop an ontology which will disclose how language is possible and on the basis of which more finely grained difficulties emerge. As we have already noted, the development of this ontology is thoroughly speculative. Heidegger's mission becomes the statement of the conditions which must be met before the essential properties of language are discernible.

What Heidegger has himself published on language is in no way to be construed as the last word on the subject. An indication of this caution is found in the title of Heidegger's principal work on language—*Unterwegs zur Sprache*. Heidegger is "on the way" to language in the sense that his arguments are still "on" that "way," that is, that his arguments are provisional, yet requisite "as far as they

6

go" towards an explicit development of the sense in which it is possible to ground language ontologically. Heidegger's entire output on language can be crudely restated as a directive of the sort that says, "Look at language this way and then inquire into what you have experienced." Such a directive is either successful or unsuccessful rather than true or false. It is successful if Heidegger's arguments lead to an experience which illuminates more of the essential characteristics of language than have been recognized to date, unsuccessful if they do not.

It will be useful here to consider an objection to such procedure, one reminiscent of an important moment in a similar context in Plato's *Meno*. Thus, how can one search for an essence when one does not know what aspects of that essence one is searching for? How does Heidegger know what the essence of language is until he finds it? And how can he find it unless he already knows what he is looking for? The answer to this objection is that Heidegger does not believe that the desired essence is in toto different from those properties now found to be essential to language. But there is the strong possibility, for Heidegger a palpable reality, that philosophers have not recognized all the dimensions of that essence just because of their concentrated concern for solving problems derived from properties already discovered. Some provisional work must be done to stimulate an awareness that there are other ways to experience the essence of language. We should note that Heidegger's use of the term *essence (Wesen)* does not imply belief in Platonic or Husserlian entities, although we shall discover that that which he construes as essential is in an important sense oblique to several forms of philosophical justification. In fact, Heidegger will attempt to explain what he apprehends of this essence in terminology which is necessarily that of the essence of language as now conceived. There is no latent intention to subvert all presently accepted linguistic concepts and distinctions, only to deepen their roots in what Heidegger believes is a necessary ontological grounding. In some respects, then, the essence of language is at present out in the open; Heidegger intends to express that essence as comprehensively as possible, and this goal necessitates a provisional exploration of an ontological sort.

The result is a methodological hesitancy, so to speak, in stating the conditions which allow the recognition of the essence of language. Heidegger cautions his audience to read his writings on language as a collection of hints toward "the possibility of undergoing an experience with language" (*US*, p. 159).[1] Now, an argument to promote an experience of the essence of something must be approached differently than an argument declaiming what that something is. And the respective evaluative stances will vary accordingly. For example, it appears relevant to object that the experience might be promoted using any means whatsoever. Hence, if the intent is merely to stimulate an experience, there will be no criteria for asserting or denying the correctness of the promotional means employed. And surely the means employed to stimulate the apprehension of an essence will influence, perhaps decisively, how that essence is finally defined. To illustrate the force of this objection, consider the essence of love. One might ponder one's own boudoir experiences, firsthand reports of the boudoir experiences of others, or Plato's *Symposium* and Genet's *Our Lady of the Flowers*. To stimulate an experience of the essence of love using some or all of these means is to contribute significantly to the final statement of that essence. All the above cited sources may be relevant to the essence of love, but are some more or perhaps most relevant? The claim that only the writings of Genet expressed the essence of love could be falsified by consideration of, say, the *Symposium*. But what if the Genet adherent asserted that only Genet will be used to instigate an experience of the essence of love? It seems clear that the response should be that such a starting point is legitimate as a starting point, but that other sources must be consulted before that essence can be finally voiced, assuming that it can be voiced at all. Thus, the means used to stimulate an experience with an essence are detrimental to the expression of that essence only if those means are themselves one-sided (and perhaps Plato is no less one-sided than Genet) and remain uncorrected either by the consideration of other means or by adequately extended reformulation of the original means used to engender that experience.

An experience of the essence of language does not imply that other experiences are not just as licit and rich as that from which Heidegger himself will draw insight. And regardless of the type of experience considered, there is no a priori guarantee that the search for such an essence will be successful (*US*, p. 161). But the attempt must be made, nonetheless. Heidegger does not specifically assert that there is one and only one unique experience which contains the desired revelatory dimensions required to apprehend the essence of language. This potential multiplicity must be kept in mind when we

8

consider that the means Heidegger selects to implement his thinking toward that essence are his studies of poetic language. Although Heidegger does describe poetic language as "pure" (*US*, p. 16), this does not imply that other forms of language might not be equally pure, although presumably in different ways. The fact that Heidegger feels at home dealing with the utterances of poets should, by itself, be neither a point of rebuke nor an occasion for praise of his humanity. What matters is the extent to which Heidegger's own conceptual developments can contribute to our understanding of language and being, regardless of the source of these illuminations. Also, even if Heidegger fails to bring to light any essential insights through his poetic searches, this does not imply that poetry is not the way, or at least one of the ways. All it implies is that Heidegger—not poetry—has failed.

The speculative aspect of Heidegger's investigation into the essence of language is apparent in two different forms. There are hypostatizations—e.g., the fourfold—which will perhaps run counter to the sensitivity of those who prefer philosophizing without such apparently arbitrary creations. In this instance, however, the notion of the fourfold is absolutely crucial for understanding Heidegger's project. And there are also a number of nicely wrought distinctions intended as directives illustrating what must be the (ontological) case in order for language to function in the first place. These distinctions employ terms which are found in other philosophical vocabularies—*name, word, speaking,*—but the sense attributed to them by Heidegger is, in its own way, just as speculative as the fourfold, as we shall observe in due course.

Heidegger's speculation does not end with the establishment of the transcendental possibility of language as such. His analyses of language are frequently directed toward a specific end, that of experiencing the entities we refer to in their status as *things (Dinge)*. Heidegger senses an intimate connection between the language used to describe and explain our experiences with entities and the nature of those entities "in themselves." As a result, a strong normative undercurrent flows through much of Heidegger's writings on language. The intimation is that if man more adequately understood the language which expresses his interactions with entities, then it would follow (in a way difficult to accept at this point without further argumentation) that our practical experience of these entities would be significantly if not drastically altered. Some of the most crucial illuminations of poetic language focus on how that language expresses our experience of an entity and, by inference, how such expression should be incorporated into our understanding of the ontological nature of that entity. Incorporations of this sort would thus serve as a provocative source of insight into an important facet of contemporary man's link with nature—his relation to entities.

The preceding brief sketch outlines what I take to be the most appropriate avenue of interpretation toward Heidegger's understanding of language in general. We now consider some more specific interpretive problems arising from Heidegger's treatment of language insofar as it is poetic. Since Heidegger's discussion of language in any form nearly always originates from a consideration of poetic texts, his own hermeneutical techniques and those of literary critics are frequently at odds. But at the very outset of the fourth edition of the Hölderlin lectures, Heidegger clearly states his position with respect to literary criticism. His writings on Hölderlin are not intended to be contributions to "literary and historical research"; but are rather a series of reflections which arise from the needs of thinking *(Denken)*. [2] The assumption is warranted that this claim holds not only for the Hölderlin lectures but also for all Heidegger's discussions of poetic language. If so, then it is evident that when Heidegger ascribes a certain meaning to a word, phrase, line, or poem, this meaning should not be evaluated under the criteria of standard literary *Wissenschaft*. Heidegger himself provides a methodological distinction to describe the tenor of his technique. An "exposition" *(Auslegung)* possesses some, and perhaps all, of those factors considered necessary to "lay out" the elements of a poetic text in the accepted scholarly sense. An "illumination" *(Erläuterung)* is the development of an exposition so that the language of poetry yields insights into problems which belong to the special province of thinking *(EH,* p. 8). If a given illumination is to approximate this end, then the content of the illumination is, as a rule, controlled by the standard canons of exposition *(US,* p. 38). In no sense does Heidegger advocate a completely freewheeling mode of interpreting poetic texts, as some literary critics doubtless believe. Now, although the two techniques are clearly different, Heidegger rarely signals his shifts from exposition to illumination. The result is that literary critics are offended (at times to the point of publishing "refutations" of Heidegger) by what they take to be arbitrary assertions in an exposition when in fact what they face are illuminations intended to contribute to the formulation or solution of a philosophical problem.[3] It may well be possible to refute what Heidegger says in an exposition, but it does not follow that such a refutation will reduce the force or the insight of the illumination derived from that exposition.

My conclusion is that there is no apparent reason why Heidegger should not be allowed to attempt such practices; in fact, there may be much value in them if new philosophical dimensions are thereby disclosed. But even if we grant the distinction between an exposition and an illumination, it is still relevant to ask what is credible in an illumination and what is not. One thing is certain. The criteria for evaluating Heidegger's results should not be set by literary criticism but should be strictly philosophical. But given that Heidegger has called into question the entire tradition, which criteria emerging from that tradition can be applied with minimal distortion to his thought? I suggest that the criteria which should control his conclusions from the illuminations are the minimal ones of consistency and comprehensibility. Thus, if it is possible to derive interpretations of a given poetic text which are contradictory to the interpretation Heidegger presents, then any doctrinal position based on such an interpretation is questionable. It is true that for Heidegger logic is merely an extension of metaphysics, a metaphysics which has traditionally distorted the relation between language and being (*EM*, p. 94). To rectify this distortion, if it can be rectified, is one reason why Heidegger must embark on this poetic voyage in the first place. We find Heidegger, perhaps as an initial step in the confrontation with the supremacy of logical principles, maintaining that an essential characteristic of poetic language is that it be "ambiguous" (*mehrdeutig*). Here and elsewhere, the word *ambiguity* indicates "multiple" meaning rather than a "confusion" in meaning. Given such multiplicity, Heidegger may well allow contradictory interpretations in order to make the claims for poetic language that he does. But surely contradiction must be retained if we want to assert that what Heidegger says is inconsistent and possibly false. If this principle is not preserved, then Heidegger becomes a prophet, or perhaps a seer, but not someone whose reflections are subject to the limits of rationality as we now know it.[4]

Heidegger would perhaps respond that these very limits have been too tightly drawn and that a general recognition of this restriction is one of the primary goals of his work. Thus, the "seer" aspect of Heidegger's thought should not be completely discounted, especially with respect to the criterion of comprehensibility. Heidegger intends to present a new and difficult perspective on the fact of language, and he feels constrained to employ a large number of new technical terms, new meanings for old technical terms, and new configurations of thinking, all to convince his audience that there are crucial reasons for looking at language as he does. We should not expect to comprehend his drift immediately, nor should we weigh the tensions present in Heidegger's distinctions against the comfortable certitude of reigning notions without expending considerable effort toward discerning order where there appears to be only chaos. In fact, of the two criteria, the search for comprehensibility should override inconsistencies that arise as "obvious" to those accustomed to conceiving language in the traditional manner.

There are three other main sources of possible misunderstanding related to the literary-philosophical framework Heidegger has adopted. The first source, itself two-pronged, concerns (a) whether Heidegger intends to establish criteria by which to determine questions of aesthetic value regarding poetry and poets; and (b) how Heidegger can defend himself against the charge of arbitrariness in attributing to Hölderlin (also, to a lesser degree, Trakl, George, Rilke, and others) sufficient value to justify the claims based upon their work. In a book entitled *Aspects of Criticism*, L. L. Duroche asks whether a criterion has been offered by Heidegger "for differentiating . . . genuine poetry in which truth occurs from a poetry in which there is distortion." Duroche's reply is a resounding no! This criticism is relevant only if Heidegger's project includes establishing such criteria. And it is evident that Heidegger is not concerned to do literary theory. This is not to say that it is impossible to *derive* incisive critical principles from what Heidegger has written,[5] just that it is inaccurate to assume that Heidegger is implicitly describing the differences between "true" and "false" poetry whenever he makes general claims about poetry or based on poetry.

Heidegger maintains that the type of poetic language he deals with is "great";[6] it then appears reasonable to question the grounds on which Heidegger decides that, for example, the greatness of Hölderlin is greater than the greatness of Goethe. Given Heidegger's proclamation, it is natural to anticipate some statement as to what constitutes greatness in general. But must Heidegger provide such declarations? First, Heidegger's appeal to greatness could be completely justified without Heidegger (or anyone else for that matter) being able to stipulate in a necessary and sufficient sense in what that greatness consists. Great art may be no less great when its greatness is impervious to discursive analysis. Second, the preferential value judgments implicit in Heidegger's choices for exposition and illumination are less crucial than the results he obtains from these choices. In fact, from the strictly philosophical point of view (cf. the genetic fallacy) it is irrelevant whether or not Heidegger chooses great poetry and also why he selects the poetry he selects. The result he achieves from the poetic language he does consider is the important point, regardless of the source of that language. Even if it could be somehow demonstrated that all the poets and poems Heidegger dwells upon are in fact superseded by greater poetic language, we would still be faced with interpreting what Heidegger has said through his own development of the language in these poems.

The second possible source of misunderstanding concerns the character of the claims Heidegger derives from poetic language. A currently viable aesthetic postulate concerning poetry is that its ordered sequences are merely expressions of the poet's feelings or emotions. Such expressions are not of the same sort as cognitive assertions, assertions whose meaning can be based on some form of verification inapplicable to the expressions of poetry. The distinction is, of course, arguable from a number of standpoints, but regardless of the various refinements possible, most entrenched Heideggerians would immediately respond that the level reached by Heidegger's illuminations is much more fundamental than the derivative dimension represented by the emotive-cognitive distinction. Heideggerians are prone to this type of rejoinder, but they usually fail to stipulate what fundamental means. One suspects they feel that those in the know will know, those not in the know are helpless to understand. Now, I agree that the point of what Heidegger is after will probably be overlooked if assessment of his arguments remains at the level explored by the emotive-cognitive distinction. But it is surely prudent, if not humane, to provide some middle ground for those philosophers who deal exclusively with that distinction when they think philosophically about matters poetic.

The sense in which Heidegger's illuminations are more fundamental is of course speculative. And for now, the following brief sketch of his position must suffice. The source of both the emotive and the cognitive elements in language is located in the human factor

13

in spoken language. But Heidegger believes that the essence of language entails the specification of ontological perspectives which are independent of the fact that language as spoken is of human origin. Since the concept of language as either cognitive or emotive is itself based on some conception of human nature, the distinction as a whole will misrepresent language, if we allow the feasibility of Heidegger's approach to language. The cognitive-emotive distinction has the advantage of focusing on the spokesman of language in terms appropriate for understanding, at least to a certain degree, differences between various types of discourse. Thus, the burden of proof, or perhaps the burden of possible legitimacy, is on Heidegger to demonstrate that, as well as how this supposed more fundamental character of poetic language exists. But the burden is possible to bear, I think, and we should at least give Heidegger the opportunity to bear it.

A similar note should be included for the third possible source of misunderstanding, that based on the prescriptive-descriptive distinction. After illuminating a certain poetic text, Heidegger at times makes assertions which would strike a reader with some awareness of ethical analytical literature as starkly prescriptive, when the context of the assertion appears to allow only propositions which are descriptive of the meaning of the passage. An example is the notion of "steadfastness" (*Inständigkeit*), which plays an important role in *Gelassenheit*. Heidegger will make claims using the notion of steadfastness which intimate the presence of a morally prescriptive force, such as "one ought to be steadfast" in some yet to be defined manner. But, so the objection might run, is it legitimate to move from apparently descriptive developments of poetic language to an apparently prescriptive if inchoate ethics?

Once again, the Heideggerian would reply that we are now operating at a more fundamental level, and once again this is basically correct. But in this case explaining how Heidegger's position is more fundamental covers more territory than the explanation offered for the cognitive-emotive distinction. As noted, the latter distinction is grounded in a conception of human nature, while the moral sense of *ought* implicit in the prescriptive function of language includes not only all values based on human considerations but also, as in the Platonic world view, values which are such by reason of knowledge of extrahuman reality. Now, Heidegger's illuminations appeal ultimately to a complex notion of being (*Sein*). This notion of being must be kept in the background of all the apparently prescriptive claims Heidegger puts forth. If the designation *prescriptive* is at all applicable, it functions only as an indicator that it is being which prescriptively grounds how men should act. Why being selects the morally determinative ways that it does must remain an open question at this point. Also—and this is equally vital—the perhaps less controversial notion of the descriptive function of language must be transcended as well. Heidegger will contend that the notion of language as a vehicle of description is based on modes of representation *(Vorstellen)* which, by their very nature, distort, or misrepresent, the being of what is represented. Again, the burden will be on Heidegger to demonstrate the tenability of these far-reaching revisionist proposals. They shall be considered in due course.

Let me now summarize the key methodological steps taken in this study. (1) When Heidegger writes about poetic language, he is presenting his own interpretation of language through a series of reflective studies in which he feels free to manipulate the various parts of poems in seemingly random fashion, but directing the total interpretation toward a preliminary sketch of ontological dimensions which have been overlooked, at least according to Heidegger. The fact that Heidegger's presentation is aimed primarily at philosophical concerns implies that the criteria invoked to evaluate his results should be philosophical as well. And these are the criteria which will be applied to the arguments discussed later. Furthermore, the question of aesthetic value is set aside as irrelevant to the issue of determining the meaning of the illuminations Heidegger educes from poetic language. (2) The cognitive-emotive and descriptive-prescriptive distinctions are both held in suspension during the course of this study. This fact in no way implies that these distinctions, and others of similar form, are naive or irrelevant to the peculiar ontological grandeur of Heidegger's work. It is simply sound methodology to begin a study of this sort by establishing an attitude of openness (insofar as this is possible) without a preconceived, and rigid, set of categories and distinctions with which to attack anything philosophically strange or novel just for the reason that it is strange or novel. An attitude of openness is not a mandate for "anything goes." However, any understanding and evaluation of Heidegger's project should begin only after presentation of that project is complete in terminology and argumentative structure derived as far as possible from its own set of problems and concerns.

Some wisdom from another important speculative mind may be pertinent to close this introduction. Toward the conclusion of *Adventures of Ideas*, Alfred North Whitehead cautions that "the speculative methods of metaphysics are dangerous, easily perverted. So is all Adventure; but Adventure belongs to the essence of civilization." Whitehead's notion of Adventure is technical, but the ordinary sense of the word fits well the scope of Heidegger's work on poetic language. And of course, whether any adventure is successful or a misadventure can be determined only after its completion.

PART I

Language as an Ontological Phenomenon

1. Word, Name, and Thing

W E SEEK AN EXPERIENCE which leads into the essence of language, an experience which must be approached with minimal philosophical preconceptions. But any experience as experienced is mute, even if the experience is itself linguistic. The content of the experience must therefore be translated into terminology of some sort. Heidegger develops this terminology in many places and in many ways, although the dominant chords are struck in his later works on language. The fact that early Heidegger had also dealt with language should not, however, be overlooked, as Heidegger himself reminds us (*US*, p. 137). The contrast between the approach taken in *Sein und Zeit* and that of the later Heidegger is important to keep in view. An outline of his earlier position will serve as a useful historical and conceptual background to the later and more complex development.[1]

For the Heidegger of *Sein und Zeit*, language plays an important role in determining the unique place of man as a being in the world. Understanding the world is an essential aspect of man's ontological nature. Man expresses this understanding in and through language, principally language as *assertion (Aussage)*. Assertions have many purposes, but as far as understanding the world is concerned, their primary purpose is the utterance of truths. From the very outset of Western reflection on language, the notion of assertion occupied the "primary and authentic 'locus' of truth" (*SZ*, p. 154). Heidegger also based the *Sein und Zeit* analysis of language on the notion of assertion. He distinguished three essential aspects, surrounding his discussion with the bold claim that "in their unity" may be found "the complete structure of the assertion" (*SZ*, p. 154). Assertion is defined as that "showing forth which communicates and characterizes" (*SZ*, p. 156). As an example (my own), consider the assertion, "The hammer is heavy." That which is shown forth is not, for Heidegger, a meaning, but rather an entity—a hammer—which is of a certain weight. That which is characterized is the hammer insofar as the predicate "heavy" is ascribed to the subject "hammer." That which is communicated is an expression which grants publicity to the manner in which the asserter relates himself to the hammer, since it is the asserter who notices the fact of the hammer's weight. This enumeration and development of the notion of assertion is concise, relatively straightforward, and perceptive. But twenty-five years later in *Unterwegs zur Sprache*, Heidegger will maintain that the "essence of language" refuses to come to language (i.e., become capable of expression through language) in the assertions *(Aussagen)* we make concerning language (*US*, p. 186). And presumably this sweeping claim includes assertions *about* the ancient notion of assertion itself.

Heidegger suggests a reason why confidence in his earlier position was premature. In his own mind, the "fundamental lack" of *Sein und Zeit* was that "I dared advance too far too soon" (*US*, p. 93).[2] This self-admonition does not necessarily imply that the views argued in *Sein und Zeit* are false. But it does imply that more should have been said before the conclusions of that work can be asserted as either true or false. For example, during the period from *Sein und Zeit* (1927) to *Unterwegs zur Sprache* (1959), Heidegger lost faith in the concept of assertion as a vehicle to provoke an experience with the essence of language. The *Sein und Zeit* analysis of assertion went too far too soon in the assumption that the concept of assertion was an automatic entry into the essence of language, regardless of the subtlety of the analysis. Even in *Sein und Zeit*, however, it is possible to discern an awareness, perhaps still dim, that more was involved in apprehending the essence of language. Heidegger had noted at that time that whenever an assertion is made, some "prior conception" *(Vorgriff)* is always latently present, since "language conceals in itself a formed mode of conceptualization" (*SZ*, p. 157). Gradually Heidegger realized the pervasiveness of such conceptualization, and it eventually spurred the attempt to state those conditions which describe how such conceptualization could be present in language in the first place, a statement which was not made public until the appearance of *Unterwegs zur Sprache*.[3]

To execute this intention, the Heidegger of *Unterwegs zur Sprache* posits a number of polar concepts which control the direction of his quest. No longer will Heidegger merely apostrophize language as the "house of being" *(Haus des Seins)*,[4] the trope verging on the notorious, which Heidegger himself soon found to be "clumsy." Nevertheless, as in *Sein und Zeit*, the central project of determining the connection between language and being *(Sein)* remains the primary consideration. This connection is so vital that it cannot be overemphasized. In the process of approaching anew the phenomenon of language, Heidegger will erect categories which cut across presently accepted conventions concerning the manner in which language and that to which language refers are related. His purpose is to suggest in a more precise sense how language is the house of being. For this reason, Heidegger begins his revamped analysis with the apparently oblique gambit of asserting that language is "in its essence neither expression nor an activity of man" (*US*, p. 19). The implication is that "the essence of language cannot be anything linguistic" (*US*, p. 114). Initially, the claim that language is not a human activity appears to be a typically perverse Heideggerian dictum. Surely it is precisely insofar as human sounds emerge as meaningful that philosophers have found this activity interesting and important. But Heidegger does not maintain that language as humanly spoken is philosophically irrelevant. His point is that the *essence* of language can be experienced only if human speech is seen in connection with what is other than the act of speaking.

Heidegger's notion of essence is obviously important in this context, particularly here at the outset of the argument; since he does not bother to describe its character, we must suggest the approximate manner in which the notion applies. The principle involved is that the essence of something cannot be found simply by describing the intrinsic components of that something. Although appeal must be made to such descriptions in order to erect relations between the parts and factors external to these parts, the essence is not the simple conjunction of parts but consists in the relations between the parts (as a unity) and what is other than this unity. If we recall that Heidegger intends to instigate an experience with such an essence, then the search for such an essence becomes a realizable endeavor. Evaluation of this essence will be based on the extent to which Heidegger can relate language in itself (i.e., as presently conceptualized) to whatever extralinguistic factors constitute the ontological content of the traditional linguistic notions. Heidegger's strategy thus becomes clear. He will distinguish aspects of linguistic activity—at times employing the traditional terminology (without the traditional meaning of those terms), at times introducing his own—based on the manner in which these distinctions can provide insight into the relation between language in itself and the being of what is other than but ontologically related to such language. According to this interpretation, it follows that the greater the knowledge of the essence of language, the greater the experience of being, the ultimate ground of this essence.[5]

Each of these distinctions will revolve around the basic notion of the word *(Wort)*. The word is characterized as the medium which grounds the "saying of the being of beings" (*W*, p. 349) or, from a different perspective, what "first bestows being to the thing" (*US*, p. 164). The connection between word and thing provides the "properly thoughtful" content for which defining characteristics are still lacking (*US*, p. 194). As a result, no evident "word for the essence of word" (*US*, p. 236) can be determined. At this juncture, Heidegger's goal is to approximate a solution for this lack by registering those conditions in virtue of which a word can become functional.

We may begin the approximation with some remarks on the notion of word as taken in abstraction, without reference to its implicit ontological function. Heidegger carefully distinguishes between a word as isolated term (e.g., as an entry in a dictionary) and a word as occurring contextually in an assertion (only here can the word be present in a relation to being). The former, words as terms, are only "the residue which falls from the word as such" (*W*, p. 349).[6] The distinction emphasizes that the latter, words as such are ontologically significant only in contexts. Now, not all contexts are equivalent in ontological fertility. Nor are all words equivalent in their capacity to reveal being. Already in *Sein und Zeit*, Heidegger had observed that "in the end it is the business of philosophy to preserve *the power of the most elementary words* in which human being [*Dasein*] expresses itself" (*SZ*, p. 220—italics in original). Some of these "most elementary" words may be found in the historical vocabulary of Western philosophical literature. But Heidegger is convinced that some of these words—and they are especially crucial for the contemporary epoch—must be found elsewhere. Given this lack in philosophical language proper, Heidegger has found it necessary to reflect thoughtfully on the language of poetry.

In this contextual and ontological sense, it is possible for *das Wort* to designate a single word. More frequently, however, the German usage of *das Wort* carries the connotation of a phrase, a proposition (as in the title of Heidegger's own essay "Nietzsches Wort 'Gott ist tot' "), or even a set of propositions. How then to translate *das Wort?* Given its multiple dimensions, the English term *saying* seems a reasonable candidate, since its meaning frequently includes both phrases and propositions. But saying will be reserved for Heidegger's technical term *Sagen* (discussed in chapter 2). Therefore, *das Wort* will be rendered simply as "the word," but with the important proviso that its referent is often one or a set of propositions, in some instances an entire poem. We here confront Heidegger's first extrapolation of the ordinary meaning of a term, and the result is conflict both with that meaning and with some contemporary philosophical interpretations of that meaning. Analytic linguistic philosophy points out with justifiable care that the properties of words in propositional contexts are on a different logical plane from the properties of propositions as such. Why willfully collapse this distinction? Such procedure must be accepted as a prelude, and only a prelude, to the task ahead:—the determination of the relation between language and being. The current standards of precision in linguistic philosophy are, for Heidegger, based on an unexamined ontological and logical structure. Heidegger does not necessarily want to sacrifice these standards but, as noted earlier, to subordinate them for the sake of new and vital perspectives on all possible aspects of the problem and nature of language.

We may now begin to describe the connection Heidegger sees between word and thing *(Ding)*. The thing which is granted being through the word is any entity "that in any way is" (*US*, p. 164). But not all words make entities into things. The word must be "found" before the thing is a thing (*US*, p. 164).[7] Thus, the existence of the entity Sputnik was not dependent on the set of letters which eventually served as this entity's name. But the *being* present in Sputnik is, according to Heidegger, dependent on the term *Sputnik* insofar as that term is realized as a word. This connection is so fundamental that it can be illustrated only by initially paradoxical claims such as "the word itself is the relation" between being and the thing (*US*, p. 170). The word is not a term taken in isolation, nor is it merely an arbitrary ascription with no real significance with respect to the being of the entity named. The word is itself the relation in the sense that being is determined only by considering how the word and the thing are related as an essential unity. Thus, "when we go through the forest," we go through the word *forest* even when "we do not utter this word and do not reflect on anything linguistic" (*H*, p. 286). This sylvan and idiosyncratic example may appear to border on the mystical, but it is merely a vigorous attempt to indicate the nature of the relation between entity represented and word as name representing. The relation *as a whole* is denoted by the notion of word in Heidegger's sense. The problem with such a position, and it is obviously crucial, will be to explore this whole by isolating those features which contribute to being, while preserving as far as possible the differences between the notion of word as a linguistic concept and the notion of thing as an extralinguistic entity. The forest and *the forest* are hardly identical even in an ontological perspective.

As just described, the word is the most basic concept for grounding those distinctions which detail the ontological possibility of language. But Heidegger must introduce correlate concepts to develop the sense in which the word accomplishes this end. The most important of these concepts is that of *the name (der Name)*. Although "there is no thing which lacks the word, namely the word which names the given thing," the relation between word and thing does not by itself explain how the word functions as a name. Heidegger asks "what does 'naming' mean?" (*US*, p. 163). The question is answered in this important passage: "Names are originating words. They present what already is to the act of representation. Names attest to their measure-giving command over things through the power of origination" (*US*, p. 225).

Consider the name for a hammer. The hammer exists, an entity usable for pounding. The entity must exist before there is a need to name it. No entity hammer, no name for hammer. The cognitive relation between the hammer as entity and the name *hammer* Heidegger calls representation *(Vorstellen)*. We represent the hammer to ourselves and to fellow speakers when we use the term *hammer*. The fact that other terms are possible to name the entity hammer does not invalidate the point that there must be some term, and whatever term is used performs this representational function. It is at this point where the distinction between word and name becomes operative. Before the name for hammer can be employed as a vehicle of representation and communication, the entity hammer must be presented so that it can be represented as named. The transition from bare entity existing prior to the actual event of spoken language—nothing in the *in se* existence of the hammer compels it to be named in a language—to entity capable of being expressed and represented in language is possible in virtue of the ontological dimensions implicit but proper to the word. When this foundation is completed, the word presenting the entity hammer becomes a name for the hammer. The term for the entity hammer remains the same

24

throughout this process, but the respective functions of word and name are very different, as Heidegger is at pains to demonstrate.

Only because all names are words in this originative sense can names bestow what Heidegger calls a measured command over entities. The measure is the extent to which any given name is a locus wherein may be experienced relations between the being of the entity named and being as totality. The relation between the being of a hammer and being as such is different than the relation between the being of a jug and being as such. But the names for these entities must be considered before the difference in their respective modes of being is fully recognized. Heidegger's forceful term *command* is justified because of the set of heterogeneous connotations inherent in almost every name, connotations which frequently disclose the manner in which we react to the entities named. Once *hammer* becomes the name for the entity hammer, that very name commands how that entity is represented and experienced when we discourse about that entity. Even when we use the hammer, the context of the event of actual use is intimately connected with the name for hammer. There is obviously a difference between the use of a hammer and the use of the name *hammer*. Heidegger does not want to maintain that a man could not use a hammer unless he had a name for hammer. But he does maintain that the actual event of using a hammer is always accompanied by the name for a hammer. This presence may be consciously attended to or completely ignored; in either case, however, the connection between entity and name is an essential factor in the illumination of being.

But consider a world which is identical to our world except that it lacks a name for the entity hammer, a type of entity which exists in that world. Surely any ontological considerations derived from the hammer in this possible world would not suffer just because the name for hammer is wanting. Heidegger seems to impose an aspect of language as necessary when it is merely accidental. In general, Heidegger's style of philosophizing is not amenable to objections of this form, so we must improvise a response. I suggest an appeal to the factual existence of language, where an argument pointing to the logical possibility of a world without terminology of a certain sort becomes a world both artificial and remote. Thus, we must accept that Heidegger's argument, here and elsewhere, assumes the existence of a world well-stocked with entities and equally well-stocked with names relating to those entities. The fact that some possible worlds, or even cultures in this world, lack hammers, and therefore perhaps names for hammers, is not damaging to his intent. All cultures (in this world) possess some entities and have some way of describing or referring to those entities, and this is sufficient for Heidegger's argument. There are, of course, possible worlds where language would not exist at all or would exist without those names present in the world we experience. But such possible worlds are comprehensible only relative to our world, where many different kinds of names denote many different kinds of entities. It is this world and the actual presence of living language found in this world which concerns Heidegger.

The distinction between word and name is therefore fundamental. But, perhaps by design, the distinction engenders more problems than it solves. The most important of these problems is the specification of those ontological considerations which are involved in the transition from word to name. For Heidegger, the dominating tendency in philosophical inquiry concerning language has been directed toward difficulties arising from language conceived at the level of representation—e.g., how names represent or refer to entities—rather than toward the much more fundamental matter of how language can present entities in the first place. The next phase in Heidegger's project will consist in analyzing a number of pivotal names and their respective commanding modes of representation until the properties present in the ontological domain of the word grounding these names can be found and described.[8]

To illustrate the effect the distinction between word and name had on Heidegger himself, consider the fact that he refused to give a name to his own philosophical efforts during his middle and late periods when his attention had been drawn more and more to the problems of language and its relation to being. If he uses the name philosophy of language, then his audience will likely compare and assess it in terms of the English version, and we have seen enough already to know that Heidegger is after results far different from his Anglo-Saxon counterparts. If he uses the name metaphysics, then his audience will tend to introduce comparisons with the history of metaphysics, and this too will deflect the force of Heidegger's cardinal principle that the history of metaphysics has inadequately apprehended the connection between language and being. And if he uses the name ontology, then the audience conversant with Heidegger will tend to compare his work on language with his own "fundamental ontology" in *Sein und Zeit*, but perhaps without realizing the need to experience in light of his later work the content of the difficult concepts of that time. These three names (and doubtless other possible candidates) are all subject to the potential dangers of rigidification present in the representational function of language. Hence, what Heidegger is doing in *Unterwegs zur Sprache* and allied works will be without self-designative nomenclature. In the conversation with his Japanese friend in *Unterwegs zur Sprache*, Heidegger concludes that he must abandon his "way of thought to namelessness" (*US*, p. 121) and that his own thinking must be altered so that it advances "without a name" (*US*, p. 138). The point here is not Heidegger's sui generis pretensions concerning his own efforts, but only the warning that we should not study his work as if it were just another in the ongoing industry of philosophical reflections on language. The intention is to argue a position without the same sort of historical and representational preconceptions as his predecessors, a position "without a name."

Heidegger now attempts to show the way between word and name by introducing notions which suggest the structure of the elemental ontological power implicit in the word. The most important of these notional guideposts is what Heidegger calls *der Wink*. Again, a unilateral translation is difficult, since the German term *Wink* may mean a wink of the eye, a wave of the hand, or a hint expressed verbally. The last of these three possibilities appears most apt, since it alone suggests language as normally understood, and it is the translation adopted here.

Heidegger indicates the approximate function of the hint in relation to word and name, but the most vivid clarification of the hint is not through discursive development as such but rather through the actual literary experience in following the course of Heidegger's thinking. We shall examine a striking example of such an experience after some general remarks on what Heidegger wants the hint to achieve. Heidegger is convinced that we will not experience language in its essence until we accept the fact that one of the residual properties in the representational stance of the name is an implicit but ontologically ultimate reference to the space-time which grounds entity named and naming word. This space-time is, apparently, peculiar to the sought-after ontology of language. Heidegger informs us that the hint belongs to an "entirely different essential space" than the representationally oriented notion of the name as a "sign" in the sense of "mere signification" (US, p. 117). A term is a sign as mere signification if it denotes the entity named without conveying the vital ontological insight that the name could not name unless the entity capable of being named became present in space-time in the first place. The hint functions by indicating the presence of this space-time. If an ontologically fundamental experience with language at the level of the word is to be at all possible, Heidegger must establish a spatio-temporal framework or continuum within which the word can function as a name and into which we must enter if we wish to understand how a word functions in all respects.[9]

Both our practical and theoretical experience with names (as vehicles of representation) is so pervasive that "it is rare and difficult to receive a hint" (WD, p. 91). The proof of this difficulty, if proof is required, is the fact that we consider names in themselves to be without spatio-temporal considerations. Names can represent temporal segments, e.g., the name hour. And the utterance of the names for temporal segments itself occurs in time. But surely the name as such is atemporal. Here Heidegger objects. Names are not temporal in the way that the hours named are temporal, but the existence of a name implies a spatio-temporal dimension which must be present to ground the ontological possibility of a word and the purely linguistic relation between entity named and the name itself.

This space-time is in some respects dissimilar to the customary conception of space and time insofar as they provide the containers of our lives and relations with entities. Heidegger approaches its description cautiously. Thus, the hint is "enigmatic," but not enigmatic in the sense of a defect or something to be rectified; rather, enigmatic means that a hint "hints toward us" and "hints away from us" (US, p. 117). The element of motion is therefore essential to the hint and to its space-time, and more must be said about the type of motion and the nature and limits of what is moved in that space-time. Heidegger first provides literary evidence illustrating how the hint moves "toward us" and "away from us." One of the chapters in Unterwegs zur Sprache is entitled "Aus einem Gespräch von der Sprache." The conversation is between a Japanese and a questioner, who in time we learn is Heidegger himself. The discussion turns to the topic of hints and how they function. The questioner begins to assert an obviously important claim about the hint. He stops in mid-sentence. His assertion is then concluded by the Japanese. The questioner asserts that hints "need the widest oscillating-sphere," and the Japanese adds and concludes that this sphere is one which "mortals only slowly draw toward and away from" (*US*, p. 119).

This conversational separation-and-completion is a stylistic ploy which should not be divorced from the total impact of Heidegger's presentation, just as the dialectical interplay of a Platonic dialogue is itself crucial to the total significance of what is explicitly *said* by the characters in the dialogue. The literary dimension of the argument displays in the living reality of the interplay what Heidegger is attempting to express theoretically in that interplay. The "oscillating" character of the "sphere" in question starts with the questioner and finishes with the Japanese. Now, the Japanese could not have finished the questioner's assertion under the conditions of normal conversation, a species of representational language. But Heidegger suggests, by apparently literary means, that he could very well finish the assertion once the sphere of the hint—the topic of conversation—had been attained. In normal discourse, a person can sometimes anticipate correctly what is about to be said and finish the beginning of the assertion on his own. But given the content of the present discussion, it is unlikely that even the most percipient Oriental could divine a typically dense Heideggerian assertion. Of course, as we have just seen, Heidegger's purpose is not to represent any actual conversation, although there is no doubt that conversations of approximately this content have occurred between Heidegger and various Japanese. The conversational literary device neither proves nor disproves anything by itself, but its purpose is to illustrate the extent of the hint as it might be experienced by two conversants. The complete specification of the space-time which the hint only hints at will establish a necessary condition for determining the ontological relations between entity and name.

Heidegger has noticed the need for a spatio-temporal sphere of some nonrepresentational form which hints at the fundamental nature of the word. The hint-function of the word indicates a to and fro movement between entity named and naming word. Within this spatio-temporal sphere "the word determines the thing to be a thing [*Ding*]," and in this sphere Heidegger announces that "we would like to name this governance of the word determination [*Bedingnis*]" (*US*, p. 232). The etymological link between *Ding* and *Bedingnis* is lost in translation, and of course this link is itself a hint of the direction Heidegger's thought is pursuing. Before commenting on this sense of determination, we should observe the modal grammar and studied

29

hesitancy in Heidegger's introduction of the technical term *determination*. Heidegger's name is now itself a representation, required for purposes of discussion and communication with others who necessarily think in terms of a representational vocabulary. The phrase "would like" indicates the provisional character of the name, and if this name is misleading or found wanting Heidegger would doubtless be the first to endorse substitute terminology. But let us proceed with the terminology at our disposal and see where it leads.

The word determines (*Bedingt*) the entity named by the word to be a thing. The being of the thing is found "in the exhortation of the naming word" (*US*, p. 110). But in order to apprehend *how* being is manifested in named things, some differentiating guidelines are necessary. Being has been said in many ways, and we must have perspectives on how being can be said before we actually attempt to specify the properties of being. Heidegger provides these guidelines when he asserts that named things "collect in themselves heaven and earth, the mortal and the divine" (*US*, p. 22). The unity of these four sectors Heidegger names *das Geviert*, variously translated in the secondary literature as "fourfold," "quadrate," even "foursome," and meaning literally what has been "foured." The name *fourfold* seems to be the most suitable English equivalent, and I have adopted it throughout the remainder of this study.

Even for those students of Heidegger accustomed to his neologisms, the precise meaning of the fourfold is especially difficult to determine.[10] I shall assume, by way of introduction, that the fourfold is the parameter, so to speak, indicating those sectors which in their mutual interplay constitute a totality essentially related to language and being. Thus, every named thing becomes such a unified presentation of the fourfold, and the spatio-temporal dimension Heidegger discerns in the notions of word and hint now receives additional explanation with respect to its limits. In order to measure the relation between word and thing, the nonrepresentational space-time must itself be grounded in an extralinguistic reality. This extralinguistic reality will partially satisfy the requirement stated at the outset, that the essence of language is not itself linguistic, that is, that it includes relations to the referents of spoken language. According to Heidegger, these relations are found in the interplay of the four sectors of the fourfold—the heavens, the earth, the mortal, the divine. When an entity is named through the word, its character as thing is experienced when the entity is experienced with respect to each of the four sectors. All four sectors are present in the named thing. If we are immediately aware of one sector, then we are ontologically in the presence of all four sectors, even if the spatio-temporal distances representationally given make this presence initially undiscernible. For example, if the named thing is an earthen jug, then when "we say earth, we already think the other three from the unity of the four" (*VA*, p. 177). Such thinking may never be or become conscious in normal experience with the jug or any other entity—but Heidegger is not doing empirical psychology. His purpose here is to detail a schematic, a monadic focus, through which the relation between language and being can be experienced according to more adequate ontological perspectives.

Some care must be taken, therefore, not to force such an attempt to obey any already well-defined conceptual order. The fourfold is not the ultimate source of the meaning of a word, if the notion of meaning is restricted to a purely enunciated expression conveying the interplay of heavens, earth, mortal, and divine as held in distinction from the extralinguistic existence of stars, fields, men, and gods. Such an approach to the notion of meaning would subvert the force of the fourfold right from the outset, making it irrelevant to an ontology of language because of the abstract and representationally induced separation of entity from entity as named by the word. If the entity named is not related to each of the four sectors as existing independent of both name itself and entity itself, then the entity remains only an entity and not a thing. The entity would still exist, but the mode of its existence is reduced to bare natural or material components, or whatever given properties are appropriate. The principal reason why entities are not experienced as things is due to the inherent limitations in the linguistic representation of entities. In fact, we do not perceive the thinghood of things: rather, we apprehend their thinghood when entities become things through the naming word and within the contexts where such speech is uttered and acted upon. Language must educate perception and any subsequent conceptual development based on that perception, at least if perception is to serve as the gateway for ontological considerations.

The fourfold is one of Heidegger's final and most complex attempts to "give a name" to being. For this reason, clarity concerning its precise significance is of primary importance. One wants to direct a host of questions to this exotic doctrine. For example, what is the relation between the spatio-temporal sphere of hint and word and the space-time of our normal representational perception? Is the fourfold constitutive of the ontological character of entities as things or is it merely heuristic, guiding the investigator of being into the right paths for the determination of the being of entities? And if all named things are interplays of the fourfold, then how is one named thing (e.g., a jug) distinguished at an ontological level from another named thing (e.g., a bridge)? As already noted, the fourfold will serve as one of the principal organizational themes of this study, and such issues will be raised and discussed at the proper time. But for now, I would like to close this chapter with a commentary on some recent interpretations of the fourfold. This commentary is only an introduction to an adequate confrontation with the fourfold and its role in language, but it is necessary given the freewheeling and, I think, off-center character of the existing interpretations.

These interpretations all tend to focus undue attention on determining the origin of the fourfold, that is, the basis either in the history of metaphysics or in the history of Heidegger's own work for such an apparently hybrid notion. Here are three examples. For William J. Richardson, the fourfold reminds us

of the trilogy that characterized classical metaphysics: God, man, "world." This is a hierarchy of being, of course, and we are dealing clearly with Being. But is it possible that the sense of the Quadrate consists in suggesting polyvalent plenitude of (the "simple") *hen*, by reason of which it can come-to-presence in *panta*, sc. *as God, as* man and *as* "world"?

For Stanley Rosen, "Heidegger's fourfold unity is Hegel's Absolute, only recast into terms derived from pagan poetry." And for Thomas Langan, the fourfold is "the unity of the three time-extases in the one projecting *Dasein*—the mortal."[11]

None of these suggestions is elaborated to any extent. Also, I believe that all of them are misguided, even with respect to their limited aims of locating the origin of the notion in question. First, Father Richardson's solid background in scholasticism tells against him in this Heideggerian context. For it seems highly doubtful that so classically metaphysical a trilogy could have inspired Heidegger to coin the fourfold for the very reason that the trilogy is so classical in its metaphysical, and representational, heritage and content. And, more to the point, how does the fourth member emerge from Richardson's trilogy? Surely Being (as Father Richardson writes it) is not distinct from being—God, man, and world—which must be

32

the case in order to preserve the fourness of the fourfold. Second, Rosen is also guilty of an unfounded historical transfer. For why should the fourfold be Hegel's Absolute rather than Parmenides' One or Nietzsche's Will to Power? Rosen offers no reason why Hegel rather than someone else is the ultimate source of the fourfold. Third, Langan, like Father Richardson, really has only three notions to work with, and he merely hypostatizes their unity to arrive at the fourth. But four is not three plus the unity of three. Four is four, that is, there are four distinct members in the fourness of four. Also, in grounding the three time-extases in the mortal, Langan implies that *Dasein* (as the mortal) is in some sense more fundamental than the three extases. But there are no indications from Heidegger that any one sector is more fundamental than any other sector. In addition, to assume that mortal is equivalent with *Dasein* is unwarranted, given the fact that *Dasein* as man oriented is only one type of mortal being. Langan offers no argument for why *Dasein* should play an especially predominant role in the interplay of the fourfold.

As noted earlier, each of these interpretations is marked by the concern to explain the origin of the fourfold, in particular the rationale behind Heidegger's seemingly arbitrary selection of four fundamental sectors. But this concern misses the mark if directed at the numerical side of the fourfold. It makes as much sense to ask Heidegger why the fourness of the fourfold as it would to ask Aristotle why the fourness of the four causes. We criticize Aristotle's theory of causality if it fails to explain what it intends to explain, not because of the fact that the four causes are four in number. Important philosophical problems will be overlooked if discussion stalls on why the cardinal notions are numerically laid out as they are. I contend that these problems (and Heidegger's account of the fourfold is such that there are many) will become evident when the fourness of the fourfold is first accepted as a notional given and then scrutinized. Where the fourness of the fourfold comes from is of less importance than determining the function Heidegger wants the fourfold to perform.[12] I suspect that the commentators just criticized would essentially agree with this conclusion. But at least their published remarks stop short of the type of investigation required to discern that which is both interesting and problematic about the fourfold.

One of the primary goals of this study will be to approach the fourfold as a key factor in Heidegger's thought on poetic language and in this context to suggest both its philosophical value and its attendant difficulties. We have already seen how Heidegger's distinction between word and name implies that things are named through the word in a sense which includes what is named as well as how it is named. The fourfold stipulates that the nature of the thing named is determined by the four sectors of heavens, earth, mortal, and divine. What Heidegger seems to be after in his quest for "an experience with language" is nothing less than a complete (if, at this point, embryonic) cosmology, where any thing within that cosmology has being only when considered from the perspective of language and the meaning of the entity named as thing by the word. Given this quest, there is no hope of acquiring the requisite understanding of the essence of language simply in the progressive refinement of already existing concepts and distinctions as developed by contemporary philosophy of language. For all these concepts and distinctions, at least for Heidegger, are based on the implicit representational character of language inherited from the Greeks and the subsequent history of metaphysics. Therefore, Heidegger considers it essential not merely to revamp purely linguistic notions as presently understood—e.g., name and word—but to suggest a restructuring of how it is possible to experience what names and words mean and denote. We have now seen in condensed and abstract form that ontological determination *(Bedingnis)* will be based on the fourfold as a fundamental condition underlying both language itself and the things spoken about in language. This notion of determination will be developed further. But for a proper appreciation of Heidegger's project, this cosmological dimension must be kept in mind as the notions of word, name, hint, and thing are now set in motion within the context of language as realized in speech. The structure implicit in the distinction between saying *(Sagen)* and speaking *(Sprechen)* is the next phase in this distinctively linguistic cosmology.

2. Saying and Speaking

THERE ARE TWO RECOGNIZABLE GIVENS in Heidegger's approach to the essence of language—the fact of discourse itself and the extralinguistic existence of entities as actual or possible referents for that discourse. No other linguistically related given is left unscrutinized. Although Heidegger adopts some traditional terminology to introduce and develop his own distinctions, these distinctions are situated within a cosmological context which, it is hoped, will brighten the path from language to and through being. Thus, Heidegger has distinguished between the word and the name so that it may be possible to determine how entities named through words are things (in the technical ontological sense). Heidegger then structures the potential linguistic experience of the being of things by establishing a backdrop cosmology named as the fourfold. Within this cosmology, an entity emerges as an interplay or reciprocity of the fourfold's four sectors, an interplay constituted in part by the word naming the entity as a thing. The confluence of word and name comes to rest when the entity named is experienced as a thing. But since the fourfold is composed of distinct and differentiating sectors, the specification of principles of motion is required, that is, how words and names move to become linguistic events within the limiting perimeter of the fourfold. Amplification of this movement will suggest how it is possible for spoken language to gather *(Versammeln)* the extralinguistic elements also residing in the fourfold. Heidegger develops this aspect of the cosmology through his distinction between saying *(Sagen)* and speaking *(Sprechen)*.

To experience the essence of language is, in part, to experience the fourfold. Man, one type of mortal, belongs to one sector of the fourfold. But although man may be the spokesman of language, the essence of language cannot be reduced to the purely human element present in actual discourse. All four sectors as unified are necessary for apprehending the essence of language. Heidegger stresses the importance of this totality when he observes that "man is capable of speaking only insofar as he, belonging to saying, listens to saying, so that in resaying it he may be able to say a word" (*US*, p. 266). Now, an obvious distinction between saying and speaking is suggested in this text, a distinction for which the boundaries are as vital as they are difficult to determine. Why then does Heidegger also maintain that "little is won" with a mere clarification *(Aufhellung)* of the distinction between saying and speaking? The reason, important for understanding Heidegger's continued hesitancy, is that a fully mapped out distinction would be governed by a series of names; consequently, what is distinguished would not necessarily be experienced solely by that named (i.e., representational) distinction alone. But Heidegger's reticence to execute a distinction does not imply that the distinction cannot be at least partially drawn. I shall attempt to do so in this chapter, keeping in mind Heidegger's injunction that, ideally, what is distinguished should first be experienced as fully as possible before being programmed into static categories.

Initial access to the saying-speaking distinction is possible through an understanding of man's relation to lanuguage. Man can speak words only to the extent that he belongs to what Heidegger has named *saying*. In fact, the activity of speaking properly understood is the essence of man—"man is man as the one who speaks" and who speaks "constantly" (*US*, p. 11).[1] The "constantly" in this assertion is not based on empirical criteria, but is ontological in character. Heidegger is not claiming that at any given moment someone somewhere is audibly speaking, an empirical claim either true or false. Nor is he asserting that any given individual can use a large variety of linguistic modes to express himself. The intended meaning may be found by considering an episode from the short and ethereal work *Der Feldweg*. While walking along a country path, Heidegger as narrator sees an oak tree and observes, almost in passing, that "the oak itself speaks" (*MH*, p. 12). Such esotericism may be dismissed as still more sylvan mysticism, but this reaction would be premature.[2] The oak "itself speaks" in that its presence can be named in language. For Heidegger, it is not self-evident, especially in the ontological domain, that the mere existence of a tree as an entity implies that language must be capable of naming that entity, much less describing it. Whether the name is *oak* or *Eiche* is immaterial. What is crucial is the fact that an entity speaks in that its mode of existence can be named through human speech.

36

Because of the bias of representational thought, the tendency is to overemphasize the conventional character of names to the point where names are looked upon as totally independent of the reality or being of what is named. Heidegger intends to correct this misconception by insisting that an oak speaks to men *before*, in an ontological sense, men speak about the oak by naming it oak. The extralinguistic existence of the oak is coupled with an inherent disposition to be represented through language, thus guaranteeing the possibility that the oak can be spoken about within human discourse. The same disposition must obtain for all other possible referents. Man speaks constantly in one way or another in the sense that ontological relations always and necessarily exist between himself and all types of entities other than himself—trees, ideas, values, states, his own thinking, God—even when man is not explicitly voicing utterances of a linguistic sort. Man attests to his nature through his constant presence within the network of spoken language which realizes these relations.

To understand the essence of man we must determine how he can speak, and to understand how he can speak we must determine the relation between speaking and saying. At this point, we have unearthed two properties of speaking—(a) speaking is always present to man, and (b) speaking relates man to all possible objects of discourse. Additional properties are derivable from the relation between speaking and saying, a relation which again includes man but is not reduced to his role in spoken language. Heidegger defines saying as follows: "Saying means showing [*zeigen*]: to let appear, the lighting-concealing setting free as offering that which we name world" (*US*, p. 200). The notion of world, which Heidegger has characterized in a number of ways in other works, is here centered on all considerations relevant to the fourfold (*US*, p. 215).[3] The essence of language now becomes language as saying, and as such it "belongs most properly to the motion [*Be-wëgung*] or reciprocity [*Gegen-ein-ander-über*] of the four world-sectors" (*US*, p. 214). This definition and explication of saying is concise, compressed, and relatively complete, but its exegesis will be difficult and extended. For now, I sketch only the most basic cosmological perspectives involved in saying and their correlations to speaking. In chapter 3, I shall explore the sense in which language as speaking is appropriated, or shown, from language as saying.

Language as Saying

Man is the voice of saying, its speaker, but as noted earlier saying as such is not reducible to its purely human properties. For Heidegger, saying occurs within that world in which entities can be shown as things. The ontological content of this world is differentiated by the fourfold. From one partial perspective, the fourfold is the extralinguistic unity of the four sectors. But from a more complete perspective, the fourfold also serves as the ground for the essence of language, language as saying, in which man (as mortal) and the other three sectors are in reciprocal motion. What are the characteristics of this motion? It must be motion which itself grounds the possibility of discursive events, thereby explaining how it is possible for discourse to refer *to* entities and to be meaningful *for* the mortals who engage in such discourse. Even if the word spoken denotes no sector other than man as mortal (e.g., if the word is "man dwells poetically"), there is still in that word reciprocal movement among all other sectors of the fourfold despite the fact that these sectors remain unnamed. As a result, words which are prima facie about men and nothing else include, at a deep ontological level, connections to each of the other three sectors. The link between these connections and man is achieved by reason of the movement proper to language as saying. Man is part of this movement in that he belongs *(gehört)* to saying as that apparently unique being who can hear *(hört)* what saying says and can say again *(nachasagen)* through speaking *(Sprechen)* the word which names the entity as a thing.[4]

The reciprocal movement proper to saying occurs in alliance with specific conditions. Only when entities interrelate within a spatio-temporal continuum bounded by the sectors of the fourfold is it possible for language to relate man as mortal with all entities referred to by men. This spatio-temporal dimension (foreshadowed by the notion of hint discussed in chapter 1) is made explicit when Heidegger reveals that, for his purposes, another word should be substituted for the term *language (Sprache)*. The word he suggests is a cognate of saying, i.e., *die Sage*. This new word means "saying and what has been said and what is to be said" *(das Sagen und sein Gesagtes und das zu-Sagende—US*, p. 145). The German *Sprache*, as perhaps most or all other words for language, lacks specific reference to those spatio-temporal conditions which must be present to ground the possibility of language. For Heidegger, past and future space-time are essential components for the reciprocity marking the interrelation of the sectors of the fourfold. What will be spoken in future saying is, of course, unknown at present, but its content will be based on continuations of what has been said in the past and what is being said now. Thus, one property necessary to experience language as saying is that space-time which encompasses the past-present-future totality of time, ranging over all entities and all relations between and among entities inasmuch as these entities and their implicit ontological characteristics are capable of being brought to expression through spoken discourse at any given moment within that totality.

We now infer some consequences from this spatio-temporal dimension and their effects on the linguistic apprehension of entities.

First, for Heidegger, many standard grammatical concepts are devoid of this space-time. For example, while verbs are tensed and thus temporally indicative, nouns may denote temporality of some measure but are not themselves temporal. This separation of time from the noun, the "name word," tends to distort the temporal mode of existence of what is named. The sentence "acorns become oaks" includes temporal and spatial considerations with respect to the relation between the being of the acorn and the being of the oak. But given our attitude toward the grammatical timelessness of nouns, these relations are only apparent through the verb. They are invisible with respect to the nouns as such. Even nouns which name entities in terms of time—e.g., baby, teen-ager, year—do so in virtue of discrete segments of the temporal continuum. In the same vein, while gerunds denote activities happening through time—e.g., writing, walking—they do not convey the requisite ontological sense of how the continuum is present as continuum rather than merely as a sort of receptacle containing the activity named by the gerund. The notion of saying implies that names are as denotative of spatio-temporal considerations as the verbs used to activate these names, that nouns and modifiers register at the appropriate ontological level the spatio-temporal relations inherent in things at least to the same extent as the verbs which traditionally have denoted these relations.

Second, the spatio-temporal character of saying has repercussions not only for the mode of existence of what is named but also for the meanings attached to assertions about those modes of existence. Thus, the meaning of what has been spoken in past saying has not been exhausted by the sum total of interpretations of that speaking. A prime example are the writings of the pre-Socratics, whose works

Heidegger has done so much to place in new and ontologically more revealing perspectives. What is unknown about (a) the content of future saying and (b) the meaning of what has been spoken in past saying become vital elements in what *is* known about any occurrences of speaking in saying. Since this double negative component is as important as the positive characteristics of saying, Heidegger names it *the unsaid (das Ungesagte)*. It follows, then, that the unsaid is "no lack and no barrier for saying" (*H*, p. 87).[5] In a sense, the introduction of the concept of knowledge into the notion of saying and its complement is a misnomer, since the unsaid describes a state of affairs which could not be otherwise and which is independent of human cognition as such. The unsaid is not unsaid because of our ignorance, either of what is in past or future time, but because of the necessarily unspoken relations connecting what has and will be said to what is actually being said in present speaking. The unsaid complements and fulfills the spatio-temporal character of language as saying by providing a necessary condition for the continuation of meaningful sentences spoken in virtue of saying. More is involved in the negativity of the unsaid than its relation to meaning, and we shall examine the notion again shortly in connection with Heidegger's difficult discussion of silence and its role in saying and speaking.

To summarize, three properties of saying are now apparent: (1) the presence of a contextual bond uniting all entities within each of the sectors of the fourfold to all other sectors of the fourfold as a whole; (2) the dispositional characteristic which allows the extralinguistic existence of entities in the fourfold to be represented by meaningful language spoken through naming words; (3) the space-time within which all entities are capable of being named so that meanings of sentences referring to these entities include essential connections to this space-time (connections hidden, e.g., in the grammatical concept of noun). Saying becomes the ultimate grounding notion describing that set of conditions which guarantee that extralinguistic entities interlocking in the fourfold can be named and thus reveal their ontological character. This emphasis on the extralinguistic explains at least in part Heidegger's conviction that "if we question language, namely on its essence, then language itself must already be granted to us" (*US*, p. 175). The essence of language is derivable from an experience with the fourfold. But the fourfold includes four sectors populated by extralinguistic entities named and represented in spoken language and realizing the many diverse ends for which language is used by mortals. Therefore, the scope of saying includes both the existence of entities and the stipulation of the conditions whereby relations emerge between entities and the words which name these entities as things. If either the entities, the words, or the relations joining entity to word are lacking, then on Heidegger's principles the determination of the ontological nature of language and beings named by language would be impossible.

Heidegger puts considerable stress on the relational character of language, and his position on the notion of saying may also be summed up from this direction: "Language is, as saying which moves world, the relation of all relations" [*das Verhaltnis aller Verhaltnisses*] (*US*, p. 215). Any derivative linguistic relation not demonstrably open to its roots in saying is tentatively misleading if the relation—regardless of its apparent usefulness in some contexts—continues to conceal these roots. Thus, a reference relation between the name *oak* and the oak tree is not for Heidegger ontologically primordial; there must be relations existing among all possible referential members (of the fourfold) before any one of those relations can be isolated and investigated as *a* reference relation. As a result, language as saying becomes the "relation of all relations," that relation from which all derivative relations draw their linguistic and ontological significance.

LANGUAGE AS SPEAKING

The distinction between saying and speaking was introduced by calling attention to man's place in the actual realization of language. Man defines himself by speaking, but it does not follow that speaking itself can be explained solely in terms of properties derived from the act of human speech. Heidegger insists that the meaning of human speaking rests "in relation to the speaking of language" (*US*, p. 51). And since saying is the basic coordinator of those ontological features inherent in language which Heidegger wishes to make visible, the meaning of human speech will be determined by delineating the sense in which the properties of saying (as outlined above) contribute to language as speaking.

As we have already observed, the distinction between saying and speaking must be crucial, since its formulation will explain, or at least help to explain, the relation between those conditions which ground the possibility of language and the diversification displayed in given instances of speech. But we should not expect the specific

41

properties of speaking to be readily available. After mentioning again the peculiar motion involved in saying, Heidegger affirms that "it remains dark how we should think this essential motion, completely dark in what way this motion speaks, but most dark what then *speaking* means" (*US*, p. 201—italics in original). But Heidegger is positive that saying and speaking are distinguishable: "Saying and speaking are not the same. One can speak, speak endlessly, and all of it says nothing. On the other hand, someone who is silent does not speak and can in this not-speaking say much" (*US*, p. 252).[6] There is an air of paradox surrounding the conjunction of these two texts, since if the meaning of speaking is "dark," then how can Heidegger maintain that saying and speaking are not the same? We must seek some interpretive parameters to remove the paradox, assuming that in principle it can be at least partially resolved.

Heidegger has claimed that (a) one can speak and say nothing and (b) one can speak nothing and say much. Let us assume that the notion of speaking entails sentences or utterances formulated according to traditional guidelines. Given this assumption, one can then presumably speak endlessly and say nothing when the sentences spoken are cut off from the ontological properties of saying, e.g., when the content of such speaking cannot be related to all four sectors of the fourfold. A specific example would be an ordinary-language assertion about an oak tree and its relation to the sources of growth, the earth—in Heidegger's technical terminology, speaking which names an entity and its corresponding fourfold sector. Now, in terms of the intentions of the speaker, there are obvious pragmatic reasons why such an assertion and all assertions of similar type need not contain explicit references to the other sectors of the fourfold. But, for Heidegger, it would be a fundamental mistake to infer that simply because these references are not readily discernible within most spoken linguistic contexts, that such references are not present. Even strictly pragmatic levels of spoken language (as well as aimless chatter) would be impossible unless language as saying provided the basis for this and all other types of individually motivated speech. Since the essential relation between the pragmatic character of most spoken language and its sources in saying is concealed, spoken language as such is opaque to the being of what is named in such language. If instances of spoken language are to serve as suggestive sources of philosophical inquiry, they must always be studied with saying as the necessary linguistic and ontological backdrop.

Saying and Speaking

The force of (a)—that one can speak and say nothing—becomes the warning that although spoken language is certainly adequate for most human purposes, such language may not testify to its ontological roots in language as saying. But the problem of describing speaking as such still remains. Its solution, insofar as a solution is possible, will be found in an analysis of (b)—the claim that men can speak nothing and say much. If, as Heidegger has already asserted, men speak constantly, then how is it possible for them to speak nothing? Several interpretive options appear feasible. One is to transpose the context from language to action, that is, Heidegger is making an implicit appeal to the bromide that "actions speak louder than words" and intends to connect a linguistic event (itself a type of action) to those actions we perform in virtue of what and how we speak. This option cannot be ruled out, but there is an alternative route more compatible with the purely linguistic direction of the previous investigations. To pursue this alternative, we must introduce some important additional concepts.

A suitable point of departure is this difficult text in which Heidegger connects naming with the interplay of speaking and saying: "Every originative and proper naming says the unspoken [*Ungesprochenes*] and in such a way that it remains unspoken" (*WD*, p. 119). Note first the parallel juxtaposing the unspoken and speaking with the unsaid and saying. Clearly this conjunction of complementary opposites is intentional and important. But how then can proper naming be of that which is unspoken, since it seems essential that naming denote something spoken? The answer is embedded in the difficult relation between the unspoken and the spoken. Heidegger writes that "what has been spoken originates in many ways from what is unspoken, whether this be the not-yet-spoken or that which must remain unspoken in the sense that it is withheld from speaking" (*US*, p. 25).[7] It is important to observe how Heidegger places linguistic and ontological priority on the negation of speaking. Speaking originates *from* the unspoken. For Heidegger, the relation between speaking and the unspoken is destroyed if the unspoken is understood as the mere absence of speech. This relation is crucial and will give insight into Heidegger's equally cryptic claim that language as saying "has its origin in silence" (*NI*, p. 471) and the subsequent inference that "authentic saying" is "simply to be silent about silence" (*US*, p. 152).

How does the introduction of negation with respect to both

speaking and saying pertain to a description of speaking as such? We have assumed that speaking implies ordinary discourse in the usual sentential sense. But this assumption has not by itself advanced our grasp of the notion of speaking. I suggest that the key to the notion is to be found in the significance of negation in the parallel notions of the unsaid and the unspoken. Consider first the claim that every instance of proper naming says the unspoken so that it remains unspoken. "Proper" naming is naming in the most fundamental ontological sense. As such, proper naming has no "improper" counterpart on the same ontological level. Naming must be proper to be naming at all. Improper naming is still naming, but naming which disperses or covers up these constitutive relations to the saying which animates the name (through the originative word). Thus, naming must say *(sagt)* because saying grants the possibility of the word; naming merely brings into representation what is capable of being said through the word. But how does naming say the unspoken so that it remains unspoken, when it appears obvious that names *are* spoken in the event of actual discourse?

The notion of the unspoken includes two different types of negative domain. On the one hand, the unspoken is that which has yet to be spoken in the sense of future speaking which is not yet but nonetheless potentially real in contexts of present speech. On the other hand, the unspoken is what will never be spoken because speaking as the linguistic vehicle of representation necessarily lacks the capacity to express, by itself alone, those ontological (or said) aspects and nuances present in the interplay of the fourfold. Consider a conversation as an example of spoken language illustrative of the first sense of the unspoken. The course of a conversation is normally an ongoing ensemble of variations on what has just preceded, with the future content of the conversation always difficult, if not impossible, to predict. Conversations may be interpersonal, familial, scientific, poetic, philosophical—in every case what will be spoken depends in many ways on what has already been spoken. This first phase of the unspoken is relatively straightforward, based as it is on the contingent futural content of spoken language. The second sense is more helpful in articulating the uniqueness of speaking itself.

In this second sense, Heidegger maintains that speaking *never* reveals everything about the being of what is said in language as saying. From the ontological perspective, language as speaking attests to the fact that aspects of language as saying *must* remain unspoken. This limitation in speaking in no way implies a structural imperfection which could somehow be rectified, a lack of perspicacity which could or should be present but is not. We should also observe, perhaps as anticipation of possible pertinent criticism, that the derivative character of speaking and its foundation in saying does not address the fact that differences exist *within* that dimension of language Heidegger has named speaking, differences which may well be philosophically important. Heidegger does not seem interested in detailing these differences. His concern is to provide an ontological basis for the possibility that language of whatever form may speak, mean, and refer. Meticulously cataloging the nuances of ordinary language found in the diverse activities of speaking mortals is not a scheduled stop on his own personal way to the essence of language.

A summary argument for this important epistemic conclusion about speaking may be sketched as follows. Speaking essentially involves the utterance of names. But names are derivative media because of their representational stance with respect to the being of the entity named through the word. The unspoken is itself a name and describes the extent to which men can speak about the being of entities. Now, if names are proper, they will preserve the necessarily unspoken connections between being as represented by the name and the nonrepresentational being of the thing as such. For Heidegger, if names and their coincident epistemology are deemed exhaustive of the being of what is named, then the nature of an authentic name has been misconstrued and the unspoken has ceased to be unspoken, although not in any sense known for that reason. Although approaches to being do exist from the names used to represent the being of entities named, the representational character of these names precludes any linguistically complete apprehension of being as it *is* in these entities.

If speaking originates from the unspoken (and if the above account of the meaning of the unspoken is approximately correct), then the speaking-unspoken relation is dependent on saying as the ground for language and the unsaid as the set of limiting conditions for whatever is expressible through language. From this important conclusion, it is possible to suggest the general differences between saying and speaking. Saying (plus, of course, the unsaid) describes the total ontological conditions requisite for language—the fourfold, its

45

spatio-temporal continuum, the disposition of an entity in the four-fold to become represented in the naming of language. Speaking (and the unspoken) describes the partial epistemic limitations on the extent to which language can divulge the being of the entities named representationally in language. Heidegger illustrates the distinction between saying and speaking when he writes that "not everything said is also something spoken" (*VA*, p. 243). Also, Heidegger's earlier warning that "little is won" by clarifying the distinction between saying and speaking now takes on added significance. For in order to implement the distinction through some traditional conceptual understanding, we must return to precisely those notions about being—in this instance the especially crucial relation between entities and how language represents the being of entities—which distort the revisionist strategy behind Heidegger's own terminology and argumentation. One might object that the insinuation of such nonlinguistic connotations places too great a strain on the meaning of the terms *saying* and *speaking*. But, for Heidegger's purposes, to realize the need for such strain is precisely the point. Only if language is taken back to its roots in being (the notion of saying) and how being is apprehended as the representation of named entities (the notion of speaking) can the relation between language and being become accessible.

Ontological and epistemological positions nearly always shade into one another, as they do here for Heidegger. But an indication of their respective limits is worth attempting in order to detail more precisely what language can reveal about the being of entities named and, by implication, for insight into Heidegger's oblique use of negations as concepts. The latter is important not just to impose some meaning on obscure texts, but to recognize an important perspective on the mode of existence of entities in relation to language. There is no question about the obscurity of the texts, especially those in which Heidegger borders on an almost reverential solicitude for the negative elements suggested by the word *silence*. We have already seen him maintain that authentic saying is simply "to be silent about silence" (on which more shortly). In the present context, Heidegger asserts that "language speaks as the peal [*Geläut*] of stillness" (*US*, P. 30). And the connection between the silence of saying and the stillness of language as speaking is adumbrated as follows: "We name the soundless calling through which saying [*Sage*] sets in motion and collects the world-relation—the peal of stillness" (*US*, p. 215).

Saying and Speaking

We must keep in mind the dominant perspective guiding Heidegger's approach to an experience with the essence of language. This perspective is enunciated in Heidegger's frequently used expression "language speaks" rather than the customary (and, for Heidegger, fundamentally misleading) "man speaks." The essence of language can be attained only from an understanding of the relation between human discourse and the being of its referents and not just from its spoken source, man. Consider now the phrase "the peal of stillness" as exemplifying the speaking of language. The name *stillness* suggests the lack of sound, whether of human or nonhuman origin, as in the stillness of a summer night. How then can there be a peal of stillness, since peal normally refers to the momentary (or longer) sounding of bells, thunder, or laughter? Heidegger provides the clue when he notes that, as a word, *stillness* "is in no way only the soundless" (*US*, p. 29). I suggest then that peal names the *sound* of the spoken relations existing among all named entities within the interplay of saying (*Sage*), and that stillness names the *prelinguistic* mode of existence of all those entities insofar as they are linked together within the limits of saying.

This interpretation of stillness can be both corroborated and expanded by considering Heidegger's related development of rest (*Ruhe*). Heidegger asserts that "rest, properly thought, is not the cessation but the collection [*Versammlung*] of motion" (*SG*, p. 144); also, "rest is a mode [*Art*] of motion; only what is capable of motion can be at rest" (*W*, p. 312). And finally, "rest has its essence in the fact that it stills" (*US*, p. 29.)[8] Rest and motion are correlative concepts representing complementary states of affairs, but Heidegger insists that rest (and its linguistic counterpart, stillness) be construed not just as the abstract absence of motion but as the collection of all entities (or, in fourfold terminology, the interplay of the four world-sectors in complete harmony with one another) with respect to the *onset* of motion. Such a stasis may never occur empirically, but ontologically it must be present in order to guarantee the possibility of motion among whatever sectors of the fourfold are named and spoken. Thus, the significance of rest must be recast into a totality-condition on the same level with the fourfold as such. Heidegger infers that stillness and silence serve as essential counterparts to their complement, spoken language, just as rest is complementary to motion. The dictionary definition of silence is the "absence of any sound or noise; stillness," but Heidegger maintains that such an absence does not imply the nonexistence of sound, or of sound as language that is meaningless or nihilistic. The notions of silence and rest must be understood in conjunction with one another and in complementary relation to their respective opposites. The intended correlation is that stillness (and, in its own way, silence) is to saying and speaking as rest is to motion.

Several of Heidegger's critics have argued that the introduction and emphasis of the words *silence* and *stillness* implies a virulent form of nihilism, a nihilism which for these critics spreads from Heidegger's approach to language to all aspects of his philosophical writings.[9] This interpretation is incorrect, and the principal reason why it is so frequently tendered is because of the failure to recognize the contextual complexities which surround the developments of silence and stillness. As noted, silence is not the mere negation or absence of sound or of meaningful discourse; it names the requisite mode of existence for all entities capable of being spoken about insofar as they exist prior to any actual event of speaking. Thus, the phrase "peal of stillness" juxtaposes the sound of speaking with the fact that the mode of existence of entities with respect to speaking contains only the disposition permitting those entities to be named.

A similar analysis will be helpful for Heidegger's characterization of authentic saying as "simply to be silent about silence."[10] The "to be silent" thus becomes primarily epistemic in tone (as such, in harmony with the general outlines of speaking) and is addressed to the human component in the speaking of language; the "silence" is, again, the prelinguistic condition of all entities in the fourfold (in harmony with the general outlines of saying), prior to the motion whereby the fourfold exists in the representational naming of language. The "to be silent" in no way implies either that men ought not to speak or that speaking is basically meaningless. Its purpose is to emphasize that the relation between language and being can be scrutinized only if we first bracket concrete speaking as such and then examine (in a state of silence, as it were) how beings are established through the actual process of naming representation. The introduction of *silence* as a technical term integrates an aspect of the complete context of a linguistic event which is customarily overlooked, especially in a technological world where the absence of sound is rare. When there is silence, everything is silent, and the eruption of sound by one entity breaks the silence for all entities,

48

thus affecting the sound relationships for all these entities and establishing the possibility that human sound can become meaningful as language. Finally, the paradoxical phrase "simply to be silent about silence" refers to the recognition that the realization of language at the level of human speaking derives from the extent to which man, that mortal who makes linguistic noise, can correlate himself as speaker to the primordial silence of the fourfold in its prelinguistic state.

According to this interpretation, the emphasis Heidegger places on the negative complements of saying and speaking—the unsaid and the unspoken—becomes more comprehensible when these complements are read together with Heidegger's understanding of such notions as stillness and rest. Heidegger needs names for such ontological priority, names which bring out the pliancy and yet the ultimate recalcitrant character of entities insofar as their being can be expressed and revealed through language. There is a crucial transition from entities in that mode of existence exemplified by rest, stillness, and silence to the entry of entities into saying (an entry expressed by the word) and the representational medium of speaking (mediated explicitly by the word as name). To articulate this intimate connection, Heidegger formulates the notions of the unsaid and the unspoken and then places the ontological pressure on these negations rather than, as one would intuitively expect, on their affirmative counterparts. The illumination of being will then be sought from the being of the referent—in Heidegger's terminology, the named entity as prospective thing—rather than from the implications of those semantic and syntactic rules which represent how we picture to ourselves our language about those entities. The emphasis on the negations of saying and speaking is also consonant with Heidegger's tactic of writing about language so that we may have "an experience" with its essence. To grasp the sense of the *un*spoken and the *un*said, we must attend to all that is *other* than both speaking and saying, but at the same time attending to the content of that other *in relation to* the linguistic properties of saying and speaking as outlined by Heidegger. Ignoring this relation will distort the resultant interpretation of their significance—e.g., that they imply or even mean nihilism. Correct interpretation will require us to reconsider language in closer proximity to the being of that which is referred to by the naming proper to speech.

SAYING AND SPEAKING

If the analysis offered above is approximately correct, Heidegger still faces the problem of linking the unique holistic character of saying to the diversity of representational speaking. Both saying and speaking delimit different aspects of the same fundamental relation binding language and being; the problem is to schematize speaking to saying—the Kantian overtone is not entirely inappropriate—so that the actual event of discourse can occur and be open to ontological investigation. Heidegger recognizes the problem of uniting what has been distinguished, and his proposed solution is initiated in the form of a conversation *(Gespräch)* between man as the spokesman of language and language as saying. Thus, "a speaking from language could only be a conversation," so that wherever "the essence of language as saying would address (announce) itself to man it would occasion the authentic conversation" (*US*, p. 150). This conversation is a "saying correspondence" *(sagendes Entsprechen—US*, p. 151) in which the speaking *(Sprechen)* of the correspondence *(Entsprechen)* need be neither "written nor spoken" as long as it "remains coming" *(im Kommen bleibt—US*, p. 152). A conversation, even the Platonic dialogue of the soul with itself, is always relational and involves at least two conversants. For Heidegger, these conversants are distinct but related linguistic domains. Language at the fundamental ontological level of saying funds the representational revealment of beings as they are spoken by men, thereby concealing the being of these named entities through that very revealment. Human speaking is what it is to the extent that it a correspondence with the primordial nature of saying.

As long as the conversation between saying and speaking remains coming, spoken language will attain the ends men intend through such language as well as be open to in-depth ontological investigation. In "what has been spoken speaking does not cease" (*US*, p. 16), that is, speaking keeps coming because of the fundamental connection between what has been spoken and the totality-conditions present in language as saying. But only "in the exhortation [*Zuspruch*] of the naming word" (*US*, p. 110) can this coming be realized. The entity related from saying through speaking must be exhorted before a word is produced which properly names and represents that entity as a thing. This emphasis on exhortation sustains Heidegger's concern that the significance of being as discoverable in representational

50

language is not readily accessible and must be carefully studied if it is to yield ontological truth. In order to prepare for this possibility, Heidegger has been attempting to describe those conditions which stipulate how the essence of language may be experienced. We have seen some of these conditions, but at this point only the more cosmological properties have been discussed. The introduction of such notions as the conversation between saying and speaking and the exhortation which allows a name to represent an entity focuses our attention once more on the need to implement these directives. This attention must return again to man insofar as he is the medium through which language speaks.

In Heidegger's linguistic cosmology, man as speaker of language is beholden to language as saying, that is, the four sectors of the fourfold as circumscribed by their unique spatio-temporal continuum. Only because this ontological framework of relations and entities is maintained in and through language can man speak at all. Heidegger must now indicate how the speaking of language is realized or schematized through its human mouthpiece. We see Heidegger attempting such schematization in the following claims on the role hearing plays in language. Heidegger maintains that "whenever we hear something, there is that hearing, the letting-saying-say-itself [*Sichsagenlassen*] already maintaining all perception and representation" (*US*, p. 255). Whatever speaking does result is, in a sense, "a *prior* hearing" such that "we not only speak the language, we speak *from* it" (*US*, p. 254—italics in text).

As developed here, hearing is on the same ontological level as silence and is more fundamental than what is usually named hearing, the result of aural sensory stimulation. In fact, in this context Heidegger is prepared to assert that such hearing can maintain "all perception and representation."[11] Hearing is not an especially privileged mode of perception from which all other modes of perception take their cue; rather, hearing implies being able to listen to what saying says so that perception (as an essential adjunct to representation) and representation itself (as the principal bearer of conceptual and practical knowledge) can function. Thus, "we do not hear because we have ears. We have ears and are corporeally fitted out with ears because we hear" (*VA*, p. 215). Hearing, as by inference all modes of perception from this perspective, is like speaking and saying in that its ontological roots go much deeper than the physiological media which implement or occasion it.[12] It follows that Heidegger's ontological analysis of perception, as indicated by his treatment of hearing, must be connected to the cosmological analyses more obviously directed at establishing conditions essential for the possibility of language. Meanings will occur only if the perceptions and representations which lead to language—the sound I describe when I hear, the object I describe when I see, the concept derived from my reflection—are spoken as the result of the fundamental saying inherent to the fourfold. We hear and speak (in the technical sense) before we perceive, before we know conceptually or practically, before we act in any capacity. If what is said is not heard in the act of speaking, then there is no possibility that an inquiry into the meaning of what is spoken will accurately depict the being of what is named by that speaking.

This analysis of hearing is incisive as far as it goes, but it is only a relatively small part of a much larger problematic whole. The problem may be set up as follows: If saying describes the limits of language with respect to being, then how is it possible for man as the spokesman of language to move among the sectors of the fourfold, to keep them distinct from one another, yet hear what is there to be heard? How, for example, does the space-time of saying contribute to the conversation whereby things are presented and individuated through human speech? Specification of these cosmological components is crucial for describing how man moves within the fourfold and thus keeps speaking coming from saying. Heidegger names this process of movement the appropriation *(Ereignis)* of language, appropriation which allows "saying to come to speaking" *(US,* p. 260). Appropriation provides the schematization enabling man to speak and activate the concrete relations speaking bears to saying and to being as such. The notion of appropriation is crucial, and our attention now turns to its description and explanation.

3. The Appropriation of Language

A REMARKABLY CONDENSED and initially puzzling assertion occurs toward the conclusion of *Unterwegs zur Sprache*. Heidegger writes that "saying and being [*Sage und Sein*], word and thing belong together in a concealed, hardly considered, and inexpressible manner" (*US*, p. 237). At first reading, this claim seems to border on skepticism. But if so, why has Heidegger exerted such effort to delineate nice distinctions between word and name, entity and thing, saying and speaking? A more fitting response to the claim is not that the problematic "belonging" compels skepticism, but that the indicated connections are so pervasive and so difficult to determine that all the basic notions mentioned must be placed in fresh contexts. Note, for example, the conjunction of thing and being with language as saying and language as word, a constant thematic unity throughout this phase of Heidegger's thought. Any ontological investigation necessarily becomes a linguistic investigation; an adequate ontology must traverse the linguistic modes in which being of whatever sort is expressed. And the relation is symmetrical. An examination of what appear to be linguistic problems must in the last analysis include ontology as it pertains to the being of what is named and represented by language.

The essence of language must be experienced and then disclosed in order to reveal, as far as revelation in language is possible, how being is both illuminated and hidden by that very language which expresses being. But if the analyses already executed are not to become mere conceptual exercises tending toward a skeptical dead end, then Heidegger must provide additional directional pointers schematizing, as it were, what being as such is like. These pointers will bridge the gap between language and being by relationally connecting elements in each domain so that each constitutes the nature of the other while at the same time remaining distinctively linguistic and distinctively ontological.

The later Heidegger accomplishes this end for the linguistic perspective, and for all other perspectives on being, principally through the notion of appropriation *(das Ereignis)*. In general, "what determines time and being in their propriety, i.e., in their association, we name: *appropriation*" (*SD*, p. 20—italics in original). Time is the key factor in this assertion, and considerable attention to the meaning of time will be given in ensuing discussions. In determining the proper relations between time and being, appropriation stipulates those conditions through which "man and being reach one another in their essence" (*US*, p. 102). Although the German name *das Ereignis* typically means event or occurrence, Heidegger specifically repudiates these meanings as oblique to the sense intended. Appropriation is to be understood as a technical term and only in the singular (*ID*, p. 101). Appropriation serves as "*the* law, insofar as it collects and holds mortals in that which is appropriate to their nature" (*US*, p. 259—italics in original). One and only one set of conditions account for the proper realization of relations between man and being.[1] While there may be certain events in history—e.g., the work of Parmenides, Hölderlin, Nietzsche—when the structure and force of appropriation are perhaps more readily discernible, these events are effects and not causes. Appropriation guarantees the possibility of such events; thus, only if the structure of appropriation is out in the open can the ultimate ontological significance of the historical events which it occasions be determined.

The structure of appropriation is present in various types of experience, but one domain is especially privileged: "Language is the most sensitive and therefore the most susceptible oscillation holding everything in the suspended structure of appropriation" (*ID*, p. 102).[2] Thus, language generates both the source material and the solution for the ultimate philosophical problem—how man makes being his own within the limits described by the oscillating relationships between man as mortal and the being of all that is other than mortal. As noted, the formulation of this key assertion suggests that there are other, perhaps less accessible or less obvious, modes of activity through which the mutual appropriation of man and being is accomplished. Heidegger's reticence to introduce these other appropriative modes here (while intimating that such modes do exist) does not mitigate the importance of language as the most vital appropriative mode. Regardless of the content of other appropriative media, the role of language must be recognized as a necessary (if not sufficient) condition for a complete ontology. The problem now is to

54

discern and establish relations of appropriation between the linguistic notions Heidegger has made available and the extralinguistic entities and states of affairs which are named by those notions.

We begin with the connection between saying and appropriation: "Appropriation collects the design [*Aufriss*] of saying and unfolds it into the structure [*Gefüge*] of manifold showing" (*US*, p. 259). The notion of showing (*Zeigen*) now becomes the pivot which controls the possibility of a distinctively linguistic appropriation between man and being—"the essence of language is saying as showing [*die Sage als die Zeige*]" (*US*, p. 254; all in italics).[3] Being is shown through spoken language when entities are named and determined as things. An analysis of showing should account for both ends of the relation between entities and names for entities, thus specifying more closely the necessary ontological conditions for the possibility of a linguistic event. The most important of the discriminating characteristics of showing is the "letting appear" and "giving freely" as a kind of "lighting-concealing" (*erscheinen lassen, lichtend-verbergend freigeben—US*, p. 200). The direction taken by this *giveness* has already been stipulated. It is, for Heidegger, the restoration of the manner in which entities as things exist *in* the flux of a temporality more in tune with being than that temporality presented by the representational character of time. To situate time thus is one of the primary functions of the notion of showing. From the linguistic standpoint, showing will indicate that an entity must be freely given *before* it can assume a referential status in spoken discourse. But exactly what is freely given, how is it given, and in what sense is the result both illuminated and concealed simultaneously?

The structure of showing can be indicated by describing how the relevant extralinguistic factors function against the linguistic background laid out in the previous two chapters. My distinction between linguistic and extralinguistic has been up to now and remains heuristic, since the way in which this distinction should be drawn is precisely the matter at hand. The point, and it bears repeating given the radical character of Heidegger's project, is that an adequate comprehension of the relations between (what we now call) language and (what we now call) entities insofar as they are named through language is possible only if this entire complexus is first approached as a unified whole and then reexamined from the ground up with a minimum of representational bias. We resume this reexamination by describing two primarily extralinguistic domains as they are essential to the showing of saying: (a) space-time as a necessary condition of language and, now, as the medium (a misleading but difficult to displace metaphor)—within which man and being are appropriated; (b) the relation between world as ground and thing as entity emerging from that ground, its determination as thing from that emergence, and the properties of things insofar as these properties determine the thing by being shown through language. (This ordering appears to be the most congenial as far as coherent development is concerned. As noted in the Introduction, Heidegger never lays out these areas in neatly circumscribed discussions. His own mode of exposition is never systematic in any obvious sense; thus, the hierarchical positioning employed here may not be what Heidegger intends. But in lieu of any ordering, the following may serve as a useful guideline in determining some of the essential appropriative relationships between language and being.)

Space-Time

The concept of showing initially implements appropriation by requiring that whatever is shown appear in the "plays of space-time" (*Zeit-Spiel-Räume—US*, p. 258). Since, for Heidegger, the central distortion in Western metaphysics is its failure to acknowledge correctly the presence of time in being, this failure carries over into all that is conceived in relation to time, and this of course includes space. When he writes that "being becomes determined as presence [*Anwesen*] through time" (*SD*, p. 2), he does not intend to restrict the determination of being to temporal considerations, if temporal means time apprehended as completely independent of space. Nor does he want to collapse all distinctions between space and time; his intention is to bring into the open any assumptions underlying such distinctions so that the ontological (i.e., nonrepresentational) character of space-time can be more adequately experienced.

The space-time which grounds showing is, at this point, undifferentiated with respect to the saying and speaking of language. Heidegger attempts to remedy this abstractness in consecutive one-sentence paragraphs joining time and space to saying:

> Of time, it can be said [*sagen*]—time temporalizes.
> Of space, it can be said [*sagen*]—space spatializes. [*US*, p. 213]

Heidegger plays on the etymological proximity between subject and

56

verb to emphasize that the space-time of "time temporalizes" *(Zeit zeitigt)* and "space spatializes" *(Raum räumt)* is not equivalent to an objectively measurable time and space but is a space-time through which language can show being. This interrelation between space-time and saying is essential to the ontological character of each. Entities are capable of being named as things, thereby realizing their incipient relation to being, only if a space-time grounds that which is freely given as this determinate thing. Every event of spoken language exists in virtue of this requisite spatio-temporal dimension. And as we shall see, some instances of spoken language (especially in poetry) are themselves amenable to analyses, or illuminations, through which the properties of this space-time are more readily apparent than in more representationally bound discourse.

The burden is on Heidegger to describe how such temporality is possible.[4] He begins by discerning a primordial "simultaneity" *(Gleich-Zeitige)* which is coextensive with the limits of language as saying. The "times" which are "alike" in this simultaneity are "what has been," "the present," and the "present which waits toward us and is usually named the future" *(US*, p. 213). Space-time in its totality now names that openness which is located in the "interpenetration [*Einander-sich-reichen*] of future, past, and present" *(SD*, pp. 14–15). In such simultaneity, time remains "still" with respect to itself and with respect to the dispositional character of entities to be named. An event of spoken language breaks the stillness and thrusts entities into their reality as things. Time "moves" *(be-wëgt)* man and all other entities through such simultaneity by "granting" (*einräumt*—the pun on *Raum*, space, is lost in translation) that space-time which ensures the possibility that spoken language may establish entities as things in the act of naming those entities.[5] Every linguistic event is derivative from saying and its primordial space-time, not (for time) in the grammatical sense in which verbs are tensed according to a discrete past-present-future temporality, but insofar as appropriation makes such temporal distinctions possible in the first place.

The principal purpose of this assertion is not difficult to determine. Space-time grounds the appropriation of language through a comprehensive presence *(Anwesen)* which plays into all those reaches of time representationally cast as the past, the present, the future. Since Heidegger is convinced that presence includes the past and the future in this sense, his strategy is to rethink time so that both past and future may be apprehended as a kind of present. But he also wants to preserve the distinctive characteristics of pastness and futurity with respect to our experience of an ever-flowing present now. This preservation of difference in sameness is, of course, the core of the problem. My remarks here will concentrate on that aspect of presence which is applicable to the meaning of utterances spoken in past and present time.

For Heidegger, the limit of the past insofar as it is present (*gegenwärtig*) in presence is the epoch of the Greeks, in particular the pre-Socratic Greeks. The notion of *logos*, so crucial to the Greek language and to Greek thinking, contains in its myriad of meanings the paradigm for all thinking and all language—"the Greek language, and it alone, is *logos*" (*WP*, p. 12). Only from an understanding of the word *logos* and its properties is it possible to experience the assembly of being: "Being is collection [Versammlung]—*logos*" (*WP*, p. 13). *Logos* "names that wherein the presence of that which is present is appropriated" (*VA*, p. 227). The entire history of language, if understood in its proper ontological setting, is contained in *legein*, the verbal infinitive of *logos*, insofar as it "unfolds early and in every unhidden and fulfilled way as saying and discourse" (*VA*, p. 212). Finally, "for the Greeks, saying is: 'to make open, to let appear, namely the appearing and the essence (of things)' " (*WD*, p. 6).[6] To determine the ontological significance of what is spoken in virtue of such saying is the goal of Heidegger's own investigations into language.

Heidegger never directly considers whether the pastness of presence depends on any non-Hellenic factors. From a purely historical perspective, there is little doubt that this unsupported preference for the Greeks and their language is biased. But for our purposes the question is whether such a bias damages the argument. Do the non-Greek eras have a significant effect on the history of Western language as that language grew out of the Greek experience, especially in terms of that space-time which grounds meanings and which allows utterances occurring in the past to continue as meaningful into the present? Since Heidegger has asserted that being is *logos* and that *logos* is the Greek language, it follows, apparently, that any experience not expressed or expressible in the Greek language or in a language derived from Greek is either impossible ontologically or irrelevant to being. This is surely an assumption of considerable magnitude. Let us grant for now that it is at least trustworthy, if not true, since there are other difficulties even if this assumption is basically sound.

How, for example, is the Greek past as past still present in the presence of space-time? Let me sketch an argument to render Heidegger's position more comprehensible. All linguistic events are historical in the sense that their occurrence takes place in time. Not all utterances are meaningful, but most utterances display meanings of a sort. Frequently these meanings are crucial in guiding the destinies of men, thinkers, and nations. In some cases, therefore, the meanings of utterances endure as meaningful beyond the historical context surrounding their original utterance. How then is it possible for meanings to perdure in this manner? The ground for the possibility of such a phenomenon is a necessary condition for meaningful language to exist *through* the passage of time. Now, it is evident that any past linguistic event always retains the possibility of entering into and affecting the present and the future. But this possibility can be realized only if such linguistic movement is grounded in the movement of time itself. Time itself must possess this omnipresent characteristic—the interpenetration of past-present-future as a continuous presence—before past linguistic events can persist as meaningful beyond their actual occurrence into the present and the future. Such must be the nature of space-time if the occurrence of linguistic events can endure beyond the immediate moment of the utterance of such events.

The crucial character of the Greek experience may now be situated within this conception of space-time. First, note that the adequacy of the Greek attitudes toward being is beside the point. Regardless whether what the Greeks said and wrote is true or false, the Greek experience served (for Heidegger) as the origin of Western metaphysics and thereby defined the contours of Western thinking about being and the actions taken on the basis of that thinking. Also, whether or not an account of being as we currently apprehend it corresponds with any of the Greek views is irrelevant. Any account of being, by the mere fact that it is meaningful, is structured by the presence of the Greek past in our present, regardless whether or not this source is explicitly considered in that account.

To accept this conclusion does not imply that contemporary philosophy should express itself with the gnomic inscrutability of such utterances as Heraclitus's "Fire steers all things." But acceptance does imply that our understanding of language should include the linguistic modes through which the Greeks construed their world, a difficult task for the modern thinker in view of the pressure of Western history. The history of Western philosophy has been a history of forgetfulness, beginning with the Romans: "Roman thinking took over Greek terms [*Wörter*] without the corresponding fundamental Greek experience of that which these terms said [*sagen*], without the Greek word" (*H*, p. 13). The interim epochs separating our epoch from the Romans increase the difficulty of resurrecting the fundamentally essential character of that defining Greek experience. All students of language recognize the pivotal role played by the Greek language in the formation of the technical vocabulary of Western thought. But Heidegger contends that not only our linguistic representations *for* being but also our very perception *of* being have been molded by the Greek mind and language. To reexperience things in the Greek manner and then do the requisite thinking beyond the Greek experience will obviously be difficult;[7] as a minimal prerequisite, Heidegger insists that we recognize how space-time as presence contributes to the possibility of meaning. In this way, the language of perception and representation, and by implication the language of being itself, will be educated. Philosophy as a thoughtful endeavor will then return to the Greeks in the only sense in which a return is possible, essential, and fruitful.

Given this transhistorical interpenetration of past, present, and future, the space-time of presence is such that parameters for locating entities in their distinctive spatio-temporal locations must be stipulated. And if presence is space-time other than space and time representationally measured, it follows that its measurement of entities will be different as well. Heidegger specifies this otherness with his introduction of the "near" (*Nahe*) and the "remote" (*Ferne*) as a type of spatio-temporal coordinate. The terms *near* and *remote* are also used in technical senses in early Heidegger, although in a more restricted context. We read in *Sein und Zeit* that "what is ontically nearest [*Nächste*] and known is ontologically most remote [*Fernste*], unknown, and in its onotological significance continually overlooked" (*SZ*, p. 43).[8] Ontic knowledge, that which pertains to a given being (*Seiende*), is nearest, while ontological knowledge, that which pertains to being as such (*Sein*), is most remote. When we know something of the being of beings, that very ontic mode of knowledge erects distance between being in its ontic dimension and the fullness of being, its presence. Given the *Sein und Zeit* context,

60

with its epistemic emphasis, we might interpret the names *near* and *remote* as primarily metaphorical in nature, that is, with no direct import on near and remote understood as relative spatio-temporal pointers. After all, the reason why ontic knowledge covers up ontological knowledge need not have anything to do with the proximity or distance of that which is known ontically. But this metaphorical sense, if indeed it was such in *Sein und Zeit*, is explicitly transformed in the later works into an explanatory framework to delimit the pervasiveness of presence.

Heidegger carefully distinguishes the near and the remote from any theory of space or time which provides the "stuff" for the representational measurement of distinct magnitudes, their *"Parameter-charakter"* in Heidegger's terminology. He first suggests that the near and the remote are completely disassociated from space and time apprehended as parameters: "The essence of nearness is outside and independent of space and time" (*US*, p. 210). But he adds immediately that this restriction is "overly hasty" and concludes with the reservation that nearness does not "depend" *(beruht)* on space and time as the latter "appear" *(erscheinen)* as parameters (*US*, p. 210). Space-time as a parametric is space-time in which entities can be representationally measured according to some objective standard of relative size and duration. But, for Heidegger, such measurement does not exhaust the modes in which space-time contributes to the being of the entities measured, especially insofar as their being is constituted by the naming word.

The central objection to space-time as parametric is the closing off of the present, the *now* from its source in the past and its projection into the future. Thus, "in the sequence of succession, the now [*der Jetzt*] as the element of parametric time is never a now open as facing another now" (*US*, p. 212). Each now (as each *here*) exists parametrically as a moment continuously vanishing into itself, especially when employed in the process of representational measurement. Such static reflexivity makes it impossible to discern the spreading out of the now as presence from past through present into future. The now (and the here) are necessary as the experienced ground for temporal and spatial measurements—from this here I may determine the distance to my destination. Heidegger does not question the propriety and usefulness of such designations. His point is that their usefulness as ground for parametric measurement does not imply that an ontological space-time must be limited to such parameters simply on account of the practical pervasiveness of such measurement in science and in daily life.

But near and remote are relative terms. How then to specify limits so that they may serve ontological ends while preserving their relativity as names within the sphere of a distinct past-present-future? Unless "with respect to" is added to any occurrence of near and remote, the terms remain indeterminate. For Heidegger, such stipulative conditions are met only when that totality named *world* *(Welt)* grounds the spatio-temporal determination of any one entity as a thing within that totality: "The motion of reciprocity [*Gegeneinander-über*] in the world-*Geviert* appropriates nearness, *is* nearness as nighness" *(US,* p. 214—italics in text). An entity is "nigh" (the archaic English matches Heidegger's archaic German) when nearness guarantees the presence of relations from that entity to the other sectors of the fourfold. In fact, such relations must be present in order for the entity to become a thing *(Ding)*. But the nearness of the relations is not sufficient to constitute the transformation from entity to thing. When an entity is shown to be a thing, "showing brings what is shown near and yet keeps it remote" *(EH,* p. 147). Dialectical tension is and must be present between the near and the remote, tension which must be experienced as tension in order to preserve the proper apprehension of the being of the thing. The collection and description of relations near an entity necessarily exclude some possible relations within the world totality. These relations are remote from the entity, yet they are part of being and, as such, indirectly but essentially related to the determination of the being of the given entity. Since there must be a distinction between part (thing) and whole (world) in order for the thing to be *this* thing, that which is shown must maintain both the nearness of the constitutive relations and the remoteness of the nonconstitutive but still present relations.

Even if this usage of near and remote is coherent and thus an effective blunting instrument against the fine discriminating edges of parametric space-time, how does nearness contribute to the constitution of this particular thing as *this thing*? Heidegger admits that such questions are in principle difficult to resolve because "the way to nearness is . . . the widest and therefore the most difficult" *(SG,* p. 16). The way to nearness is the widest because it includes "our usual representing" *(VA,* p. 280) and the traditional linguistic formulas associated with the expression of these representations. Our apprehension of entities with respect to being is near because of the representative character of that apprehension. Our lives are lived amid the continuity of representation. But the more the nearness of representative knowledge is scrutinized as ontologically constitutive, the farther our apprehension of being as such becomes. Thus, when "we intend nearness, remoteness announces itself" (*US*, p. 209). We always exist in that which is near, but as soon as this nearness is intended, i.e., brought to consciousness through representation, then the nearness fades into remoteness along with the nature of whatever appeared near. Heidegger will then require us to examine the nearness of a certain type of language in order to break away from the hold of representational language and to gather hints from this language in order to experience entities as things. The language which serves this end is the language of poetry.

WORLD-THING

The correlative notions of near and remote are dependent upon space-time, a continuing presence which guarantees that meanings can transcend their spoken origin and penetrate into past and future. The near and the remote are the coordinating axes of that spatio-temporal continuum in which entities are named and shown as things. But the being of entities is as much extralinguistic as linguistic, at least from an ontic or representational standpoint. The next step, then, is to describe how the space-time of the near and the remote plays into the naming of entities as things within the world *(Welt)*, a unifying totality with both linguistic and extralinguistic properties.

We may approach the Heideggerian notion of world by reflecting on a notion from another philosophical tradition. For many contemporary philosophers, an assertion is in principle meaningless until the context within which the assertion occurs is described (e.g., P. F. Strawson's use of context in "On Referring"). But what is the connection between different contexts as contexts? In fact, what makes a context a context in the first place? How can we determine what to include in the description of a context unless we can specify the relation between what appears relevant to that context and what does not appear relevant to that context? The notion of a context includes some indication of what is referred to by the assertion spoken from within that context. And what is referred to by the assertion are usually extralinguistic entities. Thus, a context not only enumerates the entities but also in the very process of enumerating indicates something about their mode of existence. If the stipulation or description of a context does not contain such ontological data, then the appeal to a context implicitly allows the extralinguistic existence of entities to have no bearing on the meaning derived from the assertion and the context. And surely such liberties are premature. How can we know a priori that the unspecified ontological details of a context are neutral to conclusions about the meanings of assertions emerging from these contexts? At this point, the notion of context breaks down, not as a neutral container of entities (for which purpose of the notion serves perfectly well), but insofar as the mere enumeration of these entities may assume relevant features of these entities with respect to the meaning of assertions about those entities.

Heidegger's development of the notion of world has the heuristic advantage of pointing directly to those conditions which must obtain if a context (in the contemporary Anglo-American sense) can be delimited without ontological distortion. We must first think the relation between world and thing as a unity. But Heidegger tells us that world and thing are not merely "coupled" to one another, rather they "penetrate" (*US*, p. 24) one another to the extent that they may be described as "thing-world and world-thing" (*US*, p. 28). But how does each become appropriated uniquely and yet bear necessary relations to its complement? Heidegger offers a name for the interpenetration of world and thing—the "between" (*das Zwischen—US*, p. 24).[9] This interpenetration is not "coalescence" (*Verschmelzung*) but an "inwardness" (*Innige*) within which world and thing each "separates itself purely and remains separated." World as world and thing as thing are retained in the unity of world-thing, yet each comes to its own nature through the separation and unification circumscribed by the between. The name *between* focuses attention on the mediating gap between the two end points of the world-thing relation. But merely naming what is between as *the between* is not by itself very informative. Heidegger thus develops the between as the "difference"—"the intimacy of world and thing realizes itself in the separation of the between, realizes itself in the difference [*Unter-Schied*]" (*US*, p. 25). This difference "lets the thinghood [*Dingen*] of things rest in the worldhood [*Welten*] of world" (*US*, p. 29).

The fundamental ontological difference between being and beings has now been transformed into the equally fundamental difference between world and thing. Heidegger writes *difference* as "*Unter-Schied*" to emphasize that which stands "among-[the]-separated." He then indicates the process in which world and thing are set in motion toward each other, thus establishing one thing (among other things) and separating any thing as part from the world as whole: "The difference for world and thing *appropriates* things in the gestating of world, *appropriates* world in the granting of things" (*US*, p. 25— italics in original). The original between is now a difference which is itself neither distinction nor relation but is, ultimately, the dimension *(die Dimension)* through which world and thing are considered in their own properties. Heidegger's rejection of the names *distinction* and *relation* is an attempt to transpose what these names generally represent into a schematic of appropriation which refers, initially, to the spatio-temporal character implicit in language as saying. The experiential blandness and neutrality in typical metaphysical distinctions and relations precludes these essential spatio-temporal considerations. The Heideggerian difference is the dimension within which are manifested the basic properties of both world and thing as realized through spatio-temporal qualities, qualities which the very name *dimension* suggests. The problem now is to erect guidelines so that these properties become mere determinate.

The notions of gestating *(Gebärden)* and granting *(Gönnen)* are the principal clues offered to explain how appropriation establishes the difference between world and thing. The thing is gestated by world, and world is only world when a thing is granted from it. To approach an understanding of how world can gestate things, we must first have some idea of the nature of world. Heidegger clearly affirms what world is not: it is not world as defined by any traditional metaphysical concept, neither as a universe of nature and history as secularly represented or as a theologically oriented *mundus*, or even as cosmos, the whole set of present entities (*US*, pp. 23–24). World initiates the process of gestating things insofar as it is the "single fundamental collecting in itself of what bears against and what bears towards" (*US*, p. 108), where the phrase "what bears against and what bears towards" names the interplay of the four sectors of the fourfold (*US*, p. 22).[10] To ask what distinguishes one world of language use from another such world (e.g., the world of ordinary language from the world of scientific language) is to misunderstand Heidegger's deployment of the term *world*. For Heidegger, the relevant ontological question is directed toward that totality which allows us to distinguish our language into different domains of use in the first place. Heidegger's world is such that it cannot itself be partitioned into subordinate or possible worlds, but is rather that world in virtue of which all other linguistic worlds are possible. This world is "more real [*seiender*] than the palpable and perceptible" world in which "we believe ourselves at home" (*H*, p. 33). The burden is on us to peer beyond the perceptible and name the being of things as they emerge by gestating from world as totality and as differentiated by the fourfold.

World gestates things in virtue of focusing its four sectors into a coordinated interplay.[11] How then is the emergence and constitution of the thing a granting or bestowal? First, that "ground character of thing, i.e., that essential determination of the thinghood of things as a 'this one,' is grounded in the essence of space and time" (*FD*, p. 12). But this space-time cannot be the parametric space-time of measurement and perception; only the "collecting which lets the thinghood of things linger" (*US*, p. 22) in space-time as presence will guarantee that things can achieve their proper mode of existence. Second, all things collect relations to the world as fourfold, and they do so through the modes in which the entity (as potential thing) receives the four sectors and reflects them back to the gestating totality. These modes originate in our perceptions and their conceptual representations, but the thing as such cannot be reduced to the enumeration of properties visible in light of these derivative media. Each entity as thing grants its particularity to the totality of world, preserving itself as different from world yet reflecting qua thing its participation in that totality. And each thing possesses properties from its place in the total appropriative dimension connecting thing and world.

Two of these properties are plainness and simplicity (*US*, p. 259). These two properties focus attention on how appropriation allows language to enunciate the presence of entities as things with regard to the attitudes normally taken toward entities as perceived and represented in metaphysics. "Plainness" translates the German *Unscheinbaren*, but a closer English equivalent may be "dullness," since the prefix "*Un*" negates the "shining" of "*-scheinbar*." At any rate, Heidegger does not intend plainness to refer to an entity insofar as it is not as shiny as it could be (e.g., an unwaxed car), but rather to the appearance of an entity as that entity immediately strikes the perceiver. The noonday sun is plain in this sense. Although it shines

66

with such intensity that even the briefest glance at its appearance is impossible, that very appearance prior to being named and spoken in language is just as plain as the drab tree outside my window in wintertime. Plainness is that aspect of appropriation which guarantees that the perceptual appearance of an entity never compels any necessary linguistic representation. Plainness allows the entity to move from its extralinguistic mode of existence to that of thinghood spoken through the interplay of relations joining the entity to the fourfold. This does not mean that plainness cannot involve the most florid descriptive speech. A description of an entity can be florid only if language approaches that entity through an aspect of appropriation which establishes that entity as plain, i.e., as a thing susceptible to the presence of the fourfold. If this condition was unsatisfied, the description of the entity as florid, bleak, lacklustre, inapt, would never be recognized in the first place.

Simplicity *(Einfachen)* also does not pertain to the style of descriptive language, but to another aspect of that appropriation which allows an entity to become a thing through the naming words of spoken language. An entity is simple (prior to being spoken about in language) if it manifests the unified (recall the *"Ein"* of *"Einfachen")* fourfold as world.[12] Such simplicity allows an entity to collect and unify as thing the four sectors of the fourfold. Simplicity does not refer to the structure of the named entity's physical or chemical components, which even in such "simple" entities as bread is extremely complex, but refers to the possibility that the entity can be invested with a naming word and appropriated as a thing. Nor does it follow that the connection between naming word and world is simple in the sense of easy to discern. Thus, a poetic use of the name *Brot* might readily assume its simple dictionary meaning, but from this meaning lead into the potentially complicated symbolic universe of the poem in which that name is employed. Simplicity is that property of appropriation which guarantees that the entity can become, as a referent, a unified single thing within the totality of world. Plainness is that property of appropriation which guarantees that the entity is open to all forms of linguistic description and thereby to all sectors of the fourfold, regardless of the entity's immediate perceptual exterior and the ingrained metaphysical tendency to describe and represent that exterior in a certain self-evident manner. Together the two properties are emblematic of the processes appropriation must engender if spoken language is to name entities and determine them as things.

The Appropriation of Language

Appropriation establishes ontological conditions which control the occurrence of linguistic events. These conditions must be stipulated in order to ensure that an experience with the essence of language is possible. To achieve this end, Heidegger's argumentation must be situated on a broad cosmological level. Only when consideration has been directed at the whole can the distinctively linguistic part be understood in its complete ontological setting. In a sense, this cosmology has dealt with a series of betweens, those concealed mediating connections between entities as traditionally represented and things as related to presence. Such investigations have been necessary to disclose hidden aspects in these relations, aspects which must be scrutinized before the possibility of apprehending the essence of language can be actualized. We conclude by outlining those aspects insofar as they have been articulated by the notion of appropriation.

1. All language begins from silence *(Schweigen)*. Therefore, the appropriation of language must indicate the movement between the totality of entities existing extralinguistically, or *in* silence, and the introduction of these entities as referents into meaningful language: "Silence corresponds [*entspricht*] to the soundless peal of stillness, of saying as appropriating-showing [*ereignend-zeigenden Sage*]" (*US*, p. 262). Heidegger joins appropriation and showing to emphasize the relation connecting each to the other as well as the implemental role played by this conjunction in actualizing through speech the saying *(Sage)* which grounds all language. At this level, there is nothing but stillness, the absence of all sound including that of speech. But stillness must be ontologically present in order for saying to collect within the movement of the four world-sectors everything in the nearness and absence of sound (*US*, p. 215). The space-time proper to the fourfold and to saying contributes essentially to this requirement by connecting all sectors of the fourfold within a total spatio-temporal continuum. The presence of these sectors constitutes the atmosphere of nearness surrounding all entities, although in the contemporary epoch apprehension of this presence is remote in virtue of the static conceptual and representational apprehension which determines the being of these entities.

2. From this cosmological silence, language originates with the onset

68

of the word: "The word signifies something, i.e., shows [*zeigend*] it lingering in the extent of its capability to be said" (*G*, p. 44). At the moment when entity is joined to word, the word becomes realized as a linguistic element, a term with significance, communicative power, and the possibility of public usefulness. But the term is a word only if its denotation exists in relation to the totality of the spatio-temporal continuum and the differentiating sectors of that continuum, the fourfold. An entity, if shown in this linguistic sense, *lingers* in this continuum and exists ontologically as a thing in virtue of this primordial oscillation. The thing as constituted by a word naming that thing always lingers in the possibility of extending its being from a present occurrence of that word back into the past and forward into the future.

3. The ontological dimensions proper to the word are channeled into the representational dimension proper to the word as name: "Naming is that which allows what is shown to be experienced" (*EH*, p. 188). Whenever we name, "we bid [*heissen*] that which is in presence [*das Anwesende*] to come" (*WD*, p. 85). The name bids the entity to come from its participation in presence into the present of representational experience. The name *represents* the entity, thus guaranteeing its position as a possible referent, and also *presents* the entity as a thing by stabilizing its oscillations within the spatio-temporal motion of the fourfold. The differences between world and thing are unified *in* each named entity, although the pragmatic concerns of living speech conceal this crucial ontological feature of language.

4. When we speak, we do so through names. Names function by bidding the entity to *be* within a coordinated whole. This quality of being is possible only on condition that the thing be specified as this thing within the interplay of the difference between the thing as part and the world as whole. Thus, "naming calls," and in the process of calling, naming "brings the presence of the as yet uncalled into a nearness" (*US*, p. 21).[13] Sometimes calling has a specific object, as when I call my father; sometimes calling lacks such specificity, as when I call for help when lost in a forest. Both senses are integral to the appropriative role played by the name when it calls. The mere bidding of an entity to become a named thing does not imply that such bidding will be realized, just as calling (in the usual sense) may or may not be successful. The fluidity inherent in calling thus matches that of the word and its

oscillation in the space-time of saying. Once this fluidity has been stabilized and determined by the spoken name, the entity can emerge as thing.

5. The nearness into which the called is bidden is comprised of the relations joining this entity to the various sectors of the fourfold. This nearness may be described as a "mirror-play of world" (*Spiegel-Spiels der Welt*—VA, p. 180), where the mirror is the thing insofar as it, the thing, collects the world-sectors as a totality within itself as thing and where the play is the interaction of these sectors within the continuum of space-time as presence. As a result, "what a thing becomes is appropriated from the circumscription [*Gering*] of the mirror-play of world" (VA, p. 180). The possibility that human, that is, mortal speaking can name this entity is a necessary condition in order for that entity to become a thing. And the sufficient condition for this process obtains only when the entity exhibits relations to all four sectors of the fourfold. The process as a whole may thus be described as a circumscription, a reciprocal movement from world to thing and around the four sectors of the fourfold. The difference between world and thing is preserved in the delicate interplay between named entity as granting thing and the gestating world which grounds the being of that thing. The delicacy of this preservation is often lost because of the obdurate quality of concepts derived from the thing in its entitative and representational guise. The thing than maintains its status as thing when its images or reflections of world become plainly and simply visible in linguistic hints for those speakers able to discern the presence of these hints.

6. Appropriation establishes the possibility that linguistic events can occur, but appropriation does not guarantee that everything which can be spoken will be spoken: "What must remain unspoken, what is held back in the unsaid, lingers as the unshowable [*Unzeigbares*] in that which is hidden, and is mystery [*Geheimnis*]" (US, p. 253). The word *mystery* occurs more than once in Heidegger's thought, but his use of it is always judicious. Here, the reference to mystery concerns that fact that in the interplay of world and thing certain phases of that play must remain unspoken. This lack is essential to appropriation, given the lighting-concealing factor present whenever language shows and determines entities to be things. The spoken name enlightens the entity named by showing it to be a thing. In that enlightenment, some of

the relations between the entity and the fourfold are disclosed. But the remaining possible relations are hidden by the very disclosure of those relations which provide the enlightenment. These relations are "held back in the unsaid"; they remain unspoken, residing dormant in "the mystery of the word" (*US*, p. 233). It follows that the meaning of what is said is always in principle incomplete in both ontic and ontological dimensions, i.e., in name and in word. Any meaning is the result of a process, an evocation of a set of relations limiting the incursion of the remaining unsaid relations. Thus, there is always more to be said about any entity, regardless of the extent to which that entity is subjected to linguistic investigation. *Mystery* is Heidegger's technical name for the pressure exerted on what is spoken by these silent but ontologically present relations. Any mystery, once recognized as such, beckons to be clarified, perhaps to the point of resolution, just as our language continuously attempts to clarify our experience of the world toward some omega point of perfect correspondence with that world. But, according to Heidegger, such correspondence will never occur because it *can* never occur. The desire to reach such a point and the reasons why it cannot be attained are, for Heidegger, a mystery inherent in the processes in which language is appropriated.

We conclude part 1, the investigation of the basic structures of language, with this summary observation.[14] There is, as it were, continuous conversation between word and name, saying and speaking, world and thing, the near and the remote; all such conversation occurs within the boundaries of presence and the four sectors of the fourfold. But this conversation as spoken in representational discourse begins to hesitate at the point where language as the lighting-concealing naming of entities confronts the proper being of entities as things. During the history of metaphysics, the being of entities has been enlightened in some important respects. But, for Heidegger, that which has been concealed in this linguistic light has become concealed to the extent that it becomes questionable whether contemporary thinkers can even recognize its problematic nature. This concealment is dependent on the temporality of being, the way in which entities as things are made determinate in and through their relations to time. Chapters 1 through 3, culminating in the doctrine of the appropriation of language, represent the intricate structure of

71

Heidegger's challenge to the supremacy of the history of metaphysical thought as that thought became crystalized around a certain conception of language. Once this conception of language has been broken down and its preconceptions made explicit, then Heidegger is prepared to listen to another kind of language about the being of entities than that provided by metaphysics. With the hints spoken by this other language, he will advance further on the way to a more appropriate linguistic apprehension of the temporality of things and therefore to a disclosure of being as it truly is. The language that speaks these hints is the language of poetry.

PART 2

The Illuminations of Poetic Language

4. Poetizing and Man

POETIZING

With the appropriation of language, Heidegger has summarized the conditions required for the possibility of undergoing an experience with the essence of language. The structure of these conditions results, as we have seen, in a cosmology with a distinctively linguistic orientation. But stipulating how language and being are proper to each other in this abstract sense is only part of Heidegger's project with language. The next phase, equally crucial, is the examination of language which has already been spoken to determine how such language may contribute to a more adequate articulation of beings and their relation to being.

All spoken language is based on language as saying. And, for Heidegger, the two most fundamental types of saying are poetizing and thinking (*US*, p. 199). Although Heidegger never directly argues the point, presumably any other type of discourse is subservient to poetizing and thinking in that the latter are always more ontologically revealing. Now, when language speaks through the word and its fundamental relation to these two types of saying, then "the word speaks only in association with the meaning in which the matter named by it unfolds through the history of thinking and poetizing" (*VA*, pp. 48–49). By the history of thinking and poetizing, Heidegger does not refer to the serial chronology of works in the domains of philosophy and literature, but to the temporality of presence as shown in the meaning of a given thoughtful or poetized word. Not all poetry or thought is historical in this fundamental ontological sense, and Heidegger provides a criterion of sorts for their recognition when he maintains that every occurrence of authentic language is, "through the motion of saying assigned to men, fit [*geschickt*], therefore fateful [*geschicktlich*]" (*US*, p. 264). Thus, a fateful linguistic event is one which has repercussions throughout the continuum of presence and within the four sectors of the fourfold, especially that mortal sector which grounds human being. Given the enormous quantity of poetry and philosophy, we should wonder whether a

75

standard controls which instances of poetry and thought are fateful and which merely fugitive. Heidegger does not say, at least not directly.[1] But the absence of such a standard need not, by itself, mitigate the importance of the insights Heidegger will develop with the poetized language he considers fateful.

Heidegger's notion of poetizing includes poetry as a type of literary language, but the scope of poetizing itself is not restricted to literature. Poetizing is Heidegger's name for a certain ontological condition which includes language as saying, the being of what is spoken in that saying, and the differentiations proper to presence and the fourfold. Although poetry (i.e., literature) is the result of poetizing, poetizing need not necessarily produce odes and sonnets.[2] For example, one could exist poetically without being a poet, assuming that normative guidelines for action could be derived from the totality-perspective proper to the language of poetizing. I mention this as a possible avenue for exploration as well as to explicate the technical meaning of *Dichten*. For our purposes, however, determining the properly linguistic aspect of poetizing will be of sufficient difficulty.

Poetizing is "pure speaking" (*US*, p. 16), and its purity consists primarily in the fact that in it "the visibility of the fourfold is first brought into appearance" ("SH," p. 193). Poetizing makes the four sectors of the fourfold more visible in the sense that the distinct presence of the interrelations of the fourfold become more evident than they do through philosophical or metaphysical thinking. The language of poetizing thus provides a vital corrective set of perspectives on the limits of representational thinking. This is why it is "necessary" that there be a "conversation" *(Zwiesprache)* between thinking and poetizing (*US*, p. 38).[3] Although both thinking and poetizing are modes of saying and therefore share in the appropriative structure of language, the two types of language are distinct, as Heidegger forthrightly states: "What has been said by poetizing and what has been said by thinking are never the same" (*WD*, pp. 8–9). I wish to postpone detailed consideration of the differences between poetizing and thinking until chapter 7. At that time, I shall attempt to relate representational thinking with thinking as *Denken*, that mode of thought which shares primacy with poetizing.

For now, let us begin to analyze Heidegger's belief that poetizing will elucidate and at least partially rectify the distortion wrought on the being of entities by metaphysical and representational thought.

Poetizing and Man

How does poetizing accomplish this purpose? My interpretation of this remedial function of poetizing is based on Heidegger's two fundamental names for being—presence and the fourfold. Fateful poetized language will name entities or properties of entities from each sector of the fourfold. Such naming will show, in the technical sense of appropriation, relations between the sector grounding that entity and the remaining sectors. The result will be the disclosure of both the being of what is named and the being of that which is related to what is named. It should be stressed at the outset that the actual texts of Heidegger's illuminations[4] do not follow the differentiations of the fourfold in a mechanical or even systematic manner. But if these illuminations are approached and analyzed with the demarcations of the fourfold as guides, the sense of these illuminations becomes intrinsically more evident and more applicable to the problem of thinking the being of entities as things. Thus, even if my interpretation is incorrect as far as the constitutive function of the fourfold is concerned, it retains the important heuristic advantage of ordering the considerable diversity and range of Heidegger's illuminations.

The fourfold has four sectors, but Heidegger offers no clue as to which, if any, of the four is the most ontologically informative. For example, the development of the fourfold in the essay "Das Ding" is such that each sector appears to have equal ontological importance. Had Heidegger listed the four sectors in a certain constant order, this might indicate an ontological hierarchy. But no such ranking is evident—Heidegger varies the order wherever the fourfold is introduced, apparently according to the contextual emphases required. Of course, if the ontological importance of each sector is equivalent to the ontological importance of any other sector, there is no reason why the order of sectors should always follow a definite pattern. But the lack of a definite sequential order does not imply that each of the four sectors is essential to the totality in the same way.

The order of my own commentary in part 2, chapters 4 through 6, depends on the cogency of this conclusion. Thus, chapter 4 will concern poetizing as it speaks about man, the most important member of the mortal sector of the fourfold. Why begin with man? The answer, in Heideggerian terminology, is that the nearness of man to language conceals the remoteness of the relation between language and the being which language speaks and determines. We take language for granted, certainly at the deep ontological level on which Heidegger is conducting his search for words appropriate to name being. Poetizing breaks down this nearness by showing how given poetized names may reveal points of access to this remoteness. What results is a greater recognition of how language relates to being by showing how the words poetically used to name our own linguistic activity hint at much more than even the poet himself is aware. Man as man, not merely man as poet, shows himself through such language to be on the way toward appropriating himself to being as such.

The next two chapters broaden this perspective by moving from man (as mortal) to the earth and the heavens (chapter 5) and finally to the divine and the holy (chapter 6). Chapter 5 considers the relation between some of the key words discussed in connection with man and words which name earthly and heavenly entities. In chapter 6, the fourfold is rounded off, so to speak, in the analysis of the connection between poetizing about earth and heavens and poetizing about the divine. Chapter 6 also contains an important discussion of the distinctive temporality that obtains in the relation between the divine and the deity. This temporality will then become part of the being of every named thing insofar as all named things are constituted (in part) by the divine sector. With respect to temporality, my contention is that the notion of presence *(Anwesen)* receives more detailed consideration in Heidegger's illuminations of poetizing about the divine than it does in poetizing about any of the other three sectors. In this sense, the arrangement of the sectors is hierarchical rather than merely taxonomical. Qua fourfold, each illumination reflects the necessity of each sector and the sufficiency proper to the unity of all sectors; qua presence, all illuminations from the three nondivine sectors lead toward the distinctive role played by the divine and the deity in determining the temporality of all things. But, in general, the two central totality-perspectives on being, the fourfold and presence, each receive considerable attention if the body of Heidegger's illuminations is looked on as a unified whole. In fact, it will become evident (in part 3) that Heidegger could not have thought what he has thought about the being of things unless he had at some point illuminated the language of poetizing.

Poetizing and Man

For Heidegger, man defines his nature through the essence of language of which he is the spokesman. But relatively few mortal

78

speakers are poets. Heidegger assumes at this point that poetic language about the activity of poetized speaking will disclose the more fundamental level of language as saying. Therefore, since saying grounds all language, it follows that to illuminate and understand poetizing about poetizing is to enter into the domain in which saying becomes speaking of whatever form. The analysis of Heidegger's illuminations about man is thus based on considerations relevant to the poet speaking about poetizing. In this way, we learn about the poet himself, the poetizing of which he is the agent, and language as it determines the poet and all other mortal speakers.

We begin then with the poet Stefan George.[5] The poem is his "Das Wort," and the specific word in question occurs in the poem's final stanza:

> So lernt ich traurig den verzicht:
> Kein ding sei wo das wort gebricht.

The poet "sadly learns" the "renunciation" *(verzicht)* that "no thing may be where the word is failing." The punctuation of the stanza is an important factor in directing the course of Heidegger's illumination. What follows the colon is not what the poet renounces, but rather "names the domain [*Bereich*] within which the renunciation must be admitted" (*US*, p. 167). Within this domain, "the renunciation of the poet does not concern the word, but the relation of the word to the thing" (*US*, p. 183). As we have seen, for Heidegger it is axiomatic that in every linguistic event, "only the word allows the thing as the thing to appear as it is and thus allows it presence" (*US*, p. 168). Yet given this axiom, the poet must renounce his prior belief "to have the word as the representing name for the posited being [*Seiendes*] under his control" (*US*, p. 228). This renunciation marks the first phase in the experience that determines the poet as speaker. If this renunciation is achieved, the poet may then bring the relation of the word to thing "into motion to that which concerns every saying as saying" (*US*, p. 232). Once this motion begins to oscillate and to surround the poet, he discovers that "renunciation gives" and that what it gives is "the inexhaustible power of the simple" (*MHG*, p. 15).

The connection between simplicity as an effective result of renunciation and simplicity as a characteristic of the thing shown through appropriation is, of course, not accidental. In fact, the connection is just one of the many instances where Heidegger is systematic in his concern to illuminate the appropriative aspects of language with poetic images and speaking. Other examples will follow. In this context, the simplicity of a thing is inexhaustibly powerful because the relation between entity and all four sectors of the fourfold is open to specification by means of this property. Each thing is simple in this sense. The naming word of the poet (and all naming words, poetic and otherwise) thrusts the extralinguistic entity into the motion of reciprocity proper to the presence of the fourfold. The name aspect isolates the entity as this thing bearing a determinate set of relations to each of the four sectors. The word aspect unleashes the totality of the fourfold and the possibility that an unlimited number of options are open to the poet prior to his representational isolation of a single naming word. The poet is privileged in that he learns, but learns to his sadness, that the representational givenness of names for the entity must be renounced before language as saying can be experienced and contribute words to name entities as things.

The resulting renunciation is not, of course, a report of George's personal feelings, or that of any other poet. Heidegger's illumination is not based on descriptive psychology. The meaning of renunciation, as well as all other poetized language, will be derived from the applications to being as said rather than to entities as representationally spoken, although it is normally the case that nuances of the spoken name are preserved in the illuminations. We may question whether the poet is the only type of speaker to learn the sadness of renunciation. Presumably the answer is yes, although once again Heidegger does not argue the point. Since no argument is offered, the poet may be identical with other spokesmen, e.g., the novelist or the historian, with respect to the renunciation required for proper application of word to thing. Heidegger's challenge is to recognize the need for renunciation as a necessary condition for poetizing and to situate this condition within the speaking of being. To be sure, there remains the problem of distinguishing the poet from others who experience renunciation, assuming that such experience is possible for nonpoets. However, from Heidegger's perspective the more important task is to institute renunciation into the relation between mortal speaking and the appropriation of being through language, a task which remains even if the problem posed above is solved.

It is therefore crucial to attain and develop the correct ontological slant on renunciation. Renunciation does not imply that the poet's craft is irrelevant to his choice of language and to the structure of his art or that the poet is ultimately a mere tool of the muse, a mouthpiece through which the sources of poetry speak. Also, and more important, renunciation does not name a psychological attitude restricted to entities capable of exhibiting such attitudes, i.e., men as speaking poets. The attempt to understand the necessity of renunciation will abort from the outset if renunciation represented as a purely human attribute is not set aside. Renunciation as a word names the domain in which ontological relations occur between poet as speaker and entities as spoken about, ultimately entities transformed into things through the agency of language. The speaking of George has translated the name *renunciation* back into its originative status as a word by connecting the feeling of renunciation with the poet's concern to join entities with language. The hint to be taken is that renunciation names both the speaker renouncing and the entity or condition renounced, a relation which must be considered to determine its ontological relevance. To facilitate the task, we will examine more closely the feelings allied with renunciation.

Renunciation names the domain in which the poet experiences the awesome power of the word. But sadness appears to name only the poet, not his environmental domain. It is the poet who sadly learns renunciation. Even here, however, the relational characteristic proper to renunciation also pertains to the feeling experienced by the poet when he discovers the necessity of renunciation. Sadness is similar to renunciation in that its ontological sense involves both the name for a distinctive psychological state and the connection between the name and the word as an indicator of the ontological dimension. Thus, the sadness experienced by the poet is neither mere dejection nor melancholy but is sadness resulting from the realization of the necessity of renunciation. In the first book of *The Prelude*, Wordsworth observes that

> The Poet, gentle creature as he is,
> Hath, like the lover, his unruly times . . . .

For Heidegger, these "unruly times" are not durations of experience which could be avoided or mitigated if only the poet had greater self-control or if the situation were otherwise. They are essential in an ontological sense; that is, they describe the condition through which poetized language is possible as language. The poet is not sad as a prelude to the toil of creating his poem or is not sad in retrospect, gazing abjectly upon its poorness in light of hopes for what it could have been. Sadness is a type of feeling, but feeling must not be reduced to a purely subjective reaction without ontological import simply because of its immediately private nature.

Heidegger grounds this understanding of feeling as follows: "In feeling, the condition [*Zustand*] opens and holds itself open in which we, at times, stand together toward things, toward ourselves, and towards men with us" (*NI*, pp. 62–63). This interpretation of the nature of feeling turns on the meaning of the "condition" we find ourselves in when we feel. For Heidegger, feeling should not be subsumed under a more inclusive class of attributes, e.g., affection or disposition or attitude. A feeling is a different and unique kind of state. Once this difference is accepted, it will be possible to derive ontological considerations from feelings which have remained hidden because of the unexamined belief that feelings are merely instances of some more general property of "being human."[6] Given this understanding of feeling, sadness becomes a name for a distinctive type of relation between man as mortal and anything other than man.

This claim must be amplified, however, since it is I who am sad at the death of a friend, not the friend or the state of affairs, "death of a friend." Heidegger would insist, in the face of this objection, that to restrict the scope of a feeling to the entity actually experiencing the feeling is, from the standpoint of the ontology of language, to reduce arbitrarily the content of feeling as a word to feeling as a name. The cause of sadness need not be specified for sadness to be present and experienced; there must be some cause, however, and this necessity must be included in determining the ontological meaning of the word *sadness*. But even if this relational aspect is granted, one might object that the distinctive feel of sadness begins to fade, since presumably any other feeling will also share this relational characteristic with sadness. Here we must keep representational language and ontological language distinct, even though the two dimensions converge in a single name, *sadness* in this instance. Heidegger can preserve the uniqueness of sadness and justify this extended use of its name if he can distinguish between sadness and other feelings at the ontological level presented through *sadness* as a word. If these distinctions are forthcoming, then objections based on the absence of the represented feel of a given feeling may be set aside. From the perspective of language as appropriated, the context has now been shifted from the psychological to the ontological, from the meaning of the name (as spoken) to the meaning of the word (as said). Feelings as expressed through words are to be construed as complex ontological markers, and what they show must be defined, argued, and evaluated as such.

The condition of sadness is proper to the poet, that mortal speaker of language who experiences the need to renounce the representation of entities by their customary names. As poet, he is situated in the motion of the fourfold, the originating source of an apparently limitless supply of words from which the being of those entities may be appropriated. But the attribute of sadness does not completely describe the condition of the poet in his confrontation with the relation between word and thing. In an epigram, Hölderlin writes (*EH*, p. 26):

Viele versuchten umsonst, das Freudigste freudig zu sagen,
Hier spricht endlich es mir, hier in der Trauer sich aus.

(Many have sought in vain to say joyously that which is most joyous,
Here it finally speaks to me, here in sadness.)

As we shall see in more detail later, according to Heidegger, Hölderlin is the definitive spokesman of poetic language for our epoch, and Heidegger will be attentive to almost everything Hölderlin speaks. Here, his poetizing has united sadness with joy. Therefore, we should anticipate Heidegger's attempt to elicit relations and differences between these two psychological (now ontological) opposites. The fact that George spoke about sadness and not joy while Hölderlin speaks about their conjunction does not hinder Heidegger's quest to reveal the implications of such heterogeneous speaking by tracing its roots to the primordiality of language as saying. As noted in the Introduction, the differences between George and Hölderlin—individual poets with divergent interests, styles, and techniques—are not as crucial as the fact that both are poets who speak from a common ontological source.

Heidegger illuminates the connection between sadness and joy as follows: "Yet the more joyful the joy, the purer the sadness lying dormant in it. The deeper the sadness, the more beckoning the joy resting [*ruhende*] in it. Sadness and joy play into one another. The play itself that attunes both to each other, in that it allows remoteness to be near and nearness to be remote, is *pain*" (*US*, p. 235—italics in original). This conjunction and development of sadness and joy as opposites is Heidegger's attempt at rethinking the saying illuminated through the poets' speaking. We note how sadness and joy complement one another and how each plays into the other. Heidegger then names the play itself as "*pain.*" Three distinct feelings have now been interrelated, and each must be distinguished from the other. Thus, why is the play of sadness and joy named as pain? As far as the possible origin in poetic speaking is concerned, the source may be a verse from the work of Georg Trakl:[7]

> So schmerzlich gut und wahrhaft ist, was lebt
> (What lives is so painfully good and true)

Pain is here spoken so that it names only those entities which live (including the poet himself). And the sadness and joy previously spoken refer to a domain which must also include nonliving entities. But, in order to develop the complete ontological sense which Heidegger intends for pain, some nonpoetic language must first be introduced.

Heidegger's interest in pain as a word may come from an etymology from the Greek, together with the implications illuminated from instances of poetic speaking: "The Greek word for pain, namely *algos*, would then first come into speaking for us. Presumably *algos* is cognate with *alego* which as intensive form to *lego* means intimate collection. Then pain [*Schmerz*] would be the most intimate collecting" (*W*, p. 232). First, a reminder that this etymology, as all of Heidegger's etymologies, may or may not be correct from a philological point of view.[8] But the interpreter's task is to determine what Heidegger does with the etymology, regardless of its soundness. And after all, even if the etymology is unfounded, Heidegger's conclusions may themselves still be true. At any rate, it will become evident that the meaning of pain as derived from the speaking of the Greek language and the Trakl poem is vital for comprehending how such words contribute to the ontology of feelings, in particular the feelings of sadness and joy as felt opposites.

Heidegger reminds us that "we are not permitted to represent pain anthropologically as sensation" (*US*, p. 27), thereby inferring that the significance of pain must be determined on an ontological level similar to that of sadness and joy—similar, but not identical. For pain is in one important respect even more fundamental than these or any other feelings, since "pain is the difference itself" (*US*, p. 27). With this stipulation, as with the earlier instances of renunciation

84

and simplicity, Heidegger again connects the context of poetic speaking about pain with the linguistic cosmology based on the fourfold, in particular the central notion of the difference. But how can the name *pain* and the intense experience it represents illuminate a notion as abstract as difference?

Heidegger discerns an etymological connection between the Greek word for pain *(algos)* and the Greek word for speaking *(lego)*. The connection between pain and speaking was explicit in the Greek language (assuming, of course, that Heidegger's etymology is basically sound), but it remained implicit in language as saying until the poet Trakl reminded us of its presence by again speaking pain in conjunction with "all that lives." But the speaking of Trakl is itself only a hint. The passage of historical time has dimmed this sense of pain, so much so that "the pain which must first be experienced and wrung out is the insight and knowledge that this neediness is the highest and most hidden need, which is first necessitated from the most remote remoteness" (*VA*, p. 90). The "most remote remoteness" is the location where being as such can be experienced and spoken by mortals. The "highest and most hidden need" is the fact that mortal speakers are not presently aware that being has been and is concealed. The need cannot be met until the need is first recognized as a need. One way to specify and divulge that need is to return to the primordial Greek language and to experience anew the hints from the now hidden connection between pain (as a feeling) and speaking (as a mortal event).

But how can this connection be determined given the popular reduction of the meaning of feeling to the subject in which the feeling inheres and the accumulated historical influence of all such conceptual representation? Heidegger has asserted that "pain is the difference itself." The difference is the unthought relation between being and beings. Pain now names this relation, in a sense hinted at by the saying of the Greek language. The Greek *algos* names both the subjective feeling of pain and the objective (in a wide sense) cause of that feeling. A blow from a hammer results in pain, but the hammer is itself painful in the sense that it was the instrument by which the pain was caused. This complete relational sense is what Heidegger intends. Pain names an ontological relation binding entity feeling pain with the source occasioning the pain felt. But why pain and not some other sensory phenomenon?

Even the most drawn-out pain is in itself never static. Such pain is always in motion toward its own dispersal by signaling the restoration of the member or entity in pain to the healing completeness of unity. Normally, pain is temporary and contingent. Although we may assume that every living entity experiences pain of some sort at some time, this fact does not appear essential to the nature of these entities. A mortal entity is no less an entity for having never experienced pain, at least in the negative unpleasant sense in which pain is normally represented. But for Heidegger, all such understandings of pain remain only at the threshold of pain as a word of ontological import. The Heideggerian notion of pain is a constant and is not a condition which could be avoided, such as the pain resulting from a toothache or a hammered thumb, where the entity feeling pain would remain just as whole regardless whether or not that entity ever experienced pain.

Pain, insofar as the Greek language hints at its ontological function, includes not only the movement from unity to separation but also the corresponding movement from separation back to unity. Thus, "pain rips [reisst] splinters from and into one another; it cuts, however, so that at the same time it draws everything to itself, collects everything in itself" (US, p. 27). In pain, there is movement from unity to separation. This movement is not merely the state wherein parts which should be unified are sundered, but also the continuous process preserving this state of disharmony while itself tending toward self-resolution by moving toward the wholesomeness of health. There are two important implications from this ontological sense of pain: (1) this process is a necessary condition for any form of language—ontological, pragmatic, playful; (2) the process is continuous and actively embraces totality in the interplay of the fourfold as that interplay is collected in named things. Let me attempt to develop each of these implications.

(1) There is a hidden alliance between the Greek words for pain and speaking. The evidence for this alliance is the fact that, as soon as any linguistic formula is applied for purposes of, e.g., referring, the being of the entity named is cut off from being as such. The being referred to is no longer what it was simply by the fact that it is referred to as *this* being, a being which is other than being as such. Now, we do not normally experience pain when we speak—there is no evidence that the Greeks did either. But the Greeks were aware in the saying of their speech, as apparently non-Greek speakers are not, that the very attempt to denote a being as distinct from other beings

86

is to sever its relationships with the ultimate being of the fourfold. And, for Heidegger, this severance is magnified when subsequent non-Greek speakers attempted to link spoken utterances in accordance with a "logic" which was considered necessary for rationally comprehending entities and their relation to being. The point is that even for language controlled by logic, the process of speaking and rationally relating what is spoken is painful in the sense that the unity of being and beings has been ripped apart into diversity and separation. The extent to which mortal speakers of language are aware of this pain is the extent to which the pain can be, as it were, mitigated (but, of course, never removed) by attending to what is spoken in terms of its relations to the unity of being. Pain is real at this ontological level, just as real as physical or psychical pain, but the evidence for its reality is located in the gaps between how we linguistically represent the being of entities named and how those entities ought to be named to preserve the unity from which their being originates. The problem is to know how these gaps should be approached and experienced *as* painful in the ontological sense.[9]

(2) Since the bare attempt at speaking or naming entities wrests these entities from being and since speaking is essential to the process of living, such pain will always be present as a necessary condition for the realization of language. But its relation to other feelings named at the ontological level can aid in directing this pain toward the restoration of being in the approximate wholeness which being displayed in the saying of the Greek language. The key is found in placing the linguistic designation of a feeling (or the appropriate entity) in the midst of the motion of the fourfold, then in stabilizing this motion by determining the relation between the representational content of the name and the ontological dimensions of the word insofar as the word names the entity in a more complete ontological setting.

This placing in motion has been partially accomplished for pain as it has been spoken by the Greeks and by the poet Trakl. The ontological dimension of pain in this sense is perhaps Trakl's central vision, at least from the viewpoint of experiencing being as such from spoken poetizing. Heidegger has himself codified the potentially thoughtful content of this language. He contends that the totality of saying in Trakl's work is directed toward the one who is parted, and that such *apartness (Abgeschiedenheit)* thoughtfully names Trakl's poetical insight into pain's connection with language and

87

ontology. Apartness "collects that which belongs together, however, not subsequently, but in such a way that it unfolds in its already governing collection" (US, p. 58). Apartness is, initially, the consequence of the renunciation of the poet's control over names. The poet is apart from the entities of his environment to the extent that he experiences the pain of affixing mortal speaking to what will always be other than him, that is, whatever is named in his poem. In general, the pain involved in naming entities is a consequence of the continuous presence of the other, regardless of the nearness of the relationships established by spoken language.

To be apart is the direct result of the pain essential for the speaking of language. The spatio-temporal measurement indicating the extent to which the speaker is apart from the referent of his speech includes the complete continuum of space-time, for example, beginning with the meaning of a Greek word and extending to the cognate meaning in our more refined but, according to Heidegger, less ontologically sensitive vocabulary. Apartness is necessary in order for discrimination among entities to be possible; only if such discrimination obtains can the distinction between the being of entities and being itself be preserved. To describe the various modes of this distinction is the principal task of ontology, a task which requires apartness before such discrimination can even be attempted.

We are now in a position to comprehend more adequately the ontological scope of pain as feeling and to analyze the feelings named earlier—sadness and joy. Prior to being named as things, entities exhibit a mode of existence capable of being experienced by the poet through the sadness and joy present in naming and speaking. This mode of existence, as an apartness, must be prior—and thus painful—as a necessary condition for the ontological feelings of sadness and joy to occur. Although these feelings are derivative from pain, they remain ontological in character. But in what sense? Heidegger has connected them to the notion of nearness and remoteness (US, p. 235), so we should seek their significance in the interplay of these distinctive spatio-temporal coordinates. Given the analysis of pain just concluded, we may infer that sadness and joy are similar in that they are not static states: sadness is the process of being sad; joy is the process of being joyful. An instantaneous sad or joyful mood is only an abstraction. The poet, for example, becomes and continues to be sad in the process of realizing the need to relinquish control over the word. Also, the process of being sad always moves toward its opposite, the process of becoming joyful, and vice versa. In fact, these processes interpenetrate to the point where a given duration of the one includes aspects of the other. But what then distinguishes the two feelings at the ontological level to which Heidegger has raised them?

The poetized relation between sadness and joy has been thought as follows: "The deeper the sadness, the more summoning the joy resting in it." As we saw in chapter 3, rest is the extralinguistic equivalent of that silence which marks the existence of entities prior to the advent of speech. Joy names the process in which extralinguistic entities move from rest through saying and into the discrimination of human speaking. Joy follows upon linguistic attunement to the nature of being insofar as beings bear spoken relations to being. Joy is the mortal response to the summons that beings be named and spoken *properly*, that is, in the unity of the spoken with what is spoken about, where each is fulfilled in the process of fulfilling the other in their ontological completeness.[10] In terms of the near and the remote, joy describes the movement of mortals from the near to the remote, from the representational content of names to the ontological completeness of words.

But the vivacity of joy is directly proportional to the severity of sadness; the more joyful the appropriation of the being of entities through proper language, the deeper the sadness and the greater the chance of misconstruing that being through the continued reliance on a given set of words. Even the most revealing words necessarily become reduced to names of a definite representational cast, and the more that such words are relied upon, the more being becomes progressively distorted. Sadness is the essential counterpart to joy, since sadness is the fate of any word as soon as it enters the public domain, especially if that domain is the parlance of "professional" philosophers. For Heidegger, all technical terms conceal as much as they reveal. Thus, "the more joyful the joy, the purer the sadness lying dormant in it." Joy may be increased and refined in this ontological sense, but regardless how narrow the gap between the near and the remote, the remote always remains remote from the near. The joy of naming the being of entities through words is marked by the purity of that sadness which continually reminds mortal speakers of the essential gap between the ontological significance of their words and the inadequacy of these words in spoken thoughtful or even poetized discourse.

To summarize, *joy* is the name for the movement from the near to the remote, the movement from representational speaking to ontological saying; *sadness* is the necessary correlative movement from the remote to the near, the movement from the completeness of ontological saying to the incompleteness of representational speaking. *Sadness-joy* names the linguistic relation which connects being to entities in the sense that an account of the ontological possibility of language is expressible through the interplay of these apparently opposed psychological conditions. But sadness-joy exists, at this level, on condition that the pain involved in the differentiation of speaking can determine the modes through which being is apprehended and developed in such apparently silent aspects of mortals—that is, their ability to experience feelings.

The poetic texts just selected and developed are both emblematic of the type of utterance Heidegger illuminates and are also, it seems to me, pertinent to the general problem of the relation between poetizing and thinking. My goal here (and also in the next two chapters) has not been to give a complete inventory of all the poetic speaking which could be construed as relevant to enlightening a given sector of the fourfold but to render more precise the extent to which selected texts are amenable to relatively prosaic commentary. But the selection is exactly that, selective, and the result is far from a complete poetized picture of the function of man as mortal in the interplay of the fourfold, much less of the thoughtful repercussions such poetizing entails.

The commentary does, however, suggest one of the directions in which poetizing is essential. We have learned to recognize hints concerning the ontological significance of feelings. And we received these hints not from an empirical or conceptual account of feelings, but from the language of poets speaking about feelings. The peculiarly suggestive conjunction of names for feelings with apparently unrelated states of affairs is a special province of poets and is one reason why their language must be considered as an essential complement to representational speaking about feelings.

It is true that the expression of feelings has been one of the traditional bailiwicks of poets. But even the most refined and perspicuous treatment of a feeling, any feeling, is usually interpreted by both literary critic and sympathetic philosopher as basically a personal and ultimately private report. If the report is accepted as having some more universal significance, then that significance is rarely developed. But Heidegger contends that attention directed toward the way poets connect words to entities and states of affairs as felt will allow feelings to become open to important, indeed essential, ontological considerations. The peculiar poetic capacity to capture experiences as they are experienced, insofar as they are still on the way, is a type of linguistic presentation divergent from philosophical thought with its imposition of nontemporal representational structures and categories. The efficacy of such poetized language about feelings with respect to the limits of thinking is the conjunction of possible linguistic connections with the silent prelinguistic openness of saying. The apparent arbitrariness which results when poets ascribe such language to experience or entities then becomes a virtue in that it compels the thinker (assuming poetized language is taken seriously) to readjust his views concerning what kind of language is appropriate to describe and explain the *complete* mortal experience of being.

This is in many different respects an important position to take. It forces us to wonder whether the apprehension of being by mortals should be restricted to the customary epistemic channels. Thus, feelings need not necessarily be mute, need not be subservient to knowledge, if it is possible to indicate and describe the modes in which they reveal being. Given the possibility of such revelation, an analysis of feelings will be just as vital to the being of entities as felt as the analysis of knowledge about the being of those entities as known. But the problems with this potential revelation are many. For example, how is the ontological structure of feeling developed so that the spoken results which constitute that structure (especially with its necessarily poetic scaffolding) are not arbitrary? Also, how is this structure integrated with the more traditional and supposedly better understood modes of knowledge?

The process of knowledge seems by its very nature to be more amenable to retroactive introspection and elucidation than the process of feeling. We may study how we know with more perspicuity than we may study how we feel sad or joyful, because the process of knowing is more detached psychologically than the process of feeling. The same detachment may be found in speaking about knowledge as opposed to speaking about feelings. The speaker about feeling must to a certain extent cease to be in the state of feeling prior to enunciating verbal expressions pertaining to that feeling. Although the same is true of the verbal expression of the processes of knowing, this self-distorting feature is apparently more pervasive in the language of feeling than in the language of knowledge. Nevertheless, this difference between feeling and knowing should not by itself affect our comprehension of the language of feeling and our comprehension of the extent to which feelings contribute to the structure of the being of entities. The burden, and it is a heavy one, is to discern which relations joining names for feelings with the entities or states felt are merely idiosyncratic and which are properly ontological. The fourfold differentiation of the fourfold is heuristically helpful in this respect and perhaps is an ultimately constitutive guideline sufficient for testing the reliability of such poetized speaking. The central point, however, is to accept the feasibility of this project as suggested and controlled by the utterances of poets and the illuminations Heidegger has offered for this speech.

Heidegger has presented some of the conditions which define the nature of man as mortal insofar as that nature has been poetized. But man is man only to the extent that he assumes his place within the mortal sector and in the unity of the fourfold. Only when man experiences himself as one type of entity within that unity will he comprehend both himself (as poetically spoken) and that unity in its ontological wholeness. To isolate man as mortal even in his poetized appearances is to misrepresent Heidegger's intention, if the conclusion is drawn that man as mortal man can be understood in distinction from his relations to the earth, the heavens, and the divine. The key to restoring man's mortal membership in the fourfold is to connect the previously discussed attributes of man with poetized speaking which relates these attributes to the other sectors of the fourfold. Thus, in the next chapter we will see Heidegger follow the speaking of the poets and illuminate the relations joining pain with earthly stones and joy with heavenly clouds. The chapter begins by suggesting how man as mortal serves as the medium, the between (*Zwischen*) of earth and heavens. In this respect, man is related to the earth and the heavens at least as much through the way he feels toward them as through the way he conceptualizes their nature. The analysis of poetized feelings is thus essential to fulfilling an ontology which aims at restoring the completeness proper to man's interaction with his "natural" environment. We will then be in a position to move from man as such to the exploration of the special relation joining earth and heavens within the comprehensive contextual unity of the fourfold.

5. Earth and Heavens

For Heidegger, Friedrich Hölderlin is an epochally definitive poet, and the epoch defined by his work is still our own in several essential respects. The principal reason why Hölderlin's poetizing is epochal will be discussed in chapter six, which deals with the relation between the divine and the deity and the function of this relation within the fourfold as a whole. But Hölderlin also conveys essential influence with respect to the relation between earth and heavens. We will now consider those themes from Heidegger's essay on Hölderlin's phrase, *"dichterisch wohnet der Mensch,"* which are pertinent to this relation.

Heidegger illuminates the key word *poetic (dichterisch)* to name the "fundamental characteristic of human existence" (*VA*, p. 189). This characteristic does not mean merely that some mortals are capable of producing verse, but that all mortals dwell *(wohnet)* on the earth in a manner which is entailed by poetizing as a naming word of considerable ontological scope. The notion of dwelling is therefore crucial for understanding how man as mortal relates to being, especially being in its earthly and heavenly dimensions. In this chapter, we consider those aspects of dwelling directly connected with these two sectors of the fourfold, with man as mortal serving as the intermediary focus.

The locus of mortal human existence as poetized occurs in that openness in which man can cast a glance upwards to the heavens, a glance which "spans the between of heaven and earth." Heidegger names this between the *dimension (Dimension)* and, significantly, leaves "the essence of dimension without name" (*VA*, p. 195). Describing the sense in which this dimension emerges as the between will reveal those earthly and heavenly conditions which, as poetized, determine man's existence in the fourfold, i.e., his dwelling *in* being as such. In the appropriation of language, *dimension* is Heidegger's technical term for that relation between world and thing which determines the most basic ontological properties of each. Therefore, to

93

leave the essence of dimension without a name is consistent with earlier principles. If a name more explicit than dimension were affixed to this relation, then the representational weight of that name would restrict the openness essential for realizing the ontological connection between earth and heavens. Since "presumably we dwell thoroughly unpoetically" (*VA*, p. 202), the naming words for the dimension must come from poetized speaking of sufficient caliber to penetrate the representational boundaries of available language. Can such incisive discourse be found?

The dimension is nameless for the present, but it is possible to stipulate a focal point from which to begin the search for the proper words. In Hölderlin's poetizing, man locates his essence when "he measures himself . . . with the godhead" *(Gottheit)*. The godhead, or the deity, is one source (perhaps even *the* source) of the measure *(das Maass*, in Hölderlin's spelling) with which man reckons "his dwelling, his stay on the earth under the heavens." The taking of this measure *(Vermessen)* is an essential factor in determining the essence of man insofar as that essence is determined by poetizing. The notion of measure is not equivalent to measure in any scientific sense, but it does include reference to a standard. This standard is found in poetizing itself—"the taking of the measure is appropriated in poetizing" (*VA*, p. 196). And Hölderlin's poetizing names this standard. The standard is "the deity, by which man measures himself."

Why a deity? Heidegger gives no direct reply here, except to point out that man exists as mortal and that only he can die *(nur der Mensch stirbt)*, i.e., only he can know what death means in relation to life. Thus, God could be the measure of man in the sense that God cannot die in the same way that man dies (if, of course, it makes sense to claim that God can die in the first place). In chapter 6, we shall consider in greater detail man's relation to the divine and the holy insofar as these two interlocking media are a necessary prelude to any mortal experience of the deity. For now, we will examine how Heidegger implements this difficult and obscure notion of measure by specifying those aspects of earth and heavens which constitute the conditions by which man can measure himself with a godhead.[1]

Heidegger continues to illuminate Hölderlin's words. The poet asks whether God is unknown, and he answers this question with another question: "Is he manifest like the heavens?" Hölderlin's response is that "this I rather believe," i.e., that God is manifest *through* the heavens. He then adds that God, as manifest through the heavens, is "the measure of man" *(Des Menschen Maass ist's)*. Heidegger illuminates the poet's speaking by asserting that measure exists in the manner in which "the God, remaining unknown, is manifest as unknown through the heavens" *(VA,* p. 197).

We have now reached a crucial junction, one from which many interpretive directions are possible. One obvious direction would lead into a discussion of the relation between the manifestations or appearances of the deity and the nature of that deity. Is Heidegger trying to say something about the existence and nature of God? This aspect of the problem will be discussed, as already noted, in chapter 6. For present purposes, we must determine how the appearance of an unknown deity constitutes the measure which defines our mortal dwelling, as poetized, between earth and heavens.

The notion of measurement may be defined as follows. First, to measure means to preserve the relation between the deity and the poetized appearances of the deity, even when the deity appears as unknown. Heidegger states this principle when he describes poetizing as that which names the appearances of the heavens (in this context) in such a way that "the self-concealing directly appears and, indeed, *as* the self-councealing" *(VA,* p. 200–italics in text). The appearances of the heavens are self-concealing in that they conceal the deity at the same time that they disclose the deity as unknown. The heavens appear as heavens, but their self-disclosing aspect is necessarily self-concealing in terms of the deity with which these appearances are related through poetizing. Appearances must be preserved as appearances (regardless of the problematical mode of existence of what appears—hence the crucial role played by the "unknown" deity in this context) in order to constitute a sufficient condition for that poetizing which determines things according to the differentiation of the fourfold.

The second essential property of measurement depends on this sense of preservation but is a generalization from the particularity of the deity to all entities that appear. In epochal poetizing, the saying of images "collects the brightness and sound of the heavenly appearances into unity with the darkness and silence of the alien" *(US,* p. 201). Thus, to measure man's relation to the deity, the language of poetizing must connect the images of the heavens to images in sectors other than the heavens, i.e., the earth, the mortal, and the divine. These images may seem to reside in darkness and silence—as such, they are unsaid and must be spoken in order to determine the deity as a thing. The images may even be "alien" to the spokesman of images. If so, their initial incompatibility must be structured into an appropriate unity so that the deity can be transformed from an entity spoken about to a thing said in poetizing. And the conditions which must be satisfied to measure the deity also apply to every entity. The appearances of an entity must be said in conjunction with all four sectors of the fourfold. Thus, the deity is the source of that standard of measurement in the sense that its mode of existence indicates (a) how appearances must be apprehended and preserved and (b) how appearances must be related to appearances of nondivine sectors. The "between" which is the dimension of mortal dwelling also is a necessary medium in which appearances of entities are poetized in such a way that entities can be determined and measured as things by such poetizing.

We return to the appearances of the heavens. The dimension is bounded by the heavens, but not only by the heavens. The name *dimension* denotes an extended relational quantum of some sort, and Heidegger finds this quantum in the earth as the essential counterpart to the heavens. Thus, "the earth is earth only as the earth of the heavens, which in turn is the heavens only when it is brought down to the earth" (*EH*, p. 161). Within the total interplay proper to the fourfold, there is a privileged connection between the heavens and the earth, privileged perhaps because they are the only "natural" sectors among the fourfold's differentiation. But although this connection may be privileged in uniting two diverse sectors as a natural whole, "earth and heavens and their connection [*Bezug*] belong in a richer relation [*Verhältnis*]" (*EH*, p. 162). *Bezug* and *Verhältnis* are clearly distinct, but in what sense? *Bezug* is translated as "connection" to emphasize the difference between isolating any two sectors of the fourfold, *(Bezug)* and the interplay *(Verhältnis)* relating each sector to every other sector. Thus, all relations are connections, but not all connections are relations. At the most fundamental level, however, there is only one relation in this linguistic cosmology; it is that relation of all relations in which each of the four sectors is constituted by its presence with the other sectors and the unity of the four sectors is equivalent with the unity of being as such. Connections are possible between any two sectors of the fourfold, but the determination of ontological properties of a given connection must consider those properties in relation to the totality of the fourfold.[2]

The reciprocity between heavens and earth requires that the appearances of the heavens must be extended to the appearances of the earth so that their connections contribute to the formulation of the measure. The earth sector of the heavens-earth connection will be discussed first, in order to ensure a certain ascendancy toward what I interpret as the apocalyptic character of the fourth sector, the divine. Starting from the ground up, as it were, and then moving toward the heavens will provide some assurance that those characteristics of the divine which may prove to be inaccessible will be approached with a full complement of poetized speaking based on what *can* be spoken about the other three sectors.

EARTH

Mortals live their lives on the earth. But living does not imply that mortals dwell on the earth. The increasing consumption of the earth's fuel stores is just one signal that the fact of living as mortals have conceived that fact need not imply dwelling, if dwelling means consonance between increasing mortal needs and decreasing natural resources. To dwell on the earth, mortals must "first be able to save the earth as earth" (*US*, p. 41). Thus, the nature of the earth as earth is dependent upon the connection between man as mortal and the earth. Presumably there would be no need to establish the reflexivity of the earth—the earth as *earth*—unless there were some other kind of entity which entered the ambit of the earth's own natural properties and characteristics. The problem is to relate to the earth so that it yields whatever is essential for the preservation of the earth as earth. Once again, Heidegger heeds the poetized speaking of Hölderlin, in this case a portion of a late fragment:

> Die Erde . . .
> Grossen Gesezen nachgehet, die Wissenschaft
> Und Zärtlichkeit . . .
>
> (the earth . . .
> follows great laws, science
> and tenderness . . .

The core of Heidegger's illumination is that "tenderness, its rejoicing-extending [*erfreuend-reichendes*] and at the same time simple-receiving essence, holds open the earth to the heavens, along with science, the thinking which allows appearances to return. Both

97

form the connection (*Bezug*) of the earth to the heavens and are thereby at the same time heavenly" (*EH*, pp. 167–68). Heidegger names two aspects of the "iaw of tenderness"—the joyousness present in reaching toward the entity described by a law and the simplicity which joyousness receives through such reaching. The "law of science" is that which allows appearances of earthly or heavenly entities to "return" to man, the prime perceiver of such appearances.

Tenderness and science have been poetized in connection with the earth. But because of the ontological reciprocity between earth and heavens, the lawlike character of tenderness and science is established with respect to both earth and heavens. In what sense are the "laws" of tenderness and science laws? I suggest that they are laws in that they express a necessary condition for deriving the measure whereby the appearances of earth and heavens contribute to the dwelling of mortals. The poetized name *tenderness*, in Heidegger's illumination, includes both joy and simplicity. Joy has already been discerned as an integral factor in the appropriation of language by mortal speakers of that language; simplicity is one of the cardinal categories in the process whereby entities become appropriated as things. (Once again we notice Heidegger's development of important technical terms in the course of an apparently arbitrary illumination.) Joy results from successfully transcending the representational restrictiveness of names: extension is the movement from the entity named to the words for the entity as a thing. The simplicity received is the nature of the thing insofar as the words showing that thing contribute to the thing's relations to being as such. Tenderness is required both for joy and for simplicity so that the entity may appear as it is (where *as* refers to heretofore hidden ontological relations) and with the purity which will permit the ontological joy to be experienced as joyful.

But tenderness in this sense must be complemented by another equally fundamental law, that of science (*Wissenschaft*). Science in this context names the set of attitudes required so that entities may appear in such a way that these appearances indicate their status as things. As such, science is a necessary complement to tenderness, since only through science would tenderness have the perceptual manifold from which to determine the character of thinghood present to a given entity. But tenderness transforms the undirected funding of science by structuring that which appears according to the demands of linguistic appropriation and, ultimately, to the overall completeness of the fourfold. Tenderness and science thus become poetized naming words for those regulative conditions which guarantee the preservation of appearances faithful both to what the appearances are of and also to the relations comprising the interplay of appearances among all four sectors of the fourfold. Tenderness as a name lacks definitive criteria for application. But, for Heidegger, this lack is incisive rather than defective, given the tendency of representation to reduce the appearances of entities to signals for applying these entities to purely pragmatic ends. An appearance gathered through tenderness will be an appearance which is free to resonate from the entity appearing to entities in the other sectors, thus transforming the entity into a thing.

We will now examine two instances of poetized speaking about specific earthly entities and Heidegger's subsequent illuminations. The two entities are very different, and reflection on their similarities and divergences may be useful in determining the nature of the earth as earth with respect to appearances of earthly entities. The examples are taken from poetizing which shows how rejoicing occurs during the simple experience of appearances granted from the earth, thus providing a more concrete connection between man, that entity capable of rejoicing, and earth, each understood now as parts of different sectors of the fourfold.

The first example occurs in Heidegger's essay on Trakl. Heidegger notes that the image of the stone *(der Stein)* is named more than thirty times in Trakl's work. After citing the verse

> Une leise rührt dich an ein alter Stein:
>
> (and an ancient stone softly touches you:)

Heidegger connects the stone with the image of pain as spoken in another verse from the same poem:

> So schmerzlich gut und wahrhaft ist, was lebt;
>
> (Whatever lives is so painfully good and true;)

Heidegger illuminates the connection as follows: "The ancient stone is pain itself, insofar as pain looks earthly to mortals. The colon after the word [*Wort*] '*Stein*' at the end of the verse shows that here *the stone* speaks. Pain itself has the word [*Wort*]" (*US*, p. 63—italics in original). Then, with Trakl's verse

> Gewaltig ist das Schweigen im Stein.
>
> (Silence is powerful in stone.)

Heidegger allows the stone to speak: "The stone is the mountain-sheltering [Ge-birge] pain. The stone collects what is soothing hidden in the stoneness, which pain stills in that which is essential" (US, p. 45).

The stone speaks. But it speaks insofar as it appears as painful to the mortals who look on its stoneness. The stone speaks only if man is listening and only if that which in man is receptive to pain compels man to experience the pain which, Heidegger claims, *is* the ancient stone itself. The stone speaks if and when pain has the word. Recall the results of a previous analysis. Pain *has* the word in the sense that pain permits the otherness of what is named through the spoken image of pain to appear *as* other, in this case, as earthly. Thus, the entity stone must, as a potential thing, include how it, as an earthly *(erdhaft)* entity, looks to mortals, since such looking will constitute a relation partially establishing the entity stone as a thing. This looking of the stone is a perceptual event consummated in the poetized language spoken to name such appearances. The problem is to describe how the stone looks in its ontological perspective by tracing the images spoken of the stone to their linguistic and cosmological sources.

Trakl's verse "silence is powerful in stone" becomes especially instructive for determining this aspect of Heidegger's illumination. Silence is collected in the stone as a soothing power through which the stone shelters pain. These are initially dark claims. How, for example, do stones shelter pain? Stones are solidified earth and, as such, are at rest unless disturbed by some external force. But if it is true that each entity, as prospective thing, will bear relations to all sectors of the fourfold, then even a stone in all its apparent muteness also bears these relations to the motion of the fourfold. Pain must be present in order that the stone be ripped from its earthly moorings through the painful apprehension of those mortals who perceive the stone as an entity; the stone is then established as part of the earth and yet as distinct from the earth. Therefore, the stone shelters pain in that the ontological differentiation implied by pain is preserved in the inherent obduracy of the entity stone. In so doing, the silence which grounds the possibility of a linguistic event (regardless how grandiloquent that event may be) becomes the name which most adequately reveals the sense in which the stone appears to mortals who speak. Man experiences poetized stones as an earthly appearance of the powerful silence of language. Stones in their muted state

100

of rest are a paradigm for silence and its potency to say whatever can be spoken.

The appearance of stone as pain is decisive for earth as earth by relating stone, as an earthly thing, to something other than stone—in this case, the stone experienced as pain and as the silence grounding language itself. Note, too, that if the stone is pain (as spoken in Trakl's poem) and if the powerful silence of language names the central characteristic of stone in virtue of this pain, then the twin laws of science and tenderness have been obeyed: science, in that the appearance of the silence of stone is preserved and, in fact, elevated to the highest possible ontological significance; tenderness, in that the simplicity of stone is developed by pointing to its silence as a focusing union for all four sectors of the fourfold. But how does the poetizing of stone contribute to the measure connecting earth as earth to heavens as heavens?

The poet has spoken the word which shows that any measure which is related to an earthly thing must begin with silence as a necessary factor in the determination of whatever is measured. The silence hidden in the stone collects the sectors of the fourfold but does so in such a way that we now know that any earthly entity must be named in virtue of the silence grounding the possibility of language as saying. This does not mean that all earthly things are ontologically ineffable, but it does mean that an earthly entity can be spoken as a thing and dwell among mortals as a thing only when its relations to all sectors of the fourfold are preserved. Earth as such serves as the source of measurement whenever the appearances of an earthly thing are preserved as appearances and also related to the appearances of other entities within the totality of the fourfold, for example, the pain connected to the silence of the stone. The taking of the measure provided by poetizing thus implies that appearances of any entity measured must be related to the appearances of the other sectors insofar as these appearances are specifiable through naming words spoken about that entity. Only if this totality-condition obtains can an entity be measured in the requisite ontological sense.

If the entity stone becomes at least partially determined as a thing when named in relation to pain and silence, then we should investigate another entity of a different sort to recognize the difference, qua thing, between one entity and another entity. For this purpose, we shall examine illuminations which focus on water as an entity. The first illumination, more directional than substantive, occurs in the essay on Hölderlin's "Heimkunft/An die Verwandten." Hölderlin names the Bodensee, and Heidegger affirms that if the image of this lake is reduced to a body of water between the Alps and the Danube, then the entity is thought of only as a geographical or perhaps commercial expanse. Heidegger then wonders how long the Bodensee will be apprehended in an unpoetic (*undichterisch—EH*, p. 21) manner and how long mortals will continue to hinder themselves from experiencing the being of the lake. This illumination is, as noted, only partial, since Heidegger does not announce how the Bodensee as water is to be experienced in the requisite poetized sense. But in his essay on Hölderlin's "Andenken" another body of water is named by the poet, and Heidegger does indicate how this sea can be ontologically experienced.

The verse from "Andenken" is the following:

> Es nehmet aber
> Und giebt Gedächtnis die See
> (But the sea gives and takes memory).

We should note the parallel between this passage and the stone-pain image just discussed. A connection is named between something earthly, in this case a body of water, and something mortal, the power of memory *(Gedächtnis)*. Heidegger illuminates first by paraphrasing—"the sea takes memory in that it gives. But at the same time it gives memory in that it takes." This reciprocity in the movement of the sea is the fundamental characteristic involving any man who attempts a sea-journey. The sea-journey "is permeated by a remembering [*Andenken*], which thinks back on the last homeland and forward on that homeland to be won." This "turn toward the alien as granted to the sea-journey awakes thinking to that which is proper" *(EH*, p. 142). The sea gives memory not in the sense that the sea itself remembers, but in the sense that an appearance of the remembering must be presented in language as poetized. The appearance in question is not the fluidity of the sea, but the sea as something to be traversed, an expanse between two coasts. The liquid factor is of course still present—presumably a desert (as in the novels of Saint-Exupery) could serve equally well as something to be crossed, but a desert does not present the constant give and take of the moving water that is part of the nature of the sea. In the absence of wind, a desert, unlike the sea, is still. The sea may be stormy or calm, but the sea as sea is always in motion within its own boundaries.

When mortals cross the sea they do so for a purpose, and this purpose is the link which, for them, joins one coast to the other. Mortals leave the *"Heimat,"* the familiar source providing the ground for what they have been, and turn to the *"Fremde,"* the unknown occasion for what they are not yet. But the actual passage over the sea names a time when mortals can realize that their existence is just a series of passages—birth to death, sickness to health, sadness to joy, and for some, the search for being through beings. To dismiss the passage over the sea as something to be gotten over is to overlook what the sea *is* as a fluid expanse. The stuff of mortality is found in crossing the waters of the sea, from one shore to the other. This is the give and take which Heidegger considers, via the poet's experience, essential to memory and which expands our awareness of what the sea is as a thing spoken by poetized language.

The sea as sea becomes the appearance of the sea as the giver and taker of memory. The poetized sea thus becomes a temporal as well as a spatial entity: it is the earthly counterpart to the time involved in remembering the past in the present, and the movement required to transcend the present and recall that moment in the past which is to be remembered. The reason for remembering is poetized as the shore to be reached, the approaching boundary of the sea as opposed to the receding boundary, the source of the moment for which the act of remembering was initiated. To experience the sea as an aspect of time is the justification for addressing the sea (after Hölderlin's poetizing) as the giver and taker of memory. And there is the hint, a hint which must remain undeveloped at this point, that the unity of the sea which underlies the undulations of its give and take is an important aspect of the time which is present to memory *(Andenken)* and which Heidegger will eventually integrate into thinking as such *(Denken)*. Memory is of *one* time just as the immediate configuration of waves is of *one* sea.

Let us assume that the connection *(Bezug)* between an undulating sea and memory is an essential factor in the constitution of the sea as a thing. We now want to determine, if possible, the difference between the stone and the sea, given that each of them, qua thing, is identical in that each bears a spoken relation to the earth. The spoken connections joining stones to pain and silence name the stone as an entity at rest, but with appearances linguistically depicted which direct that rest toward mortals and thus toward the primordial motion of the fourfold. By contrast, the sea as an entity is never at rest, always in motion, and the thinghood of the sea is constituted, in part, by extending this motion from the purely spatial appearance of the sea to the spatio-temporality of presence *(Anwesen)* as an essential aspect of memory. Can these results be generalized about the ontological character of the earth as such, thus providing a standard to distinguish ontologically between things which are things (in part) because of their relations to the earth? The problem may be posed by asking what is the earth *as* earth? The answer seems to be that the earth *as* earth is the ground for the appearances of earthly entities as these appearances are open to specification with the nonearthly sectors of the fourfold.

This conclusion is something less that satisfactory, and it points to an important problem, assuming criteria are desired according to which earth as earth can be distinguished at a fundamental ontological level from heavens as heavens and from the other sectors of the fourfold. The problem is simply that such criteria seem difficult, if not impossible, to secure. But perhaps the quest for criteria of this sort is itself another vestige of representational thinking, that type of thinking which Heidegger is so anxious to counteract and redirect toward a thinking more adequate to the demands of being. But even if this quest is misguided, then the problem is not so much resolved as relocated, now in the domain of thinking *(Denken)*. For surely it is not in vain, or at least not self-evidently in vain, to inquire into whether there are specifiable differences between earth as one sector of the fourfold and any other sector of the fourfold.[3] This problem and others related to thinking will be considered in the concluding chapter. The difficulty is worth introducing now, however, to indicate both the problematic nature of thinking and the resident opaqueness surrounding the interpreter's attempts to reformulate Heidegger's illuminations according to the structural requirements of the fourfold.

EARTH AND HEAVENS

The isolation of earth as earth is, in a sense, artificial, since Heidegger has clearly stipulated that earth and heavens are mutually fulfilling ontological sectors.[4] One of the clearest poetized sources illustrating the intimate connection between earth and heavens is again found in the discussion of Trakl. Heidegger insists that Trakl's "the nocturnal pond" *(den nächtigen Weiher)* is not a mere representation *(Vorstellen)* of the pond but rather "the night sky is in the truth *[Wahrheit]* of its essence this pond. On the contrary, what we otherwise name night remains only an image, namely the faded and empty copy *[Nachbild]* of its essence" *(US,* p. 48). Heidegger concretizes the relation between earth and heavens by asserting that the night sky can be experienced as the night sky only when it is reflected in the pond and that the pond is a pond only when it receives the dark radiance of the night sky. Some may respond that Trakl is merely poetically, and therefore arbitrarily, juggling with images. But for Heidegger such response is a retreat to the "faded and empty" copy of the night sky when separated from its earthly correspondent for the sake of representational clarity. Trakl's own image "nocturnal pond" is itself not a faded copy because the name *pond* is connected to the name *night* in such a way that the corresponding sectors, earth and heavens, are fulfilled as spoken through the word *"nocturnal pond."*

The force of Heidegger's illumination is again, more directional than substantive. The presence of the connection between earth and heavens is more visible as a result of such poetic words, but the precise thoughtful content of this connection is still indeterminate. The image is substantive to a certain degree, in that the aspect of the heavens joined to the pond is the night sky, where night suggests a duration of time and also the absence of light proper to that duration. Both of these aspects—time and light—prove especially crucial to Heidegger's illuminations of the heavens as heavens.

HEAVENS

The nocturnal pond image suggests that the heavens as heavens may be approached through the image of night, or at least the diurnal cycle of which night is a part. The heavens poetized in this manner by Hölderlin offer scope for one of the most provocative Heideggerian illuminations. The passage is from Hölderlin's "Heimkunft":

> Drinn in den Alpen ists noch helle Nacht und die Wolke,
> Freudiges dichtend, sie dekt drinnen das gähnende Thal.
>
> (In the Alps there is still bright night and the cloud,
> joyously poetizing, covers the gaping valley.)

The cloud not only sets off the night sky from the valley and the mountains, but in effect provides the spur for the appearance of the night as "bright." Heidegger affirms that "the cloud poetizes" (*Die Wolke dichtet—EH*, p. 15); to do so, it must "freely go out over itself to something which is no longer it itself." In this case, what the cloud poetizes is the joyous—"the joyous is the poetized." But what is poetized does not come from the joyousness of the cloud alone, for the cloud must first be "serenified" (*aufgeheitert*) in the "serene" (*Heitere*), which Heidegger then renames the "spatially ordered" (*das Aufgeräumte—EH*, p. 16).

The serene is named the spatially ordered, that which "lingers against" (*entgegenweilt*) the cloud, thus letting the cloud poetize in the first place. Something must be lingering against the cloud in order that the cloud can be experienced. If the heavens were nothing but a continuous unbroken cloud cover, *a* cloud would never appear. Something must exist in the heavens other than the cloud before the cloud can exist as *a* cloud. What is this something other? It is the heavens as they exist serenely, i.e., without clouds. Heidegger characterizes the heavens as the spatially ordered so that only the most minimal but most essential aspect of the heavens guarantees the possibility of clouds coming into appearance, an ordered distance perceivable as such so that a cloud can be experienced within the spatio-temporal heavenly backdrop. The extralinguistic condition for naming a cloud within the open reaches of the heavens comprises the order of this space. The space itself is without sound, without commotion, without disharmony of any sort. Heidegger names it the serene, a striking word for the condition in virtue of which all that is nonserene can appear in the heavens.

The joyousness of a poetizing cloud emerges from the serene, and the power of serenity depends on the ordering characteristics of saying as related to the heavens. The serene is therefore a feeling on the same ontological level as joy, the feeling which marks a sense of oneness with totality. In this case, the unity is proper to the heavens alone, but the serenity of the heavens is paradigmatic for the fourfold as a whole. Serenity names the oneness of the heavens, while joy names the actualization of the cloud named as *a* cloud within this serene oneness. Heidegger affirms that the cloud itself poetizes—not the poet. Here, he points to the necessary existence of an extralinguistic entity, the mass of condensed water particles, which is constituted ontologically only with the conjunction of the appropriate naming word. The particular appearance of the entity in the night sky occasions the mortal speaker, the poet, to name that appearance and thus contribute to the constitution of the entity cloud as a thing. But only an entity of such appearance would allow the poetizing of this appearance through this particular naming word.

The spatially ordered expanse of the heavens lingers against the cloud. The introduction of a primarily temporal word—*lingering*—reinforces the presence of the space-time proper to the fourfold, but also performs the more explicit function of describing how the cloud is related to the spatio-temporal continuum. The entity cloud is in motion, with the heavens serving as a spatio-temporal backdrop. The cloud lingers, its shape changing variously, its motion through space taking time of a peculiarly indeterminate sort. This is a time which involves both the cloud and the heavens as backdrop. As such, the lingering bears essential relations to the totality of the sector within which an entity exists. Much can and must be said about this name, since lingering *(Weilen)* is one of the principal modes of presence. We shall find additional poetized ground for the development of lingering and its connection to time in the next series of illuminations.

Hölderlin's cloud appeared as joyously poetizing amid a "bright night." Trakl's pond was a nocturnal pond. Both of these seminal images are heavenly in that they refer to that portion of the diurnal cycle named night, or at least to the darkness associated with night. But the Hölderlin image of the bright night is a clash of opposites, since it is not immediately evident how night can be bright and still preserve night's darkness. Let us pursue a possible resolution of this clash between darkness and light by considering the intimate union between extremes, the iridescent period of twilight, the coalescence of night and day. From poetizing about twilight, it may be possible to describe the interpenetration of light and darkness and then return to the heavens as such.

Heidegger says that Trakl's nocturnal pond image appears as "the twilighting blue of the spiritual night" *(US,* p. 48). Why twilight? Because during this time in the diurnal cycle light is, so to speak, evenly divided. The "twilighting blue" is the spatio-temporal medium looking backward to the brightness of full day and ahead to the darkness of night. There is no precise moment at which one can definitively assert "now, *this* is twilight," and such temporal ambiguity fits in perfectly with Heidegger's designs. For Heidegger, twilight is "no mere extinction of the day as falling of brightness into gloom. Twilight does not in general necessarily intend extinction. The morning also twilights. With it the day expands. Twilight is at the same time an unfolding" (US, p. 42). Twilight bears the same fluid relation to the diurnal cycle that the sea bore to the movement of memory. Twilight names a distictive duration which spans all temporal dimensions throughout the course of night and day. Twilight continuously anticipates what is to come and continuously looks back on what has been, just as the sea is motion toward the alien of the future coincident with motion away from the homeland of the past. This pervasiveness of twilight, its futural and past dimensions bound in a continuous present, now becomes an essential factor in determining any part of time, especially with respect to the connection between time and light.

If twilight continuously mediates between night and day, we should expect Heidegger to place particular emphasis on both the darkness and the light which together, as an interplay, make twilight possible. Thus, in the essay on Hölderlin's "Wie wenn am Feiertage," Heidegger says of Hölderlin's cry "*Jezt, aber tagts!*" that "the awakening of the lighting light is, however, the stillest of all events" (*EH*, p. 58). Heidegger joins the distinctively visual appearance of dawning light to the aural stillness of the silence *(Schweigen)* which grounds the possibility of language. He then makes explicit the connection of day with light as experienced through the poet's language—the day comes to light as "the stillest of all events." But the fact that it is an event without sound does not imply that the light greeting the day's arrival is an appearance devoid of linguistic significance. The onset of day is all-pervasive, it lights up everything which can be lit up. Now, the tendency would be to keep the appearances of silence and light apart, at least from the representational perspective, where there is no reason to consider their conjunction. But there is good reason to do so if we examine with ontological concerns in mind the two disparate appearances. For if we admit the relevance of Heidegger's earlier analysis of silence, then a similar strategy emerges here for the dawning of light. Light must now be understood, not as a purely astronomical phenomenon, or merely as a necessary condition for the visibility of entities, but as a condition which is essential to the experience of time, just as silence contributes to the understanding of how language must begin from the absence of sound. The peculiar temporality of twilight provided the hint for this interpretation of light as itself ontologically temporal in character. Although time is always on the move in terms of its appearances as day and night, both high noon and the dead of midnight appear more as static states than as moving continua. But twilight, the play of fading daylight and oncoming nightfall, is intrinsically evanescent and impervious to linguistic description. Perhaps for this very reason Heidegger finds its appearance in Hölderlin's poetizing as an important perspective on the nature of time and its relation to other appearances which, like time, are in continuous motion.

Twilight is light as well as darkness, and Heidegger enters still deeper into the thoughtful implications of poetizing light by illuminating the fourth stanza of the poem:

> Und wie im Aug' ein Feuer dem Manne glänzt,
> Wenn hohes er entwarf, so ist
> Von neuem an den Zeichen, den Thaten der Welt jezt
> Ein Feuer angezündet in Seelen der Dichter.

> (And as a fire gleams in the eye for a man,
> when he conceives something high, so
> once more by the signs, the deeds of the world
> a fire is now enkindled in the souls of the poets.)

Fire, daylight, and twilight are all types of light. But fire is especially vivid in the light (and shadows) that it manifests. Heidegger explains the connection between light and the poet's fire in this way: "The lighting of the light belongs to fire, is the fire." But the source of the light is neither candles nor the sun, for "the fire is, as bright-glowing light, the open [*das Offene*] which already grounds presence in everything which goes forward and departs within the open" (*EH*, p. 57). Hölderlin describes the image of light as "philosophical," and Heidegger illuminates this description using Hölderlin's own terminology: "This light is that brightness [*Helle*] which, in the capacity of letting shining return [*Zurückscheinenlassen*] in the power of the reflection, bestows every thing present into the brightness of presence" (*EH*, p. 161). Light as a naming word must be understood in the most primordial sense. It is that light which first allows the between of earth and heavens to be experienced as a between and which allows any entity to be seen as a thing through mortal man's power of reflection. In fact, the visually experienced light of day can become the appearance of day only because of that ontological light which allows all that is experienced during the day, including the lightness of day itself, to come into the presence of the open.

The approach to the temporality of presence is blocked, principally because of the restraints imposed by representational thinking. To move around this blockade, Heidegger is compelled to stress the openness requisite for the recognition of presence. But the open as such is abstract without something, itself different from the open, which is allowed to exist as present within the open. Similarly, the ontological light involves something other than itself as an essential part of its own being. The third stanza of Hölderlin's "Andenken" begins:

> Es reicht aber
> Den dunklen Lichtes voll,
> Mir einer den duftenden Becher,
>
> (But someone reach for me
> the fragrant cup
> full of dark light)

Heidegger illuminates: "Not the dark light but rather the excess of brightness denies clarity, because the brighter it is the more decisively vision fails. The all-too-fiery fire does not blind only the eye, but the excess brightness also engulfs everything which is self-showing, and is therefore darker than darkness" (*EH*, p. 119). The result is that entities as things must be seen as present because of an interplay of light *and* darkness.

In what sense is light "darker than darkness"? The clue is in the connection between light and Hölderlin's power of reflection. If there were nothing but light flooding through our power of reflection, we might expect the products visible through that light to be boundless as far as knowledge of their nature is concerned. But this expectation misrepresents what light is and does. Light, in itself, is abstract; light needs darkness in order to appear as light, the bearer of visibility and knowledge. Light now becomes darker than darkness in that the very visibility bestowed by light conceals, and, according to Heidegger, necessarily conceals, the nature of that which the light has enlightened. Light in this sense must be darker than darkness, if the light (e.g., of knowledge) dissimulates to a greater degree than the relatively straightforward darkness (e.g., of ignorance). In this respect, light is similar to the darkness that the seeker of wisdom experiences in Plato's cave as he moves up and out toward the sunlight, i.e., a darkness or lack of visibility because of an excess of light (the parallel goes no further, since Heidegger vigorously rejects Plato's Good as the light's source).

110

Darkness should not be construed negatively, as the mere absence of light. In the Trakl essay Heidegger says of the "spiritual night" (*geistlicher Nacht*): "In the wandering through the spiritual night . . . the innocence [*Einfalt*] of the turning-against which perdures through pain first comes into pure play" (*US*, p. 72). Man wanders in all his activities, even when he is convinced that his goal is clearly in view. The point of the illumination is that he must wander through the darkness of night. This wandering is necessary because only through the night's darkness can man recognize how he must turn against an entity by letting that entity be scattered and collected as a thing through his own intentions and actions and also through the "pure play" of the other sectors of the fourfold. Man can determine entities as things by groping for them in the darkness; in the "spiritual night" he gropes in the same way, only in a more primordial form of darkness, where groping is more pervasive than that experienced by a wanderer lost in a forest at midnight.

Innocence is, so to speak, the armor against the ontological pain proper to determination and discrimination of things through spoken discourse. It is also the condition or attitude which allows the pure play of the fourfold to be approached through the entity as a presented thing. The fact that such pain can be mitigated but never completely alleviated finds its imagistic counterpart in the fact that darkness is an essential adjunct to light. This darkness includes not only knowledge now unrealized, but also, and more importantly, that which is concealed concerning the being of entities by the representational knowledge of entities. Such darkness is always present, even when the light is, or appears to be, the brightest, just as the darkness of twilight is present to all other periods of daylight.

This chiaroscuro effect, both in appearance and in ontological import, extends from knowledge of earthly and heavenly entities, where its influence is readily apparent, to the existence of God, where its influence may not be so apparent. We must first distinguish between (a) the existence and nature of God and (b) the divine presence of God, the aura that surrounds the existing deity and which serves as the intermediary region between the deity and all that is other than the deity. In chapter 6, this relation will be discussed in greater detail. For now, the immediate poetized connection concerns the appearances of the heavens and the divine presence. In Hölderlin's "Feiertage" ode (seventh stanza), the light of fire is again spoken by the poet, but this time it is the light of heavenly (*himmlische*) fire, a qualification which signals the transition from the heavens as such to the divine. The verses are:

> Und daher trinken himmlischen Feuer jezt
> Die Erdensöhne ohne Gefahr,
> Doch uns gebührt es, unter Gottes Gewittern,
> Ihr Dichter! mit entblösstem Haupte zu stehen,

> (And therefore the sons of earth now
> drink heavenly fire without danger,
> Yet it is fitting for us, you poets,
> to stand with bare heads under god's thunderstorms)

In Heidegger's illumination, the "heavenly fire" does not mean lightning *(Blitz)* but that fire which " 'is now enkindled in the soul of the poet'—the holy [*das Heilige*]" (*EH*, p. 70). In "Das Gedicht," the most recently published of the Hölderlin essays (1968), Heidegger cites the image "the god wrapped in steel" *(Der Gott gehüllt in Stahl)*, and after noting that steel strikes sparks *(Funken)* and is thus akin to fire, he lets the image speak: "The 'god wrapped in steel' means: the god wrapped in the fire of heavens, or in clouds. The heavenly fire blinding the eyes is no less concealing than the darkness of the clouds." (*EH*, pp. 189–90). Hölderlin's original poetizing cloud now becomes, in Heidegger's illumination, the clouds which focus both light and darkness in a direct relation to the deity. Heavenly fire pierces the cloud and in its own way shows the presence of the divine.

Heidegger then says that the "heavenly fire intends itself to the one greeting and remains near to him as that which has been present as divine" (*EH*, p. 116). The connection between the poetized image "heavenly fire" originating from the holy and "heavenly fire" remaining near "the one greeting" will be one of the key themes discussed in chapter 6. First, I will discuss the image of fire as a special type of heavenly light.

The presence of the divine must be understood in the contextual framework of the fourfold. In this instance, the divine is disclosed through its initial appearance as lightning, the fire of heavens, or as the darkness of clouds. But if the divine is concealed by dark clouds, it is equally concealed by the brightness of heavenly fire. Heidegger names the heavenly fire as that which remains ontologically near to the presence of the divine, but he could have named the darkness of the clouds with equal justification. For if both fire and clouds conceal that which makes the divine holy and therefore receptive to the deity, there is no a priori reason to choose the one image rather than the other. The relevant point is, however, that even if the divine appears as divine primarily through heavenly appearances of light, we must interpret the appearances of the divine with the same light-dark interplay as we have found in the appearances of the heavens as such.

If the rhythm of light-dark appearances is taken as one of the fundamental properties of the heavens, then it is possible to epitomize the heavens as heavens. The light and darkness of the heavens condition the appearances of any entity in the diurnal cycle of day and night with the twilight of that cycle present in every moment of the twenty-four hours. And when the light and dark are maximized, as it were, in their fusion as divine thunderstorms, the heavens collect and direct their appearances toward the sector of the divine as such. The heavens *as* heavens is that sector which provides a privileged entry into the manifestations of the divine, but it does so only by collecting and manifesting all proper appearances of all that which is nondivine. We note that the heavens as heavens and the earth as earth are alike in that poetizing which speaks about either sector conceals as much as it reveals. Therefore, we should anticipate that the brightness or light of the deity appearing in the heavens will be complemented by an essential and divine darkness.

In chapter 4, we saw the nature of man as mortal in terms of poetized speaking about his feelings toward language and toward that which is shown in language. In chapter 5, we have seen Heidegger develop the mortal sector of the fourfold as a poetized interplay in which man is determined as man not only through his feelings, but also by virtue of his place in the dimension between earth and heavens. The notion of measurement was then introduced by Heidegger in conjunction with the activity of poetizing and the function of poetizing in determining entities as things. Now, the notion of measurement entails that something can be measured and that a standard controls how the measurement is to be regulated. But if measurement qua poetizing is taken seriously (as, of course, it has been taken here) and if measurement retains any sense of nonarbitrariness, then the Heideggerian position faces a number of serious problems.

These problems may be formulated and appreciated with greater responsiveness now that we have had first-hand experience with illuminations of two different sectors of the fourfold. No one would deny that feelings and the expression of feelings in language are important properties of mortal man. Nor would anyone deny that man exists on the earth and under the heavens and that both of these "natural" sectors must be taken into account if the nature of man's relation of what is other than man is to be in any sense complete. But at this point the problems begin. We encountered difficulty in stating a principle which characterized the earth *as* earth; we would encounter a similar difficulty in stating the difference between the earth *as* earth and the heavens *as* heavens. The same type of difficulty would be met if one attempted to describe what determined a given entity *within* one sector to be a thing (as the interplay of all four sectors).

The reasons for these difficulties are readily apparent. For Heidegger, the determination of the thinghood of a given entity is not merely a function of the entity's "real" nature (i.e., its being in itself) or merely a function of the appearances of the entity, but is a function of the poetized expression of the appearances of the entity. If we assume that an entity may appear in many different ways and if we also assume that poetizing may render these appearances in many other different ways (e.g., in metaphor), then the magnitude of the problem of how to measure which poetized names are appropriate and which inappropriate becomes evident. If Heidegger's confrontation between thinking and poetizing is to be all understood, then his illuminations of pain, rocks, ponds, the sea, memory, and divine thunderstorms must be read with sympathy. But sympathy alone is not sufficient. At some point a standard must be presented in order that the apparent arbitrariness in connecting pain with stones, the sea with memory, and the divine with thunderstorms can be recognized as a necessary factor in the determination of all those named entities as things. It would be premature to speculate further about this standard, or the lack of such a standard, until Heidegger has completed the rounds of the fourfold, that is, until his illuminations of poetizing about the fourth sector—the divine—are in view. In the process of illuminating a number of abstruse poetized utterances on an intrinsically difficult theme, Heidegger may provide hints on how the appearances of the deity can relate to the existence and nature of that particular entity as thing. It may then be possible to extrapolate criteria for the required standard which Heidegger claims is proper to the measurement of poetizing.

6. The Divine and the Holy

Men have frequently sought God, or at least an approach to God, by gazing at the heavens and its ordered expanse. But for Heidegger, the God men seek to experience is as vivid in his heavenly appearances as he is concealed in the very vivacity of those appearances. In our epoch, the deity is lacking in ways in which it was not lacking in other epochs. The poetizing of Rilke suggests, and that of Hölderlin defines, the presence of this lack. Hölderlin's recurring theme of an absent or lacking deity antedates both Nietzsche's famous cry that God is dead and the lesser-known proclamation of the same event toward the conclusion of the chapter on revealed religion in Hegel's *Phenomenology of Spirit*. Thus, the poet anticipates the thinking of Hegel and Nietzsche on the reality of God in the contemporary epoch. Heidegger finds Hölderlin's poetized speaking about this reality essential for understanding the problematic existence of God and the subsequent relations between that mode of existence and all that is other than God.

At this point, the images Heidegger has illuminated are directed upward and onward to the presence of a deity made manifest through appearances in the heavens. For example, Hölderlin's image of the "round-dance" *(Reigen)* elicits Heidegger's assertion "the round-dance is the drunken reciprocity of the gods themselves in the heavenly fire of joy" *(EH,* p. 174). In addition to the gods themselves, Heidegger notes that the participants of this dance are the members of the fourfold—earth, heavens, mortals, and the divine. The fact that God's interaction with the fourfold is "drunken" hints that God's presence is manifest not only through the heavens, but also anywhere and everywhere, and apparently in the most haphazard and unsystematic of ways. The problem is to select in as sober a manner as possible those appearances, principally from the heavens but, if necessary, from any sector of the fourfold which name essential properties of the presence of the deity, if not the deity as such. To name that presence will confer that joy which results

115

from the proper correlation of words with the being of entities, the "heavenly fire of joy" resulting from this successful union between word and deity.

Appearances of the deity may occur most immediately in the heavens, but regardless where they occur, mortal man must be receptive to their possibility. Such receptivity runs counter, in a sense, to the normal course of man's lived existence, and Heidegger's illumination of Rilke's poetizing suggests some of the conditions which must be met before this receptivity is possible. The essay on Rilke is entitled "Wozu Dichter?" and was published in *Holzwege* (1950). The essay was originally presented as a lecture in 1946, the twentieth anniversary of Rilke's death. This chronology is relevant, since the Rilke essay antedates Heidegger's first published remarks on the fourfold by some ten years and thus may not have been intended to contribute to the fourfold and its relation to language as poetized. But the illumination of Rilke is definitely a step on Heidegger's own way toward experiencing the essence of language, as well as an approach to describing the mortal receptivity required to experience divine appearances.

Heidegger's illumination is based on a set of improvised verses collected by Rilke's editors. Here is a translation of the relevant part of the poem (the German will be cited in the subsequent commentary):

> Just as nature cedes their essence
> To the venture of their dull pleasure
> And grants nothing special in soil and branches,
> So we also at the ground of our being
>
> Are not dearer; it ventures us. Except that we,
> Even more than plant or beast
> Go with this venturing, will it, are even
> More venturesome (and not from selfishness)
> Than is life itself, more venturesome
> Than a breath . . .

Heidegger begins by affirming that the word *nature (die Natur)* means "the being of beings" *(das Sein des Seienden—H* p. 256) and that Rilke's name for the being of beings is "the will." Heidegger then expands this synonym for being by considering Rilke's "it ventures us" *(es wagt uns)*. By interpolating the word *being* for the word *nature,* it follows that "being is simply the venture. It dares us, us men" *(H,* p. 257). At this point, Heidegger expressly admits that Rilke's poem
116

"says nothing directly concerning being as simply the venture." But he insists that "the poem says something indirectly to us concerning the venture, in that it says of what has been ventured" (*H*, p. 258). The next step then is the specification of the connection between the image of venturing and being as such.

Rilke poetizes that "nature ventures us" and adds that, contrary to plants and animals, we (as men) "go with the venture, will it" and at times are even "more venturesome" than life itself, "more venturesome by a breath . . . *(um einen Hauch/wagender . . .)*. In Heidegger's illumination, the word *"life"* means "beings in their being: Nature." Therefore, what could it mean to be more venturesome than life, since life names the being of beings? The answer rests on the relation between the being of man and being as such. The answer is not provided by the speaking of Rilke's poem, as Heidegger admits, but is arrived at by a "thinking confrontation" *(denkend entegegenzukommen)* with the saying of this and other Rilke poems (*H*, p. 285). In a word, what men venture is "the area of being. They venture language" *(Sie wagen den Bezirk des Seins. Sie wagen die Sprache—H*, p. 286). But Rilke has named men as *more* venturesome. Heidegger then asks whether man possesses language by his very essence, thus necessarily venturing language if man is to be man. The answer is yes. But how then can man be more venturesome if his very essence is bound up with the venturing of language?

It is true that every man who wills anything in the usual way already ventures saying, since man must will in order to act and all actions are by their nature thrust into the dimension of language at its most fundamental level. But the willing requisite for that which is more venturesome results in saying proper.[1] Heidegger concludes that the "more venturesome are they who are what they are only when they are saying more." (*H*, p. 291). Although all men are implicitly involved in saying, only some men say more *(Sagenderen)* "in the manner of the singer." These singers, the more venturesome, are the poets *(Die Wagenderen sind die Dichter)*. But, according to Heidegger, the more venturesome are poets whose task is specialized, given the demands of being as a whole. That part or aspect of being which comprises this special province is the deity, in particular the relation between the deity and all that is other than the deity.

Heidegger names this crucial intermediary region *the holy (das Heilige)*. Insofar as they are more venturesome, poets are "on the way to the trace of the holy because they experience the lack of the holy as such." These poets "bring mortals the trace of the flown gods," and they do so in virtue of the fact that "the holy binds the divine" and "the divine supports the deity" (*H*, p. 294). Such poets are more venturesome "by a breath," where breath means, according to Heidegger's illumination, "the word and the nature of language" (*das Wort und das Wesen der Sprache—H*, p. 293). Heidegger then concludes, with little explanation, that it is not accidental that an ellipsis follows this passage in the poem, for this device "says what is kept silent." This breath speaks "a blowing in the god. A wind" (*Ein Wehn im Gott. Ein Wind—H*, p. 292).

I suggest that the key to appreciating the thrust of Heidegger's illumination may be found in the image of breath, this breath which trails off into the grammatical silence of the ellipsis. It is, in fact, a brilliant stroke to illustrate Heidegger's position. Rilke has named this breath as a "blowing in the god," and Heidegger experiences this breath, the sigh of the more venturesome poet, as the saying of "what is kept silent" about the god. If we assume that the fourfold and its linguistic configurations are implicit in Heidegger's thoughtful illumination of Rilke, then this silence (indicated by Rilke's spoken ellipsis) assumes the technical meaning of that prelinguistic harmony of the fourfold from which saying and speaking become realized.

As we have seen, silence in this sense refers to all four sectors of the fourfold. This is important to note, for otherwise the brunt of Heidegger's essay might be taken as an injunction upon poets to bear the mark of the "flown gods" to the exclusion of poetizing about all other sectors of the fourfold. Rilke himself speaks, and thus connects, the "more venturesome" with "breath in the god"—Heidegger illuminates this speaking and announces an explicit bond between the more venturesomeness of the poet and what this poetic breathing is of—the holy in its relation to the deity. Such singing is saying "from the holy of the whole pure relation, and to say only this means: to belong [*gehört*] in the area of beings themselves" (*H*, p. 292). The saying of the holy can be spoken by the poet only in conjunction with all sectors of the fourfold and the beings existing in these sectors. This inference is crucial as far as indicating the range of content open to ontologically sensitive poets. Heidegger is not prescribing to poets that they devote their work to creating celestial resurrections; rather, he is situating what one poet has spoken concerning the relation between man and a flown god within a more inclusive linguistic and ontological framework.

What seems to be a purely human and perhaps arbitrary characteristic, the daredevil quality of the venture ascribed to the poet, is now established as something much more complex, similar in structure to Heidegger's later developments of joy, sadness, and pain. The apparent anthropomorphism in the utterance that "nature [which Heidegger reads as *Sein*] ventures us" is another spoken instance of a naming word ultimately grounded in language as saying. Since each sector of the fourfold is equiprimordial and since venture names one of the poet's essential relations to language, it follows that this venturing comes from the totality, the world as saying, and not just from that one sector which is, on occasion, described in representational speech as venturesome. Because man is mortal and therefore part of that sector of the fourfold, man can be venturesome (and more venturesome) and can exist in ventured relations with other entities. The power in venturesome as a naming word captures the peculiar capacity of men to chance, risk, and hazard the voicing of utterances which attempt to convey the depth of any portion or segment of the fourfold, much less that of the divine with its flown deity. This is the venture of ventures, as it were, with the poet at the vanguard of human speakers.

A second aspect of venture hints at the context of the "*Wozu,*" the poetical "wherefore" Heidegger is in the process of specifying. Although venture refers to the endeavor to use language for any of its possible purposes, it is singularly apt to name that type of language which brings the holy into existence through the naming word. This is especially the case when the deity's flight so completely saturates modern consciousness that even traces of his presence are difficult to discern. The burden of the poet in an epoch such as this is to seek and express these traces of the god, not to attempt the verbalization of the god's existence as such. Yet even this subsidiary task requires him to be more venturesome, because the traces must first be found before the deity can be approached in language. Although Heidegger does not expressly state this, one can assume that traces of a flown deity are more difficult to locate than traces of anything else; this is why the name *venture* aptly describes the poet's work rooted in being *(Sein)* as it presents occasions for experiencing the presence of the deity. Thus, the very effort to initiate a poem (much less complete it) is more venturesome, involves more of an ontological risk, than any other activity, especially when the risk includes naming the traces of a flown deity. The tragic fate of the man Hölderlin may have been connected with this risk, a fate which Rilke the man did not share. Perhaps this is one reason why Rilke's poetizing takes us only part of the way into the problem of linguistically relating mortal man to the deity and to the divine.

The ensemble of themes surrounding the notion of the poet as privileged speaker in matters divine is developed in Heidegger's subsequent writings, especially those dealing with Hölderlin. As an example to introduce the range of this development, consider this fertile but condensed illumination of Hölderlin's word *Gewitter* spoken in connection with the existence of God. Heidegger asserts that "the presence" *(Anwesenheit)* of God hides itself in "lightning, thunder, storm, and showers of rain." But "although the thunderclouds veil the heavens, they belong to it and show [*Zeigen*] the joy of God" *(EH,* p. 166). Notice that the phrase "joy of God" is ambiguous as it stands; it could mean either the joy which God himself possesses as manifested through his presence in thunderclouds or the joy spectators experience when in the presence of a God made manifest in these heavenly appearances. This ambiguity would be alleviated, if not resolved, if the joy in the beholder becomes in some sense identical with the joy in God himself, that is, if the appearance of the thundercloud reflects the same joyful reaction in both observer and observed. Let us assume that this possible identity approximates Heidegger's intent. If so, there must be some common ground between God and man, the entity who ventures to name his experience of that divine presence as joyful. This common ground exists. In fact, Heidegger has already named it in the Rilke essay as the holy, that medium through which the presence of God appears to all sectors of being, i.e., to the fourfold.

Heidegger has now introduced three notions of a typically theological cast which are intimately related but nevertheless distinct. It is vital, I believe, to possess some relatively clear understanding of these notions before any commentary on their illumination can proceed. Heidegger has provided ample prose development of these notions, and this development warrants special consideration. Thus, I shall sketch what I take to be their principal meaning, then follow that sketch with a discussion of some relevant illuminations pertaining to each of them. The three notions are: (1) the deity, or the gods, an entity (or entities) possessing being; (2) the presence

120

of the deity or, in a word, the divine; (3) the holy. In general, the three notions are related as follows: The deity exists, but its nature is concealed in certain crucial respects. Nevertheless, the existence of the deity encompasses a presence which radiates from the deity and therefore is like the deity. This presence is the ontological basis of the divine. The divine presence displays appearances of the deity as concealed, appearances which are capable of being perceived by whatever entities are open to such appearing. Since there is no limit on what form the appearances of the divine presence can assume, any entity can receive impressions of this presence and reflect that presence from itself. This totality-disposition, extradivine in character, is the holy. The holy names all entities insofar as they have the capacity to display an aspect or aspects of the divine presence. I shall now attempt to refine this general outline by considering in greater detail the deity and its properties as Heidegger has developed these properties, and the relation between the divine and the holy.

THE DEITY

In the Rilke essay, Heidegger develops an important perspective on the problem of God. There he affirms that "that wherein God is still present [*west*] is the holy. The element of the ether for the arrival of the flown gods, the holy, is the trace of the flown gods." In what sense have the gods flown? Heidegger describes the flight as a specific "lack": "The lack [*Fehl*] of god means that God no longer visibly and unequivocally collects men and things [*Dinge*] to himself and from such a collection unites world history and the human residence in it" (*H*, p. 248).[2] This assertion implies that if a God did exist but did not collect man and things in the manner stipulated, there would still be a lack of God. Therefore, this lack would be a lack relative to the nature of God as existing, not a lack in the sense that God was completely lacking, i.e., did not exist. In fact, such a lack might not lie solely in the nature of God at all. Since the collection unites God with men and things, the lack may exist because of some omission or failure on the part of men and/or things.[3] But regardless which relata is the source of the lack, to assert that something lacks a certain property or disposition is to assume that the something exists. A nonexistent deity could not lack any property just as a nonexisting

121

deity could not display any property—a nonexistent deity has only one property, that of nonexistence. Therefore, Heidegger's position in the Rilke essay and its development of the notion of the holy requires the existence of a deity (or deities). The deity must have being of some sort.

The later writings elaborate in more detail the ontological properties destinctive to the presence of a flown or lacking deity. But the connection between the deity and nondivine entities is axiomatic for that ontology. Thus, it is impossible to sever in all respects the being proper to the deity from the being proper to those mortals who are related to the deity. God, or the gods, is not something wholly other than that which is nondivine. Heidegger makes this bond quite clear when he asserts that "gods must be gods and men, men, and yet at the same time they could not be without one another" (*EH*, p. 69). There is, of course, a difference between gods and men, but the difference does not isolate the one from the other. In fact, Heidegger here makes the strong claim that the gods could not be gods unless they were connected with men in what must be some ultimate ontological relation.[4] (It follows that the gods must have existed in the past if men existed as men in the past. A similar inference holds for the present and the future. Since men exist now, although perhaps not as they ought to exist and since there is ontological necessity joining gods and men the gods must exist now, again in some sense of *exist*.)

There are numerous problems with this position from the standpoint of theology, and although these problems can hardly be considered here, much less resolved, some reflection on them will be instructive for understanding Heidegger's line of thought. One obvious difficulty is Heidegger's apparently random reference to "God" (or, perhaps more accurately, "god") and "the gods." A theology based on one deity will be very different from a theology based on more than one deity, regardless of the exact number of "the gods." Surely similar repercussions will affect the structure of an ontology like the fourfold, even though it is more secular in scope. Two points should be made in this regard. The first is that Heidegger usually follows the original poetic spokesman in referring to God or the gods. The illumination is phrased in such a way that it contains whichever referent, singular or plural, Heidegger deems appropriate for the poetized speaking under scrutiny. The second point is more important. The indifferent use of the singular of plural is consistent with that contemporary state of affairs in which God is lacking or has flown. Although "God is dead" generally refers to the monotheistic Christian deity, the polytheistic deities of the Greek epoch are just as dead. And we have no real right to presume that the traces of the divine presence will lead to one god or more than one. When Heidegger uses the word *the gods*, we should not interpret the plural as necessarily ruling out the resurgence of one deity, but rather as an openness indicative of the historical sweep of theological possibilities from the Greek epoch to the present.[5]

The deity is related ontologically to all that is other than itself, including man. And the deity does not compel man to embrace the divine presence, or for that matter even to be concerned with that presence. This inference is important for appreciating what I take to be the point of Heidegger's pronouncement that "God also still stands under destiny. God is one of the voices of destiny" (*EH*, p. 169). At first reading, this claim may seem to resurrect the Greek subjugation of deities to a destiny understood as a more primordial and powerful force. This interpretation is feasible only if the "force" is transformed into a contextual interplay where all entities possess some determinate role and where any one of those entities—including the deity—is less than the whole, even when one of these entities may have created that whole. In short, the destiny that the deity "stands under" is the set of conditions connecting God and all that is other than God so that God can make his presence forcefully felt, as it were, in his appearances. When mortal man is related to the world so that he realizes the divine presence, then destiny has ordained a moment (a moment which may last a millenium or longer) when what was perhaps at one time separated is now united in ontological fullness. The ontology implicit in the fourfold takes the deity and the history of his manifestations to man seriously, but does so in a relational and "destined" sense. This sense need not necessarily demean or destroy the traditional conception of the infinite attributes of the deity. The fact that Heidegger himself does not attempt such discourse about the deity does not imply that (a) it cannot in principle be done or (b) that Heidegger is not concerned with the possibility that his own thinking or developments of that thinking by others may eventually pursue this end. But even if the deity is infinite, his relation to that which is not infinite is essential for determining how being in all its modes is connected with beings.

According to my interpretation, the deity exists. But this deduction adds little if anything about the nature of that existence. If the contemporary status of the deity is lacking, the thinker is limited to seeking out the traces of the deity as these traces have appeared in poetizing and to following these traces as far as they lead. Thus, "the establishment of being [*Seins*] is bound to the hints of the gods" (*EH*, p. 46). Note that being is bound to the *hints* of the gods, not to the gods as such. Although hints of gods cannot exist if gods do not exist, an ontology describing being must deal only with hints if hints of a certain kind of being are all that exist. Obviously then the nature of such hints becomes crucial, not only for understanding what is understandable about the source of those hints but also for understanding being itself, since without the being of the deity being as such is truncated.

Heidegger's description of God as one of the voices of destiny is thus no mere imagistic device, especially when engendering an experience with the essence of language includes hearing the voice of the deity. In fact, the majority of Heidegger's discussions about the deity revolve around those conditions which must be satisfied so that God can speak of himself to that which is other than himself. The destiny aspect of such speaking is important for interpreting the following: "The gods could come into the world only when they themselves address us and take their stand under their address. At any given time, this answer springs from the responsibility of a destiny" (*EH*, p. 40). The "answer" of men is responsible to that moment of destiny in which the conditions are fulfilled for the reception of the deity's address. Man must listen, but regardless how attentive he may be, he cannot hear the deity speaking unless there is speaking to be heard. Thus, "only when the gods themselves bring us to language is the power of naming first allotted to the poetic word" (*EH*, p. 45). The poet can name entities as things through his word (including the divine presence of the deity), but a necessary condition for such naming is that the gods themselves exist so that their presence can be experienced and expressed through mortal discourse.[6] Through this divine presence, "God's speaking is the address which assigns to man a more hushed essence," (*US*, p. 79). Man's essence is hushed in that the silence which encompasses the totality of the fourfold also includes man and the possibility that man can speak about entities as things. Some men, as poets, have ventured to break that primordial silence and to speak hints which express the traces of the deity. But before these hints can be discussed, still more elaboration of how such hints are possible is required. Heidegger provides this elaboration through the notions of the divine and the holy.

THE DIVINE AND THE HOLY

Heidegger has named the general intermediary region between the existing deity and all that is other than that deity as *the holy (das Heilige)*. Thus, "the holy originatively decides beforehand concerning men and concerning the gods, whether they are and who they are and how they are and when they are" *(EH,* p. 76). The holy is all-pervasive with respect to the connection between gods and men. The extent to which gods and men exist (in, presumably, an ontological sense yet to be defined in all respects), who and how each is to be named (in terms of their connection to each other), and when they are (when in the sense that only through the holy is the divine presence perceived at any given moment of an epoch)—all are decided within the holy.

In some epochs, the deity has not appeared to lack as the deity lacks in our epoch. But if it is possible for the deity to appear in *any* epoch, including our own, then it follows that the holy *always* exists as a necessary condition for this possibility; for if the holy ceased to be holy, then an existing deity would have nothing *through* which to display appearances of himself. Therefore, Heidegger asserts that "the holy appears to be sure," but in our epoch the "god remains remote" *(EH,* p. 27). God exists, but the remoteness of the deity is indicated by his hidden nature—"God is present only in that he is concealed" *(EH,* pp. 169–70). The holy itself presents the conditions which allow the deity to appear, even when the appearances are of a deity who is concealed.[7] But presumably the same holy would allow the appearance of a deity who was not concealed and who was lacking in no respect whatsoever. The holy is therefore ontologically neutral, in the sense that the reality of the deity depends on at least one other factor besides the holy before the distinctive character of that reality is actualized.

Heidegger accounts for this factor by distinguishing between the holy and the divine: "The holy binds the divine. The divine supports God" *(H,* p. 294). I shall attempt to describe first the notion of the divine, then its relation to the holy. The divine "supports" the deity not in the sense that the deity could not exist without man-

125

ifesting perceptible divine appearances, but as a bridge between the self-subsistence of the deity—God in himself, as it were—and those aspects of his nature open to self-disclosure through appearances. If God is completely self-subsistent, then his attributes need not extend beyond his own self-awareness. But the fact that God is such that his nature is related to the existence of nondivine entities requires that the disposition of these entities to receive appearances of the deity be on the same ontological level as the retinue of attributes proper to the deity in himself. Only through the agency of a unique presence can the deity become present to all that is other than the deity. Heidegger names this presence the *divine*.

It is vital to keep in mind that whenever Heidegger enumerates the four sectors of the fourfold, he refers to the divine *(das Göttliche)—not* to the deity *(der Gott)*. The distinction is crucial.[8] It allows Heidegger to develop a doctrine of divine presence which includes aspects of the deity appearing within the other sectors of the fourfold without committing Heidegger to stating the nature of God in himself and apart from these appearances. This approach to the relation between the being of the deity and being as such is especially incisive if, as Heidegger believes, the deity exists, but exists as concealed. From the equiprimordial character of each of the four sectors, it follows that the more pressure exerted on seeing and speaking the divine appearances among the nondivine sectors, the more likelihood that the presence of the deity will become less concealed.

A correct understanding of the divine depends on situating its relation to the fourfold, and the same holds for understanding the difference between the divine and the holy. The holy binds the divine by allowing the attributes of the deity's presence to extend beyond the deity as a self-contained entity to the limits of being itself (i.e., the fourfold), thus projecting the possibility of apprehending the divine presence as it appears within this totality. Therefore, in an assertion reminiscent of a key passage in the *Euthyphro*, Heidegger maintains that "the holy is not holy because it is divine, but the divine is divine because in its own way it is holy" *(EH*, p. 59). The principal difference between the divine and the holy is based on a directional flow between the deity as an entity and the totality of the fourfold. The divine names the presence of the deity as something distinct from yet essentially related to what is other than that presence as differentiated by the three nondivine sectors of the fourfold.

126

The holy names the dispositional capacity in all that is other than the deity to receive the appearances of the divine presence. The divine is directed *from* the attributes of the divine presence as it appears and *to* the deity as a self-contained entity; the holy is directed *from* the divine presence of the deity *to* the fourfold as such. The divine is what it is because it is holy in that all the attributes of the deity's presence capable of being perceived must appear *through* a medium which is receptive and disposed to such appearances. This medium is the holy.

All proper speaking about the deity must originate from the holy as that totality-condition directed at disclosing the divine presence. Thus, the deity-divine-holy interplay must now be integrated into the structure of language already developed. Heidegger first assures us of the intimacy between the holy and language: "The holy bestows the word and itself comes into this word. The word is the appropriation [*Ereignis*] of the holy" (*EH*, p. 76). Appropriation must be understood in the technical sense outlined in chapter 3. Therefore, since the holy is essentially related to the fourfold and since speaking is the mortal counterpart of that saying which is fundamentally coordinate with the fourfold, then all the conditions required for the naming of any entity as thing also apply to the naming of the divine presence. The holy bestows this naming word in that the relations joining all sectors, including the divine, must be present before a word can name any one entity in its ontological completeness.

Only specially gifted speakers of language are sensitive to such ontological completeness. For Heidegger, the poet is that speaker whose language shows the being of the deity. But why is the poet in so privileged, and precarious, a position? The poet is the mortal who "stands between man and the gods as the one who shows [*der Zeigender*]" (*EH*, p. 123). The poet is "between" man and the gods in that he transcends his finitude as mortal to the extent that his poetizing enters the holy and names appearances of the divine presence. But why the poet and not the priest, or the mystic, or the devout peasant in the fields? This question is crucial, since we concern ourselves with the speaking of the poet only if there is some reason for believing that the poet should be listened to in such matters. Once again, however, Heidegger leaves this assertion naked, without accompanying argumentation. The following remarks may be relevant, but they are scarcely conclusive. Although there is nothing to preclude the priest, mystic, or peasant from experiencing the holy for what it is, there is more likelihood that the poet will be open to experiences of the holy and of the divine presence for the reason that poets are more open to all manner and form of experience. Nietzsche's irreverent aphorism, that "poets treat their experiences shamelessly—they exploit them" points up the other pertinent feature of the poetic attitude. For the poet not only experiences what all other men may experience, but he also transcribes these experiences into some form of public discourse. The poet who feels deeply but never puts pen to paper is of course no poet at all. But the muteness of a poet who does not write is equivalent *mutatis mutandis* to the natural tendency of all nonpoets to let their experiences die aborning, as it were. While not all poets direct their energies to that sector of being concerned with the divine, the fact that a few—indeed, one great poet—have done so at least partially vindicates Heidegger's selection of the poet as the spokesman for those aspects of the divine which are in some degree accessible to mortal expression.

The holy is the primordial setting for the event of poetized naming, as Heidegger reminds us in this especially condensed and difficult passage: "This advance opening is the holy, the unpoetizable poem [*unvordichtbare Gedicht*] which has already poetized beyond [*überdichtet*] all poetry because in it, the holy, all-establishing, makes secure that which is established" (*EH*, p. 148). Poetizing establishes by making entities "secure" through words, by naming entities as things and eliciting the ontological relations between one thing and another. As such, the holy is itself an unpoetizable poem, that openness grounding entities of vastly divergent form and appearance but gathering this divergency in such a way that things and the differences between things may be apprehended and spoken in relation to the appearances of the divine. Thus, as a necessary condition for experiencing the divine presence, the poet "must represent the holy in order to sense the gods themselves through his saying and thus bring them into appearance in the abode of men on this earth" (*EH*, p. 123). Only the poet who is inspired will satisfy this condition, and endowed with such inspiration, he will "preserve the stilled vibration of the holy in the stillness of its silence." The presence of the gods may be discernible, e.g., in the heavens, but the gods do not appear in the full ontological sense until this perceptual presence is translated into language. The poet must not insinuate his own per-
128

sonal view on this perception; if he does, he will disrupt the stillness of the silence, that prelinguistic state of harmony through which the holy allows the presence of the deity to be apprehended in and through poetized speaking. The "vibration" of the holy is the movement generated by the interaction between the deity and all that is other than the deity through the divine presence. But the holy as such must be "stilled," that is, extended over the totality of the fourfold so that the spoken word naming an entity in one sector emerges from the holy as prelinguistic silent totality. Such preservation maintains the connection between naming word and named aspect of the divine in such a way that each element is shown in its ontological completeness.

For Heidegger, Hölderlin is the definitive spokesman of the holy in our epoch: "Hölderlin's word [*Wort*] says the holy and thus names the single space-time of the original decision for the essential structure of the future history of gods and humanity" (*EH*, p. 77). "Word" here means everything, including fragments, that has come down to us from Hölderlin's pen. Hölderlin's poetized speaking is, in this sense, equivalent to language as saying; hence Hölderlin "says" the holy. But Hölderlin must speak in order to say, and the fact that speaking and saying are never equivalent in all respects holds here as well. The poet's speaking shows the limits of what can be spoken about the divine presence in this epoch—this is the speaking which "says the holy," and this is the speaking which Heidegger has attempted to illuminate.

Hölderlin's speaking is decisive, especially with respect to the spatio-temporal presence of the divine and the appearances of that presence through the holy. But even the incisiveness and precision of Hölderlin's naming words can show only what is there to be shown. And the rigidification that occurs in the transition from word to name in such showing also marks the speaking of an epochal poet. Thus, despite Hölderlin's hints showing the presence of God, it remains true that the lack of God persists in our epoch. But we learn from these hints that any poet who would bear the tidings of a deity no longer lacking must confront this present lack as a hard fact. Such a poet must "remain near to the lack of God without fear before the appearance of godlessness and persevere in the prepared nearness to the lack until the originative word is granted from the nearness of the lacking God, the word which names the high one." (*EH*, p. 28). The name *high one (Hohen)* is Hölderlin's and indicates the extent of our experience of the deity. As such, it is merely a directional hint for what a poet will speak and name in the future. Not only are the names themselves unspoken, but it is also impossible to stipulate the precise experiences the poet must undergo in order to be in a position to name the presence of the deity: "To name him himself, even the saddening joy does not yet suffice, although it still lingers [*verweilt*] in the correct nearness toward the high one" (*EH*, p. 27). This warning indicates that the special mortal experiences of sadness and joy discussed earlier are necessary but not sufficient conditions for revealing the presence of the deity. For in addition to sadness and joy, the poet must experience the "nearness" of the "appearance of godlessness," and this will necessitate additional experiences to ground the appropriate naming words.

These experiences are not specified as such, but rather are situated within the near-remote interplay and one important poetized hint. This pivotal passage is lengthy and must be quoted in its entirety if we are to appreciate Heidegger's emphases:

> The poet becomes compelled-by-holiness into a saying which is only a still naming.
> The name in which this naming speaks must be dark.
> The place from which the poet is obliged to name the gods must be thus; that for him, what is to be named remains remote in the present of its approach and thus exactly that which is approaching. In order to open this remoteness as remoteness, the poem must withdraw from the oppressing nearness of the gods and "name" them "only softly." [*EH*, pp. 187–88]

Why "must" the name for the gods be "dark"? The point made here is obviously important, since Heidegger emphasizes it with a one-sentence paragraph. I suggest that there are two senses of necessity implied. The first sense is the fact that no one at present knows what the name is, or at least Heidegger himself has not found any poetized speaking or speaking which can accomplish what Hölderlin himself names as lacking. The second sense is that if and when the name is spoken, it will conceal in darkness as much as it enlightens. Regardless of the proximity established by the originating word, some essential loss of that proximity will result in view of the conditions necessary for the word to be spoken as a name. While there is light at the moment when the divine presence appears and is spoken, the word naming that presence retreats into darkness, the dark gap between the entity, or presence, named and all that is unspoken in that naming. Thus, a name which is "soft" preserves the "approaching nearness" of the presence of the deity by "protecting" (*hütet*) its divine appearances from any linguistic (and representational) distortion. The "oppressing nearness of the gods" is the set of all experiences and names which have traditionally been the medium through which mortals have sought, and have attained, the divine presence. The comfortable nearness of these names conceals in darkness the fact that names which once showed the divine presence no longer have the same revelatory power. In an epoch burdened by the possibility of atomic annihilation, the bromide "God is love" has lost the meaning it may have once had, even for many sincere seekers of the divine presence. The deity is therefore remote, and in order to keep him "approaching," the poet must withdraw from conventional language and, if he does venture a name, do so softly, in a manner which sustains the motion among the silent totality of the fourfold in which the deity himself exists and appears.

The image of the gods approaching through the holy becomes the central link between the poet and the divine, especially the distinctive temporality which necessarily conditions such approaching. In general, Heidegger affirms, poets "can say only that which is prior to their poetizing . . . when they say that which precedes everything which is actual: the approaching" (*EH*, p. 114). The poet must plunge into that which approaches and mediate that flux so that it is experienced and spoken by himself as mortal and as poet. The poet cannot say the holy as such because the holy is that openness which allows him to poetize about the divine. In virtue of the divine presence which appears, it is possible to experience an entity as a thing in its progression through the flux of space-time and the totality of the fourfold. As a result, the poet must "show the remoteness which draws near in the approach of the holy [*Kommen des Heiligen*]" (*EH*, p148). The deity as an entity becomes determined as a thing within the holy and through the approach of the divine presence: "The approach is the complete infinite relation [*un-endliche Verhältnis*] in which earth and heavens belong with God and men" (*EH*, p. 175). Since this totality is infinite, God approaches the present within the flux of a past time when the gods were not lacking as they are now. This is why Heidegger writes "God" and not the usual "the divine," that is, to stress the fact that the reality of the deity in past epochs was distinctively different than the reality of a lacking deity in our epoch. The emphasis on flux is necessary, given that the epoch originating with Hölderlin's poetizing "is the time of the flown gods *and* of the approaching gods" (*EH*, p. 47—italics in original). The italicized "*and*" does not denote simple logical conjunction; it denotes "and *therefore*"—the gods in this epoch have flown, but because flown gods are still gods they are necessarily approaching in the presence proper to this epoch. The specific properties which will define the nature of this deity in relation to the divine, the holy, and the fourfold must await the proper naming words.

This chapter began by discussing several aspects of Heidegger's Rilke illumination. But the problem of determining the meaning of one aspect, the holy, is so complex that it became necessary to postpone the examination of explicit poetized texts and disentangle the meanings and relations between the holy, the divine, and the deity. In a sense, of course, the commentary on the illuminations has never really ceased, but merely been shifted onto a more abstract or thoughtful plane, since all of the texts introduced so far in this chapter have been taken from essays devoted to illuminations of poetizing. But I now return to illuminations and their immediate conjunction with poetized speech. These illuminations are ordered in an ascending scale from the earth and heavens to the presence of the deity. The purpose of my brief commentary at this stage is twofold—to suggest how these illuminations concretize the notions distinguished above by connecting these notions with entities within the context of the fourfold and to arrange these illuminations in such a way that they progress toward the central phenomenon as temporality present in those entities named in conjunction with the divine and the holy. The holy will serve as the principal focal point through which poetized images naming nondivine entities connect those entities to the divine presence.

We begin with the Trakl essay. Heidegger cites the verses:

> . . . Ein Tiergesicht
> Erstarrt vor Bläue, ihrer Heiligkeit.
> (. . . an animal face
> benumbed before blue, its holiness.)

The illumination then proceeds as follows: "The blue is no image for the meaning of the holy. The blue itself is the holy as its gathering depths first shining in its veiling" (*US*, p. 44). We see the holy when we see blueness not as an image standing for the holy, but as the holy itself, shining forth as blueness which veils in its shining. Presumably what is veiled, or concealed, is an attribute of the presence of the

132

deity as that presence appears in the holy. But how does blueness as an aspect of the holy contribute to the decision which concerns, as Heidegger has claimed, "whether and who and how and when gods are gods and men are men"? To gather hints for an answer, we pursue the Trakl illumination.

Heidegger first connects the revealing-concealing property of the blue with that light-darkness proper to linguistic experience of the holy: "The holy radiates light from the blue, but at the same time conceals itself through its own darkness." Then, after Trakl poetizes that "pain is the flaming intuition of the great soul," Heidegger connects pain to blueness and the holy: "Pain thus remains . . . the pure correspondence to the holiness of the blue" (*US*, p. 64). Because the poet must experience the blue as holiness by experiencing the blue in relation to the totality of the fourfold, the "pure correspondence" is "pain," the poetized word for the necessary linguistic conjunction of scattering and collecting in which saying becomes speaking. Blueness is an appearance of the heavens, but it is also an appearance of everything insofar as light shines through the blueness of the heavens and makes the faces of animals and all other entities visible with respect to their connections with the holy and, ultimately, with the divine presence. The pain in virtue of which all entities are scattered and collected in their fourfold unity as things implies that everything be experienced as blue, but not everything as blue in the same way or at the same time. Each thing must be experienced as blue in its own way, just as the holy itself can be named in conjunction with blueness in its own way. At this point, the holy becomes near to the divine presence in that the holy as blue appears, or can appear, in each entity as thing, including the presence of that thing which is God.

In the essay on Hölderlin's "Feiertage," Heidegger elicits a more concrete correspondence to the holy than that implicit in Trakl's image of pure pain and blueness. A Hölderlin fragment contains the words "deep shadows" *(tiefen Schatten)* and "cool-breathing brook" *(kühlathmende Bach)*, and Heidegger says that "the coolness and shadiness of calmness correspond [*entspricht*] to the holy" (*EH*, p. 77). The difference between the "*entspricht*" in this illumination and the "*reine Entsprechung*" in the Trakl illumination is the difference between the pain through which blueness is experienced as blue after its radiation among all four sectors of the fourfold and the experience of shadows and the brook as only "speaking to" *(ent-*

spricht) the holy without the poet extending those appearances to the fourfold as a whole. The shadows and brook show the holy, as it were, but in an abstract and unfulfilled sense. The calmness resulting from this experience is incomplete from the standpoint of the full ontology of things. Nevertheless, such calmness is, as Heidegger puts it, the "readiness for the holy," a readiness which the presence of deep shadows and the cool-breathing brook evokes for those mortals who have experienced them as spoken in Hölderlin's poetizing. More than shadows and brooks must be calm before the holy can be adequately experienced, however, and the emphasis on totality is lacking in this particular instance of poetized speech.

Speaking which names the color blue and the natural entities shadow and a cool brook introduces the presence of the holy. But this speaking is hindered by the very nature of such appearances from saying the holy as the necessary immediacy between mortals and the divine. Other naming words must be brought to bear. An important example is Hölderlin's image of the feast celebrating the "nuptials of men and gods." Heidegger says that this feast is "the appropriation of the greeting in which *the holy* greets and appears as greeting" (*EH,* p. 105—italics in text). The image of greeting, as appropriated in the holy, thus becomes a more appropriate name for the connection between the divine and the mortal.

How does the image of greeting show the divine presence? Heidegger's illumination begins: "In greeting, the one greeting names himself, to be sure, but only in order to say that he wants nothing for himself, but gives everything to the one greeted which is due him." Heidegger then transposes greeting to the space-time of the near and remote: "The greeting unfolds the remoteness between the one greeted and the one greeting, in order that in such remoteness a nearness is grounded which does not require familiarity. The genuine greeting bestows to the one greeted the harmony of his essence" (*EH,* p. 96). Heidegger concludes that "the pure and at the same time simple greeting is poetic" (*EH,* p. 96). And at least one occasion for greeting the divine presence occurs through the appearance of the heavenly fire announced by the poetized speaking of Hölderlin—"the heavenly fire intends itself to the one greeting and remains near to him as the essence of what has been as divine" (*EH,* p. 116).

The key element in the image of greeting is the reference to the temporality of the divine appearance which greeted mortals as heavenly fire. The heavenly fire is "near" to the one greeting as an indication of that divine presence which "has been," that is, when the connection between the appearance of fire in the heavens and the divine presence was more immediately evident than in our epoch. But the connection between fire and the divine presence "has been," with the implicit inference that it *is* no longer. The connection nevertheless remains near, and the problem becomes one of determining how such nearness is possible. Nearness implies remoteness, and this in turn implies the spatio-temporal motion proper to the fourfold. Regardless which of the many diverse images appears as an indication of the holy and its connection to the divine, any given appearance—heavenly fire, blueness, shadows and brooks—is near and greets mortals from that total temporal presence grounding all appearances of the deity. The deity itself may not be temporal, or its temporality may be completely different from the temporality of any other entity, but the presence of the deity is and must be temporally determined. Such presence becomes accessible linguistically only if the poet experiences the temporal conditions within which the approaching gods will appear as approaching and thus as present. The poet must therefore reflect the holy as the ground of the flown and of the approaching gods. And this necessity demands that the temporality which conditions the possibility of a past appearance remaining near in our present be itself experienced as a modality of presence. The central problem as far as the poetizing of the divine is concerned has now been posed: How to name temporality so that the deity can appear as the deity within the presence of that temporality?

The approaching gods greet mortals in a present moment which is determined by the extent to which this moment can contain the presence, the total temporality, of the deity. Heidegger will concentrate his illuminative powers on those poetized words which hint at the limits of such temporality. Thus, he says of Hölderlin's "*Jezt aber tagts!*" that "the '*Jezt*' names the approach of the holy" (*EH*, p. 76). The holy approaches as a distinctive now, but the now (*Jezt*) naming the holy is not a temporal now in the idiomatic sense of the "hence and now." How then is such a now to be made determinate? Heidegger elicits clues to the temporality of the now by illuminating Hölderlin's "Destiny is a lingering" (*Ist eine Weile das Schiksaal—EH*, p. 105). Only by the designs of destiny will the now as a moment of presence fulfill the divine presence.

Heidegger first asserts what lingering is *not:* "Lingering is calculated as the temporary and neglected for the continuing." But such calculation is the result of representational thinking and results in the mere dismissal of lingering as something only "temporary" and without any constant duration. According to Heidegger, lingering has its own distinctive constancy: "We seek the customary constancy in the mere advance of the and-so-forth. If the latter can indeed renounce claim to the beginning and end, constancy without beginning and without end raises itself to the appearance of the purest remaining" (*EH*, p. 106). Constancy is represented as a fluid progression of "et ceteras" and must then be elevated into an ontological constancy, one without beginning and end and raised to a state of "purest remaining." Thus, the past as past, the present as present, the future as future, all remain in a constancy which destines itself as, according to the speaking of the poet, a peculiar and distinctive lingering.

The temporality of lingering is unique, and Heidegger's illumination must be cited in its entirety to appreciate the difficulty of this uniqueness:

The uniqueness of this lingering does not require a return, because lingering as related to the past is averse to every "recapitulation." But the lingering of the unique is also not surpassable, because it lingers toward what is approaching so that all that is approaching has its arrival in the lingering of the uniqueness of what is past. Lingering is neither finite nor infinite. It lingers [*weilt*] *before* these measures. This lingering shelters the peace in which all dispensation of destiny is retained. [*EH*, p. 106—italics in original.]

This illumination of Hölderlin's word *Weile* is Heidegger's highly condensed attempt to think through past, present, and future time as a unity which lingers and thus shows the nature of being as presence. Let me very briefly suggest some implications of this illumination with respect to the divine sector. (Lingering and the notion of presence will be discussed in greater detail in part 3.) First, the priority *(vor)* Heidegger assigns to the notion of lingering is clearly an attempt to ground time in such a way that the distinction can be drawn (in representational thought) between what lasts as "finite" and what lasts as "infinite." The finite is determined as finite and the infinite is determined as infinite through a common medium in which what approaches in the future can confront what has been in the past. The unity of this medium is named by the word *lingering*, and this unity is itself unique—there is only one past and only one future when these two temporal horizons linger in the present as presence. The temporality inherent in the divine thus becomes crucial: if the temporality proper to the mode of existence of the thing (the deity) grounding the divine can be linguistically expressed, then it should be possible to develop that language to determine the temporality of all other lingering things.

Second, the "peace" that is sheltered by lingering is the name for all events that can happen during the temporality of lingering, insofar as such events can be spoken about in language. The totality, although inexpressible as such in language, is nonetheless peaceful, that is, its constituent parts are capable of being expressed in speech. Such expression would result from the experience of a mortal who remained lingering and whose speaking itself displayed the peace which characterizes the events which occur during the temporality of lingering. Thus, speaking which lingers reflects the lingering of that which is spoken about. This is the peace from which the calmness spoken of in Hölderlin's deep shadows and cool-breathing brook is possible. But it is a peace which must pervade *all* entities before the temporality of that peace can be experienced and named in lingering speaking about the temporality of the entities as things. To break the peace, as it were, is to occasion an event which, in our epoch, may destine renewed intimacy between mortal man and the deity.

Whether or not theologians find such conclusions incisive and useful for their purposes is a possibility which must be resolved elsewhere. But the provocative, and problematic, character of these illuminations as far as the philosopher is concerned requires no further demonstration. If the rounds of the fourfold conclude with the divine, then the problems of experiencing the deity, the divine presence, and the holy culminate in the problem of understanding the temporality which grounds the possibility of such an experience. Heidegger's condensed and difficult development of Hölderlin's word *lingering* is just one attempt to translate the insights of poetized saying into the speaking of more prosaic thought. But given that any entity is not a thing until the entity is related to the divine sector of the fourfold, the problematic temporality pertaining to an experience of the divine presence is essential to the determination of all nondivine things as well. [9] In one important sense then, confronting the death of God as that epochal event is poetized instigates anew Heidegger's ultimate ontological problem—the relation between being and time. Now, however, being as such includes the being of a flown or lacking deity as well as the being of all entities other than such a deity.

The second phase of my commentary on Heidegger and the language of poetry is now complete. This phase has examined explicit poetized texts and the ways in which Heidegger has attempted to illuminate those texts. In part 1, the problems inherent in thoughtfully understanding the structure of language were developed to facilitate an approach to Heidegger's illuminations of a certain type of language. Any disagreement with the implications of illuminations without taking into account the broad linguistic and ontological base which grounds all the illuminations is a fundamentally misconceived approach to Heidegger's thought. My commentary in part 2 has been intended to show how Heidegger's illuminations shed light on his own "theoretical" views about language and also how these illuminations present and develop perspectives on the being of what is named in such speaking.

I am aware of the inadequacy of my remarks on both fronts. It becomes clear to the careful and sympathetic student that the majority of Heidegger's illuminations are suggestive monadic structures. And the number of possible thoughtful worlds in each poetized and illuminated image is endless. The more effort exerted in trying to understand why Heidegger says what he does about each image, the more one understands both Heidegger himself and the being of what is named in that poetizing. Whatever results have been achieved here will be found wanting by someone with the diligence and insight to grapple with Heidegger's illuminations more rigorously than I have. However, the interpretive assumptions and technique employed I believe to be absolutely sound and the most fruitful available. And this is why it does not seem adequate to conclude an interpretation of this sort at this point. If one confronts Heidegger's thinking on poetizing, one must also confront Heidegger's thinking on the thoughtful implications of such poetizing. One aspect of such thought will be selected for more extensive discussion, but many other aspects are possible candidates. One hopes that these possibilities will eventually be explored in the secondary literature.

Part 3 of this study will focus on the theme of temporality as it has been progressively formulated in the poetizing introduced and illuminated by Heidegger. I approach this theme by describing the

138

most appropriate way to understand the confluence of poetizing *(Dichten)* and thinking *(Denken)* as this confluence is found in the experience of the divine presence and the temporality distinctive to that presence. One of the principal guiding notions for my discussion is the sought-after standard mentioned at the conclusion of chapter 5. The nature of this standard is still far from evident, but now it is clear that it must be sought for in the domain of Heidegger's reflections on the temporality of being. If such a standard is definable, then we will be that much nearer to measuring the ontological nature of man and his relation to things in the world, a world of sufficient diversity to include pain, stones, the sea, and the deity.

PART 3

The Confrontation between Poetizing and Thinking

7. Poetizing and Thinking

ALTHOUGH THE DEITY is lacking in our epoch, Heidegger posits the possibility of making contact with the divine presence as long as certain conditions of receptivity are fulfilled. Mortals may "first come to meet the gods in a brightly structured presence [*hellgefügten Anwesenheit*]" if this presence is approached and mediated through the "strictness of poetizing thinking imaging comprehension" (*dichtenden denkenden bildenden Fassens—EH*, pp. 87–88). To explicate this dark utterance, an analysis of the conjunction uniting poetizing (*Dichten*) with thinking (*Denken*) is required. Do we muse poetically on the appearances of the deity in the manner of the poet who experienced and spoke these appearances? Or do we think on these appearances in a manner distinct from the original poetized speaking so that by such thinking we understand, in some conceptual sense, what the appearances reveal? Or, as the conjunction seems to imply, do we apprehend the appearances through a unique combination of both poetizing and thinking? Even if the resulting conjunction is unique, however, the fact that it may be described as both thought-ful and poetic suggests that distinctively different properties persist *within* that unique fusion. It should also be determined whether thinking must complement poetizing for the appearances of entities other than the deity. If the mode of existence of the deity is unique, then there is no reason to extend the problems involved in ap-prehending that mode of existence to nondivine entities. If, on the other hand, the deity is not unique in requiring the conjunction of poetizing and thinking, then the problem of describing and distin-guishing the two activities becomes crucial for determining the on-tological characteristics of *all* entities.

Besides Heidegger's explicit concern for fidelity to ontological demands, the problematic conjunction of poetizing and thinking is important for other reasons. In the first Nietzsche volume, Heideg-ger notes that all "great philosophy [*Philosophie*] is in itself thoughtful-poetic" (*NI*, p. 129).[1] Now, Heidegger's work may itself

143

be great, but this greatness is not the greatness of Plato, Aristotle, and Kant. These figures, and of course others, are philosophers in a sense distinguishable from the thinkers of whom Heidegger is both protagonist and, at times, exponent. However (assuming the truth of Heidegger's claim about the history of philosophy), the point is that if the determination of the goals and procedures of present thinking requires investigation of past efforts at thought, i.e., philosophy, then our study of these past efforts must discern and preserve the same dual and apparently divergent features which underlie the needs of our contemporary epoch. Thus, every effort at thought, whether philosophical in the traditional sense or in Heidegger's quasi-revisionist sense, requires the conjunction of thinking and poetizing.

This requirement is stated in a number of ways. At times, Heidegger insists that thinking and poetizing are essentially identical. Thus, "all meditative thinking is a poetizing, but all poetizing a thinking" (*US*, p. 267). And again, "But thinking is the poetizing of the truth [*Wahrheit*] of being" (*H*, p. 343). At other times, however, he does not claim that the two activities are identical, but that each cannot be what it is without the other. Thus, "all poetizing . . . is in its ground a thinking" (*H*, p. 303). And, in straightforward fashion, "both poetizing and thinking need one another" (*US*, p. 173), and this same need more fully developed: "But it is also possible and at times even necessary that there be a conversation between thinking and poetizing, and this because both own an especially distinctive although distinct relation [*Verhältnis*] to language" (*US*, p. 38). This final passage is important for two reasons: first, it establishes a fundamental relation uniting thinking and poetizing with language; second, it suggests possible autonomy for thinking, with the conversation between thinking and poetizing needed only when thinking is itself somehow lacking.

We may summarize as follows: In some respects, poetizing and thinking are identical. Heidegger has hinted at one respect, their joint relation to language. But in other respects, there is dependency of the one on the other, that is, the one cannot be what it is without the agency of the other. But despite this dependency, the two activities are still distinct. Heidegger clearly stipulates that such a distinction obtains. While asserting that "thinking and poetizing, each in its own unalterable way, are the essential saying" (*WD*, p. 87),[2] he also maintains that "what is said poetically and what is said

144

thoughtfully are never the same. But the one and the other say [*sagen*] the same thing in different ways" (*VA*, p. 138). How then to establish the difference between poetizing and thinking?[3]

Philosophy may be gnomically characterized as the art of drawing distinctions, and drawing the distinction in question demands art of a fairly high order. This is especially true when the desired distinction appears to be readily accessible. The numerous passages in which Heidegger asserts that "poetizing is such and such" suggests that an assembly of all such passages might yield the essence of poetizing. A similar process could be initiated for thinking. After both processes have been completed, the resulting characteristics would define poetizing and thinking so that an individual instance of spoken language could be appropriately cataloged.

There are two objections to such procedure. The first objection is textual—Heidegger himself has asserted that "the poetical character of thinking is still veiled" (*AED*, p. 23) and that "a concealed affinity governs both thinking and poetizing" (*WP*, p. 30). And from *Unterwegs zur Sprache*: "We are not able to decide straightway whether poetizing is properly [*eigentlich*] a thinking or thinking properly a poetizing" (*US*, pp. 188–89). Now, an obvious objection arises when these claims are placed in apposition to the assertion of a definitive but implicit distinction between thinking and poetizing: if Heidegger himself cannot distinguish between thinking and poetizing, on what basis does he maintain that a distinction can be discerned at all?

I do not consider this objection to be especially damaging. First, the reason why the distinction cannot be drawn may be due to Heidegger's own inadequacies as a "poetical thinker." The insight that allows one to recognize a legitimate problem does not necessarily confer the insight to solve that problem. Someone other than Heidegger may succeed where he fails. But, second, perhaps Heidegger and anyone else concerned with this problem is fated to fail when attempting to draw the distinction. Why? If the distinction is in principle impossible to locate regardless of strenuous mortal endeavor, then why mention the distinction in the first place? But if the distinction is not in principle impossible to determine (surely this is Heidegger's intent), then there may be some explanation for its currently veiled status. One such explanation might run as follows: Given Heidegger's concern for the historical character of both thinking and poetizing, perhaps "the time is not ripe" for the resolution of the distinction. This explanation may or may not be persuasive; for present purposes, let us assume that it is. But its persuasiveness is based on the necessary historicity of both poetizing and thinking. And this position must surely be argued. The explanation is introduced here in anticipation of a problem central to Heidegger's view of temporality and its relation to language. The problem will be discussed later in chapter 7 and in chapter 9.

The second objection is not textual as such but is based on inferences derived from Heidegger's fundamental principles. Consider this passage from the Postscript to *Was ist Metaphysik?*, a passage which appears to suggest criteria for distinguishing thinking and poetizing: "The thinker says being. The poet names the holy" (*WM*, p. 107). The contrast which emerges from these claims seems helpful, perhaps even definitive. The assistance is in two different areas. First, the thinker is characterized as the spokesman of that medium in which language is realized at its most basic ontological level, language as saying. Thus, the thinker says being. The poet, on the other hand, remains at the representational level of language as spoken through the word as name. Second, the thinker has the totality of being for his province; the poet is limited merely to the penumbra of holiness which belongs properly to only one ontological sector, the divine. According to this text, the differences are based on *how* each speaker pursues his end— the thinker by saying, the poet by naming—and *what* that end is—for the thinker, being; for the poet, the holy. The problematic distinction therefore ceases to be problematic.

But this conclusion is premature, not to mention that it ignores what Heidegger himself has written. For immediately after this apparently definitive text, Heidegger adds that, from the perspective of the essence of being, the ways in which poetizing and thinking relate to and are distinguished from one another "must here remain open." Heidegger then suggests that "presumably" *(vermutlich)* poetizing springs from thinking because poetizing requires thinking to be poetizing. Priority is given to thinking, from which in some "open" sense poetizing finds its realization. As Heidegger has here described their respective functions, it is not difficult to understand why thinking is presumably more fundamental than poetizing. All things *(Dinge)* are derived from being, and if thinking says being then it follows that poetizing could name the holy only in virtue of the possibility that the holy is itself accessible to the saying of being. But to name anything is possible only because of the primordial saying of language, saying which in this text is asserted as the domain of thinking alone. Since speaking is what it is because of saying, poetizing is what it is because of thinking.

But let us now examine what the poet does in light of a systematic rehearsal of Heidegger's own linguistic principles. If the poet as poet names the holy and if the holy is properly an aspect of being, then when the name for the holy is spoken, the word underlying the name connects the holy to the divine and from there to the other sectors of the fourfold. But by so doing, the poet himself ultimately *says being*. For if the holy were not said as being but merely represented by a given name, then the presence of the word would either be hidden or disappear. Therefore, the holy would cease to be the holy, since its essential linguistic relation to being would be nonexistent. As a result, if the poet ultimately *says* being in *speaking* the name for the holy, then how does the thinker say being in a manner distinguishing his activity from the activity of the poet?

This conclusion is important, and its particularity may be generalized. It is not sufficient to stipulate which things poetizing names, regardless of what the thing or things may be. If the distinction between poetizing and thinking is based on considerations concerning a single named thing, then the distinctions would still ultimately rest on how this thing as named was spoken from the saying of language and of being. But how could thinking then be distinguished from poetizing, since all language, whether in the form of thinking or poetizing, must say through the world of being as differentiated by the fourfold? It is not sufficient to claim just that thinking "says being," since all saying says in virtue of being and the distinctive attributes of thinking as such are lost. Heidegger's claim that poetizing names the holy can be only suggestive and not conclusive as far as establishing the difference between poetizing and thinking. Further characteristics must be added to determine how thinking says being in ways other than that of poetizing, which names being as the holy. The matter of drawing the distinction is more complex than first appeared.

This attempt at securing the distinction was based on letting the activity of thinking stand as whole and then approaching that whole with poetizing as an apparently distinguishing part. But given Heidegger's position on language in general, the part denoted in this text could not serve as the distinguishing factor, a conclusion with which Heidegger himself would seem to concur. Furthermore, I have argued that no poetized part, if designated in the above manner, could satisfy this requirement. Let us now reverse the order by considering whether some part or aspect of thinking may prove sufficient for the desired distinction. If the lesson just learned is symmetrical, one would anticipate the results of this reversal to be equally inconclusive. But a development of Heidegger's views on thinking *(Denken)* may suggest an approach to the problematic distinction.

THINKING

What does Heidegger understand by the word *thinking*? The following is not intended to weave together all the various strands on the notion of thinking scattered throughout Heidegger's works. Nor does it fulfill a more limited but still complex end—an interpretation of Heidegger's main work on the subject, *Was Heisst Denken?*. What I have attempted to construct here is a representative account of Heidegger on thinking insofar as thinking is essentially related to poetizing. It will become evident that my results may be something less than pellucidly clear. However, the course I have followed at least partially determines thinking as Heidegger has described it.

Heidegger's initial characterizations of thinking may be ranged under the heading of what thinking is not. "Thinking is not conceiving" (WD, p. 128), and the reason why thinking does not result in concepts is because it "is no means for knowledge" (*US*, p. 123). Knowledge *(Erkennen)* is a consequence of that thinking which has been both subject and object of traditional metaphysics. Heidegger's notion of thinking is not antithetical to all types of knowing (since, presumably, it would not be inappropriate to designate the ontological apprehension of being as a type of knowing), but he insists that thinking as *Denken* be understood according to standards which do not result in knowledge in the customary metaphysical or even scientific sense. Thus, in thinking, "there is neither method nor subject" (*US*, p. 178), with an implicit rejection of a Husserlian program of phenomenological reduction or, indeed, of any method which elevates techniques of whatever form above the openness necessary to experience and speak about being as such.[4]

But these negative restrictions must be integrated with the positive attributes of thinking. Heidegger asserts that thinking is "a mode of doing. But a mode of doing [*Tun*] which transcends all

148

practical conduct [*Praxis*]" (*W*, p. 191). Heidegger does not wish to suggest that practical conduct is irrelevant to thinking, or that practical conduct may not be eventually guided by thinking or that thinking is some form of mysticism. The point is that thinking includes (a) all modes of existence of that entity capable of thinking, not merely the products and processes of the mind as the putative instrument and domain of thought, and (b) the environment or, more accurately, the ontological context which grounds the attempt to think. As a result, the stipulation of properties which define thinking must extend beyond those properties which have traditionally restricted thinking to a form of mental or practical conduct.

The chief obstacle to recognizing the nature of thinking in this holistic sense is, in Heidegger's view, that thinking which has predominated in the history of Western speculation. Heidegger names such thinking representation *(Vorstellen)*. We have mentioned the notion of representation in an informal sense often in this study; now we must determine precisely what Heidegger finds objectionable in the type of cognition denoted by representation.

Representational thinking is thinking which characterizes the entity thought and the entity thinking in a certain definite manner. Thus, "representing means to bring something [*etwas*] before oneself and have it for oneself, to have something present [*präsent*] to oneself as subject" (*FD* p. 106). And again, "representing presents [*präsentiert*] the object in that it represents the object to the subject, through which representation the subject presents itself as such" (*H*, pp. 121–22). The entity represented displays a certain temporality which exists in relation to the subject, or knower. In the process of rendering the entity accessible to the knower, the temporal constitution of the entity represented also constitutes the temporality of the knowing subject as knower. The ontological character of this mutual temporality is the most crucial characteristic of representational thinking.

The result, stated in general terms, is that "contemporary philosophy experiences the being of an entity as the object [*Gegenstand*]. The entity comes to such standing in opposition through perception and for perception" (*VA*, p. 234).[5] The process of perception is an essential part of the representational bond uniting subject and object. The notions and problems inherent in perception are based metaphysically on the same set of principles which underlie representational thought. Thus, "the perception of reason [*Vernunft*] unfolds itself as this manifold placing [*Stellen*], which is overall and first of all a representing [*Vor-stellen*]" (*WD*, p. 27). For Heidegger, this connection between perception and reason is characteristic of modern philosophy from Leibniz to Kant, and it is implicit in the doctrines of reasoned knowledge and the objects of such knowledge antecedent to modernity, as far back as Plato.[6] Contemporary philosophy merely echoes the fundamental principles of its own history. But Heidegger insists that "reason and its representation are only *one* kind of thinking" (*W*, p. 216—italics in original).

To represent is to think, but to think need not be to represent. And the possibility of thinking is real: "But that which is nonrepresentable is in no way also unthinkable, supposing that thinking is not exhausted in representation" (*SG*, p. 39). Nevertheless, *Denken* cannot simply spring forth *de novo*, bypassing completely that thinking which is representational. Heidegger recognizes this fact and explicitly integrates it into his position: "An attempt to transcend the representation of entities as such in thinking on the truth [*Wahrheit*] of being must, proceeding from that representation, still in a certain manner represent the truth of being" (*W*, p. 206). And the same point more concisely expressed, "the metaphysical mode of representation may be in a certain respect unavoidable" (*US*, p. 116). This unavoidability not only attests to the fact that the origin and development of thinking will necessarily be as historical as the origin and development of representation, but also to the partial truth of the subject-object relation and the partial reliability of the language used in statements expressing this relation. But partial truth is, strictly speaking, not truth at all, so the attempt to transcend the limits of representational thinking must be made. This attempt will require "the step back" (*der Schritt zurück*), one of Heidegger's most frequently quoted phrases. The thinker must step back behind the history of metaphysical and representational thinking and its correlative language, without entirely circumventing representational thinking. In fact, "the step back from the representational thinking of metaphysics does not repudiate this thinking, but it opens the remoteness to the claim [*Anspruch*] of the truth of being in which the correspondence [*Entsprechen*] stands and proceeds" (*VA*, p. 84). The remoteness (*Ferne*) in this passage names all the hidden attributes of the entity as thing which may be brought near if the speaking of thoughtful language corresponds to the saying hidden in metaphysical language.[7]

The way to this remoteness is long and requires considerable effort: "The step back from the essence of metaphysics demands a constancy and perseverance whose measure we do not know. This much is clear: the step requires a preparation which must be dared here and now" (*ID*, p. 117). The preparation for thinking includes the comprehensive reexamination of language as that necessary medium which shows the object of thinking, the being of entities as things. But this reexamination is only the first phase in a preparation which must be implemented in the midst of a tradition which runs counter to the intended goal of that preparation. The fact that Heidegger's subsequent claims are preparatory rather than constitutive must be kept in mind. Heidegger himself has not mastered all the conditions of thinking, nor does he feel that anyone else on the current philosophical scene has mastered them either. "We do not yet think; we all do not think, including the speaker, he first and foremost above all" (*WD*, p. 49). The situation is, however, not impossible. But it must be understood from the outset that when an entire tradition is thrown into question, no principles could serve as criteria according to which proofs of Heidegger's position could be established. Heidegger proclaims bluntly, "we need prove nothing here. All proof is only a subsequent undertaking on the basis of presuppositions" (*VA*, p. 196). And the whole burden of Heidegger's investigations into language as a medium of representational thinking is to indicate the presuppositional character of representation and the metaphysics on which it is based. Thus, how could such claims be proven, since the proofs must appeal to the very representational principles thrown into question?

Heidegger must prepare the way for thinking with special care, since his position can be plausible at best and never demonstrable. He begins by asserting that "only when we exist in that which is to be thought about [*zu-Bedenkende*] are we able to think" (*WD*, p. 1). And we as mortals do so exist: "We already are, and to be sure insofar as we are in general [*wir überhaupt sind*], in relation to that which is to be thought" (*WD*, p. 59). No mode of existence, regardless how common or transitory that mode may be, is cut off from the object of thinking: "Every human comportment [*Verhalten*] in its own way stands open" to a receptivity for an authentic apprehension of being (*W*, p. 86). There is no need to restrict thinking to epistemology in the traditional sense. Thinking includes the extent to which we apprehend being in *all* the modes in which we exist in relation to being.[8]

Thinking and being are essentially related but are not identical.

"Being is no production of thinking. Rather, essential thinking is an appropriation [*Ereignis*] of being" (*W*, p. 103). And again: "Thinking does not arise. It exists insofar as being becomes present [*west*]" (*H*, p. 325). These claims taken jointly imply that thinking is both other than and dependent upon being. The first claim asserts that thinking is an appropriation of being, with the clear implication that thinking and the language which expresses thinking are essentially related; the second claim directs thinking toward its fundamental ontological dimension, time as presence (*Anwesen*). But where and how can thinking begin to assert itself?

Heidegger has epitomized this possibility as a confluence of representational thought and *Denken:* "Thinking must think against itself, which it can do only seldom" (*AED*, p. 15). The insights of representational thinking are indeed insights relative to the principles which ground that thinking. But they become obstacles to thinking which must be met and overcome before thinking can emerge and offer its own insights. Thus, "our customary representing is the essence of nearness" (*VA*, p. 280). The relation in which an objective entity is represented by a subjective knower must be reexamined to approach that nearness. As noted above, every aspect of the subject/object, knower/known relation must be thrown into question. "The connection [*Beziehung*] of representing directed toward the thing is the completion of that relation [*Verhältnisses*] which, as a comportment [*Verhalten*], brings itself fundamentally and at times to oscillation" (*H*, p. 80). All connections between knower and represented entity are instances of comportment, but not all comportments must take the form of representation. And hints toward the ontological nature of the comportment proper to thinking are present in poetized speaking, hence Heidegger's use of oscillation (*Schwingen*) to account for its now visible, now hidden characteristic.

Thinking has a comportment proper to itself, and the oscillation of that comportment is grounded in language. For "all ways of thought lead . . . in an exceptional manner through language" (*VA*, p. 13). Heidegger acknowledges that "the language of thinking can proceed only from natural language," even though such language "is basically historical-metaphysical" (*SD*, p. 54) and thus reflects in its structure and in its primary content the presuppositions of that metaphysics. If properly understood, however, language provides the stimulus for all thinking: "When we are in accordance with language, we learn to know thinking not only in its essential fitness, we learn in this way thinking itself" (*WD*, p. 62). For Heidegger, "being and thought" emerge from "the place of stillness" (*SD*, p. 75), that aspect of the totality which grounds the possibility of all speech. Once this and the other totality-conditions implicit in language are experienced, then presumably we will know not only the proper subject matter of thinking, but also how that subject matter should be thought. Such thinking "does not use terms [*Wörtern*], but says words [*Worte*]" (*WD*, p. 88); it will thus fulfill the most basic ontological requirement for the linguistic appropriation of being.

From the perspective of ontology, language emerges from silence. The first phase of this emergence is language as saying. To the question, "What brings saying into appearance?" Heidegger answers "The presence of all that is present" (*VA*, p. 247). Whenever an entity is named and thus made to appear in language, "we bid that which is present to come in its presence" (*WD*, p. 85). Each name contains a glimmer of the presence which the word grounding that name can, if spoken properly, bring into the totality of presence as such. Determining being as the temporality of such presence is the distinctive domain of thinking: "The essence of thinking is determined from that which is to be thought about—from the presence of all that is present, from the being of beings" (*WD*, p. 149). For Heidegger, representational thinking either ignores or distorts being and its relation to temporality; thinking, however, recognizes and rectifies this crucial historical bias.

The being-beings distinction, so prevalent in Heidegger's early work, now is made equivalent to the relation between presence and that which is present. Presence—*Anwesen*—names the three temporal dimensions of past, present, and future. In the temporality of presence, "the past, the present [*Gegenwärtige*]," and the future as approaching "appear in the oneness of a united presence" (*WD*, p. 92). Thus, the temporality of a given entity is a unified presence of past, present, and future; thinking must address itself to this presence and discover appropriate names for it. Now, although any given entity is *in* presence, its particular existence does not exhaust the totality of presence. Therefore, thinking is also determined "from that which is other than a being" (*W*, p. 105), where otherness denotes that part or phase of presence which is other than the presence of the given entity. This otherness becomes "measure giving for that which is unthought and even for that which is unthinkable" (*W*, p. 268). Thinking about the distinctive presence of an entity will

153

necessarily include that which has not been thought about the entity (*das Ungedachte*) and that which cannot be thought about that entity (*Das Undenkbare*).

This convergence of thinking with what is not and cannot be thought, in addition to Heidegger's own mention of a "measure," raises the problem of the limits and rules of thinking. In *Was Heisst Denken?*, Heidegger reminds us that several crucial aspects of the question "What is thinking?" can never be answered, if by an answer we mean the statement of conceptually precise definitions "whose content may, with industry, be divulged" (*WD*, p. 9). The "most difficult" of these questions is that which concerns what must be brought into play "so that we are capable of thinking in its essential rightness."[9] The answer to the problem of criteria for thought's rightness can be expressed only in the most limited way through "statements and propositions" (*Angaben und Sätze*). Heidegger guardedly concludes that "we ourselves must come to the way" this question is to be answered (*WD*, p. 160), where presumably the way leads beyond the expressible limits of language. Although to express the limits of thinking may transcend the capabilities of language as such, the processes and products of thinking cannot transcend language. Heidegger then repeats that because thinking "is a fundamental saying and speaking of language, it must remain near to poetizing" (*WD*, p. 155). Therefore, we may conclude that whatever precision is attainable in thinking, the presence of entities depends on how "near" thinking remains to poetizing.[10]

THINKING AND POETIZING

With this brief sketch of Heidegger's notion of thinking, we have come full circle, since to determine the correct nearness between poetizing and thinking implies that the two linguistic activities can first of all be distinguished. What I have presented under the heading of thinking is systematic (Heidegger is not), condensed, and principally in Heidegger's own terminology. Both the order and its implications are defensible, I believe, insofar as they purport to represent the core of Heidegger's position. Let me now summarize that position. (1) The object of thinking is the determination of presence as found in the distinctive temporality of a given entity. (2) The medium in which thinking is expressed is language, not only the language traditionally associated with conceptual representation

154

or epistemology, but also any language which reveals the temporality of an entity. Whether this language must obey rules of argumentation, or indeed any rules, is still to be determined. (3) The context of thinking is totality-conditioned and thus, at least by intent, engenders results which undercut the traditional primordiality of, e.g., the subject/object dichotomy.

There are two interpretive alternatives at this point. The first alternative is to attempt to distinguish between poetizing and thinking with the various notions at hand. The second alternative is to develop the available notions as a totality which grounds both poetizing and thinking. The structure of the totality would then become more accessible, as well as the relation between a given entity and that totality insofar as that relation is poetized or thought. Now, even if the first alternative succeeds (and Heidegger has intimated that it will not succeed, or will succeed only partially), the second alternative must still be explored. The more we know about the whole, the more we know about the parts, especially if the relation between two different parts (poetizing and thinking) of that whole can be only partially defined.

Let us now attempt the distinction between poetizing and thinking according to guidelines suggested by the threefold summary of thinking just mentioned. First, it is evident that the distinction cannot lie within the medium, since both thinking and poetizing are based on the saying of language. Nor, second, can the distinction be based on the totality-orientation as such, since poetizing also shows the presence of the totality as the fourfold. The only condition which remains is that based on the presence of a given entity, and here we return to Heidegger's claim that poetizing names that entity which is the holy. I have already offered arguments to demonstrate that, from one perspective, this claim cannot serve as the ground for the distinction. But other perspectives may be relevant to achieve this end. For example, if Heidegger's stipulation about poetizing and the holy is generalized, the result is the following: thinking will continue to say being, but poetizing now names whatever is "out of tune" with being as such in all epochs. In our epoch, it is the lack of the deity and the resulting effect this has on the divine presence, the holy within which the divine presence appears, and all entities insofar as they relate to the divine. In other epochs, it may be other such lacks. But whatever is lacking to the totality of being is the special province of poetizing and its capability to perceive and express linguistically what other types of language overlook or are incapable of expressing.

As thus formulated, however, this conclusion has peculiar repercussions for being as such insofar as being is the ultimate ground of poetizing. For if poetizing names what is out of tune in being, then being must always be out of tune in some respect in order to sustain the reality of poetizing. If being is not out of tune, then poetizing would cease to exist as a separate mode of linguistic activity. Heidegger has suggested that thinking may do without poetizing under certain conditions, but he has never even hinted at the possibility that poetizing itself could cease altogether. And it must cease if, under the hypothesis offered above, it exists solely to name what is out of tune in being (assuming that being may become perfectly harmonious with itself).

However, a reformulation of the hypothesis covers the inference that poetizing is basically, as it were, a function of the malfunction of being. Being is both differentiated by the fourfold and in motion through presence. Therefore, perhaps poetizing names the most predominant aspect of the motion and differentiation of being. In our epoch, the predominance is the lack of the deity and the resulting ontological deviations for all other entities. According to this reformulation, poetizing will cease only when the motion of being is in such perfect harmony that no single part or phase ever predominates over the remaining parts. Presumably, the unity of being is of such a sort that this harmony is impossible, with the result that poetizing will always and necessarily continue to exist. We thus arrive at a distinction of sorts between poetizing and thinking. It is that thinking says the whole and poetizing names the predominant part of the whole, that part which determines the uniqueness of all entities within the whole for that particular epoch.

If this interpretation is sound, then pursuing the first interpretive alternative mentioned above has proven at least partially successful. But this interpretation is based on attributing characteristics to being which may or may not be proper to being. We may also mention the subsequent but equally crucial problem of determining criteria for deciding which poetizing (among all the possible types of poetical language) will name that aspect of being which is out of phase. The latter problem will be taken up in the concluding chapter. For now, the second alternative must still be explored. For even if being does go in and out of phase and poetizing does direct attention to the predominant characteristic of a given epoch, poetizing as such does not convey the precise sense in which an entity must be linguistically connected with another entity to show the effect of this predominance on the ontological nature of that entity. Such connections can only be realized from that totality-perspective which says the whole, that is, which can take the appropriate poetized hints and integrate those hints with the language thinking has at its disposal and can presumably develop for this end. In our epoch, naming the holy can guide the essential nearness of poetizing and thinking on condition that the properties poetizing speaks from the holy are extended to cover all entities capable of being thought as things.

Given that being is differentiated as presence and as the fourfold, the most important characteristic of the holy is the cluster of names describing how a thing temporally approaches in the transition from being as such to a position as a particular thing. If the deity as a thing can be discerned approaching in and through presence and the fourfold, then the temporality of any other entity as thing in that same totality can also be determined. The names showing that thing need not themselves evoke anything celestial, angelic, or divine (in traditional theological or popular senses of these terms). Such restrictions are the residue of representational limitations and are not proper to the linguistic appropriation of the holy and of the deity. The holy is an ontological dimension which includes all sectors of the fourfold so that the presence of a lacking deity can appear in all things mortal, earthly, and heavenly. Heidegger's own illuminations have partially shown how the holy plays into human will and human feelings and how this connection relates to the fourfold as a whole. The earthly and heavenly illuminations also contribute vital links uniting the three nondivine sectors and directing them toward the problematic approach of the past deity and its appearances in our present epoch.

Thinking must seek the proper names for the approach of presence amid the welter of names for many apparently nondivine and nontemporal entities and phenomena. Therefore, Heidegger must be allowed leeway to steer the notion of presence according to linguistic guidelines which may be different, perhaps radically different, from the sense of appropriateness which clings to customary temporal representations. This potentially radical shift also includes the introduction of new language, especially names of a certain sort, which may appear inappropriate to something as ontologically empty as time. But, if Heidegger is correct, this empty neutrality of time and its seeming irrelevance to the ontological constitution of things is the result of the history of metaphysics and the language of representational thinking. As a consequence, drastic linguistic measures are required to resurrect and elevate our experience of time and things in time to the appropriate level of time as presence.

THINKING AND TIME

If the connection between poetizing and thinking is veiled, as Heidegger has asserted, the veil has been lifted to the extent that we now know what the veil conceals—the temporality of presence as related to distinct entities. But can anything further than this be said? If presence can be described at all, then it should be possible to suggest what Heidegger thinks presence means and also to determine the direction subsequent analyses of presence should take. To attempt such a description is important for two reasons: first, the result will more clearly illustrate how poetized language enters into the language of thought with respect to a problem with which each mode of language is essentially connected; second, there is the possibility that hints from Heidegger's own fragmentary discussions may stimulate contemporary or future thinkers to follow Heidegger's approach in ontology. For suggestive fragments are all that Heidegger himself has so far presented in defense and explication of his own ontological convictions.

To determine time as presence is to determine what the history of metaphysics has progressively misrepresented, the being of beings with respect to (a) the temporality of a given being, and (b) the relation between the temporality of that being and the temporality of being as such. The problematic nature of time has been central to Heidegger's work from the very beginning. Early in *Sein und Zeit*, Heidegger announces that "the central problematic of all ontology is rooted in the correctly seen and explained phenomenon of time" (*SZ*, p. 18). In *Sein und Zeit*, the phases of phenomenal time as past, present, and future are named the "ecstases of temporality" (*SZ*, p. 329), the primary ways in which time "stands out." But regardless of the subtlety and incisiveness of these analyses of time, Heidegger felt certain even at that point in his development that time possessed properties which the threefold ecstatic dimension tended to conceal. The concluding part of *Sein und Zeit* was held back because, as

158

Heidegger admitted later, the thinking required for that part "did not succeed with the help of the language of metaphysics" (*W*, p. 159). His own inability to solve the problem of time with the metaphysical language at his disposal led to the conviction that this one problem was, and continues to be, symptomatic of a general misunderstanding of all ontological problems. Consequently, Heidegger has proposed that time is "presumably *the* matter of thought" (*SD*, p. 4—italics in original).

Thus, for Heidegger, time and being are dependent on one another for their ontological determination: "Being and time are reciprocally determined; however, in such a way that the former—being—is not temporal nor the latter—time—can claim to be spoken of as having being [*als Seiendes*]" (*SD*, p. 3). Here, Heidegger verges on contradictory assertions, and he is well aware of the impending logical threat to the subsequent course of his argument. But the being-time reciprocity is so crucial, yet so deeply embedded in the language of representational thought, that the process of thinking the reciprocity must take place in the very shadows of contradiction in order to ensure that all aspects of being, including logic itself, have been brought into play. This principle of reciprocal determination is more than merely directional, however, and we shall have due occasion to examine its effects on the substance of Heidegger's development of presence.

That part of being who seeks to apprehend the mutual relation between being and time is mortal man. But man's knowledge of being and time has had a checkered history, and therefore his potential for such knowledge must be channeled according to the notion of appropriation. Being and time "exist only in appropriation," and only when man is "brought into that which is properly his, i.e., when he stands in authentic time" can he "perceive being. Appropriated in this way, man belongs to appropriation" (*SD*, p. 24). The principal mode in which man is made appropriate to the relation between being and time is through the language he speaks to express that relation. The essence of language is necessarily linked with the temporality proper to presence: "Language speaks in that, while it shows by reaching into all regions of presence, it at times allows that which is present to appear" (*US*, p. 255). On those occasions when language reveals presence, it does so by allowing the ontological dimension of the word as name. Thus, the word first bestows "presence, i.e., being wherein something appears as a being" (*US*, p.

227). But since all words, as spoken, are names, "the essence of presence is hidden deep in the original names of being" (*W*, p. 205). Original means first in the order of ontological adequacy, not first in the historical sense. The "original names" may be Greek in origin and connotation, but this is not essential. In addition, the names for being as presence are not necessarily found hidden in the names for time as representationally depicted, but in the names of *being*. This relocation implies that names appropriate for presence may be inappropriate for time measured according to representational or quantified standards. Their appropriateness derives from the primordial unity of being and time, a unity which may have appropriated an essential temporal quality on words now considered proper only as names for entities apprehended according to nontemporal perspectives.[11]

Let us now begin to investigate some possible names for presence. Although the temporality of presence is not measureable or even discernible by dating, whether by "counting years" or any other measurement to delimit time quantitatively (*EH*, p. 76), it does not follow that all of the typical representational names for temporality are fundamentally deceiving. For example, consider one name for that moment of time which is right now—the present. One German word for present is *Gegenwart*, but Heidegger contends that "the present [*Gegenwart*] in the sense of presence [*Anwesenheit*] is so vastly different from the present in the sense of the now that the present as presence in no way allows itself to be determined by the present as the now" (*SD*, p. 12). Although the dimension of time known representationally as the present, the now, is distinct from time as presence, the present properly understood is one of the core notions which ground presence: "But this present [*Gegenwart*] governing in presence [*Anwesen*] is a characteristic of time, whose essence is never grasped through the traditional concept of time" (*VA*, p. 142).

What in the present now as represented does Heidegger consider deceptive and ontologically false? The present now is different from the past now and from the future now, but according to Heidegger's understanding of representational thought, "all three phases of time advance together toward sameness as the sameness in a unified present [*Gegenwart*], in a standing now [*Jetzt*]" (*VA*, p. 109). As a result, "the future *is* the 'not yet now'; the past *is* the 'no longer now' " (*WD*, p. 41—italics in text). And finally, "metaphysics names this continuous now: eternity" (*VA*, p. 109). The unity of time construed as

160

an eternal now, or as a now constantly in motion from past to present to future, is not the unity of time considered from the ontological setting of time as presence.

Heidegger does not explicitly develop objections against the metaphysical tradition in which the continuous now is named as eternity, but his point seems to be this: in viewing the past as a present which is no longer and the future as a present which is not yet and then naming the resulting continuum as eternity, the representational mode of thought has reduced difference to sameness, that is, the differences between past and present, future and present, past and future are all reduced to the undifferentiated sameness of a present now. Thus, eternity names a temporal unity which has no real ontological duration.[12] But caution is required at this point, especially for those with theological interests. In rejecting this attempt to grasp the continuum of present nows as eternity, it would be premature to infer that Heidegger is rejecting eternity as a potentially legitimate temporal notion. For example, if eternity lacks duration as representationally depicted, then it names a temporal unity which Heidegger might be willing to accept as distinct from the temporal unity imposed on time by metaphysics. The metaphysical notion of eternity reduces difference to sameness and is ontologically defective for that reason. But an eternity filled with temporal characteristics of a different order would not be metaphysical in the sense Heidegger is attacking and thus could, with some justification, be applicable to investigation of the temporality of a certain kind of being. However, the problem of relating such an eternity to time as presence would still remain.

We now have isolated one essential property of presence *(Anwesen)*, i.e., it has unity. But what does it unify? A partial answer is developed in this passage, in which Heidegger contends that "true [*wahre*] time is the arrival of what has been [*Gewesenen*]. This arrival is not the past [*Vergangene*], but the collection of what is essential which precedes all such arrival in that, as collection, it brings itself back in its own respective priority" *(US, p. 57)*. The thrust of this difficult passage is relatively clear; the details, however, are not. The main point seems to be that the temporality of "what has been" is not identical with the temporality of past time as represented. Since the arrival of something implies that something must have existed prior to that arrival, Heidegger argues that what has been *is* still in the present, at least as far as the "collection" of its essential attributes is concerned. The arrival can then be both prior and present, because its mode of temporality includes the past as past as unified in and through the present as present.[13]

But the details of this transtemporal inclusion are still far from clear. The transposition of past into present requires more development before it is evident how the pastness of past time can be present and united with the past and future in presence. An event occurring in the past may have repercussions in the present and thus the effect of the event could be present even though the actual event is itself past. This is obvious. What is not obvious is how the temporality of the past event as past can be present when, at least in appearance (and as we representationally portray the movement of time), that event itself is irrevocably past. The problem may be posed as follows: If being as such is equivalent to presence, then in virtue of what principle does some being as past continue into the present and on into the future and some being exist only in the past? This problem may serve to illustrate the tension in the original premise that time is determined by being but cannot itself be predicated of being. At this point, Heidegger's explicated position appears to verge on the incomprehensible.

If this objection can be answered, the answer must begin with an analysis of how two represented phases of temporality can remain differentiated but yet assume, as it were, a higher reality as presence. Let us return to the German name for the present. Heidegger argues that the "against" (*gegen*) in "present" (*gegenwärtig*) "does not mean the opposition [*Gegenüber*] to a subject, but the open region [*Gegend*] of disclosure in which and within which lingers that which comes near" (*W*, p. 319). The key word is *linger*: Heidegger uses *weilen* and *verweilen* alternately for emphasis. Heidegger conceives the subject-object link as a relation bound to a temporality which cannot pass beyond the limits of a present (*gegenwärtig*) now. This present now is the moment when entity X faces entity Y as subject to object. Heidegger's inference is that the being of both entity X and entity Y is foreshortened in virtue of the one-dimensional temporality which locks them into the subject-object relation. Only if a more primordial "openness" surrounds the two entities will the proper temporality of the entities be discerned and, perhaps, the proper ontological nature of those entities. *Lingering* is the name Heidegger introduces to capture the temporality of that openness. It is one of the most important examples of the language of poetizing (Hölderlin's) entering into the language of thinking.

Lingering breaks down the static ever-present character of the subject-object relation, thereby establishing the possibility that an entity can become a thing in conjunction with all three representationally distinguished temporal dimensions. But how does lingering accomplish this task of unification? In general, "lingering means to preserve, to remain still and maintain itself, namely in peace" (*SG*, p. 207). And, even more concisely, when lingering names "being and its ground," it names "preserving" (*Währen—SG*, p. 208). The peace which lingering preserves is identical in meaning to the notion of rest which grounds the silence of language as such. Here, peace names the unity of time as differentiated, both the differentiation of temporality within presence and the differentiation of temporality through the language which is part of the appropriation of this temporality. Therefore, peace names the harmonious interaction between or among distinguishable parts. What then are the parts, and how are they sustained within the totality of presence?

Heidegger asserts that "the lingering of the destiny that lingers is the measure of authentic remaining," a lingering which appears and is open to expression in thinking (*EH*, p. 105). Lingering implies the measurement of what is lingering and measurement implies limits; to determine the nature of these limits we must return to the notion of presence and the way in which the temporality of presence lingers. Heidegger describes the connection in this difficult passage: "Presence is that which ever lingers. Lingering is present as presence as the transitional arrival in the departure. Lingering is present as presence between coming forth and going away, between this double absence [*Ab-wesen*] the presence of all lingering is present" (*H*, p. 327). The coming forth and going away refer to the oncoming motion of the past into the present and the fading away of the present into the future. But this double motion in different directions, as it were, occurs from within a common base of simultaneity, thus generating an absence within the totality of presence. As a result, presence *(Anwesen)* is constituted by, as the language of representation might put it, its own opposite—absence *(Abwesen)*.

At this point, Heidegger's positive thoughtful reconstruction of the structure of presence becomes especially difficult to understand. Thus, there is motion within the interplay of presence and absence, and although the motion pervades all phases of the past-present-future distinction and appears to be regulated in a certain manner, the nature of these regulations is difficult to determine. We do know that not everything appropriated within these limits continues to exist; there is a "destiny" which preserves that which does remain in a certain state of ontological peace. However, many other problems remain. For example, if lingering collects and preserves that which is essential, then it appears that being itself is always the same. For there could be difference in being as presence only if something which was not essential did not linger but still bore relations to being. But whatever is nonessential is not preserved, does not linger, and therefore lacks being. Thus, even if being as such is differentiated as Heidegger has suggested, the result appears to be an unilluminating tautology—being is the same as itself.

Furthermore, what is "preserved" in the motion of presence? Some being is preserved and persists in and through presence, and some being is not. Why? Is the nature of that "destiny" which apparently collects what is preserved accessible to thoughtful (or thoughtful-poetized) disclosure or is it ineffable? These are questions which the enunciated doctrine of presence raises but leaves unanswered. And even the scattered but extensive analyses of lingering are often more perplexing than helpful. We should not be bemused by the incantatory power of a word like lingering, with its nuances of time whiling away in some indeterminate sense where past, present, and future melt into an undifferentiated flux. Some hard thinking remains as far as showing how lingering bridges the gap between the opposing directional flows of absence and presence found in each of the past-present-future temporal discriminations.

It seems evident that however the relation between being as such and time is construed, our experience of time is structured, perhaps in some ultimate sense, by our experience of entities *in* time. Heidegger himself admits as much when he appeals frequently to the presence of that which is present. Thus, even if presence and being as such were explained clearly and comprehensively, Heidegger still faces the problem of determining the temporality of given beings or things, as well as determining the difference between the temporality proper to things and the temporality of being as such. If there were guidelines to concretize the abstraction of Heidegger's development of presence as being, it might be possible to think the unity of time with greater precision.

To initiate the determination of presence in entities, Heidegger finds it necessary "now to name the locus [*Ort*] of the presence *of* what is present, which appears to the contemporary era as object, the state of objectivity [*Gegenständigkeit*]" (*VA*, pp. 51–52—italics in original). But objects are not things. And Heidegger maintains that "the thinghood of the thing rests neither in that it is the represented object, nor in general can it be determined from the objectivity of the object" (*VA*, p. 169). The thing in its thinghood "lingers toward [*verweilt*] the fourfold in a continuous lingering from the simplicity [*einfalt*] of world" (*VA*, p. 179). We now have an indication of the limits within which the presence of something present can be preserved, or remain in peace. The thing is present in presence (a) by lingering toward the world as differentiated by the fourfold and (b) by perduring through the oscillating motion of absence as it plays into the totality of presence.[14]

The entity becomes appropriated as thing when it lingers toward the world as fourfold. The temporality of the thing is based on each of the four sectors of world as assembled and united in one totality. Can these directional aspects of temporality now be named? In the lyrical language of *Aus der Erfahrung des Denkens*, Heidegger suggests that "every thing becomes alone and slow in thinking" (*AED*, p. 17). The slowness of the thing is its lingering quality in and through the duration of presence. The temporality of the thing is slower than the instantaneous quality of the present now which binds the entity to the knower as agent of representational thinking. And the fact that the thing is alone suggests that one thing must be isolated from another thing to preserve the difference between the two things.

Where and how is the distinction between different things to be drawn? In theory, any comportment toward the entity will yield the various relations required to constitute and differentiate the thing—"we perceive presence in every simple, sufficient prejudgmental reflection on the availability [*Vorhandenheit*] and accessibility [*Zuhandenheit*] of beings" (*SD*, p. 7). These two characteristics are obviously related to the categories of the same name which Heidegger had developed in *Sein und Zeit*. Their inclusion here is intended to remind us of their earlier appearance in Heidegger's own work and to warn us that the whole story about the being (as presence) of beings was far from told. But they are also intended to emphasize that there is no privileged perceptual or experiential avenue toward apprehending the presence of being in beings and the differences between things. As long as the correct nonrepresentational attitude of reflection is achieved, the presence of an entity is open to determination and differentiation.

But this openness only compounds the problem of determining

165

how one thing, once constituted as a thing, differs from another thing. And thinking, or at least Heidegger's own thinking, has not advanced sufficiently to detail the required differentiating characteristics. Heidegger writes that "it remains a task of thinking to determine the unconcealment of different thing-domains" (SD, pp. 50–51). It is important to realize why this particular task of thought remains unfulfilled. The English "thing-domains" is the German *Dingbereiche*. This notion is crucial, especially with respect to the temporal relations joining the thing to each of the four sectors of the fourfold. The domain of the thing is the set of limits which distinguish this thing from any other thing. There are different thing-domains because there are different things. Given that each thing is what it is because of a totality-relation to the fourfold, the only way to distinguish different things as different is to restrict the extent to which each thing enters into each sector.

The lack of the deity may be one essential reason why the domain of each thing is difficult to determine. Heidegger notes that the lack of God is a "dark condition" which lets "every being stand in uneasiness" (NII, p. 394). In other words, the absence of the divine presence affects the presence of *all* entities, not just mortal men in a theological sense, but everything in an ontological sense. Heidegger makes this effect explicit: "The lack of God and of the divine is absence [*Abwesenheit*]. However, not only is absence not nothing, but it is precisely the first appropriating presence of the hidden fullness of what has been and in this way the collected essence of the divine in the Hellenic age, in the Judeo-prophetic, in the preacher Jesus" (VA, p. 183). The absence of the deity is part of the temporality of presence in the sense that the various appearances of the deity throughout Western history (appearances which do not appear with the same efficacy in the present as they did in the past) still condition the temporality of presence—and our own moment as a present within this presence—by their very absence. The measure of presence must include the difference between past appearances of the deity and the fact that these appearances are now of a deity lacking or concealed. "The deity is present [*west*] only in that he is hidden" (EH, pp. 169–70). The absence of the deity and the absence of presence run parallel to one another in terms of ultimate ontological significance. Until the absence of the deity is accepted as part of the present, and thus part of presence, it will be impossible to measure the temporality of a thing as that thing is governed by this absence.

The language of poetizing has provided Heidegger with a naming word, *lingering*, which speaks from the fundamental identity between language and being as presence. Lingering names the common temporality underlying the gap between past and present, or any other representational temporal distinction, and also suggests the effect that one entity has on the temporality of all other entities. The being of a thing is determined by preserving that thing in its relation to all sectors of the fourfold, including that one sector which is presently grounded by an entity who is lacking. The temporality of presence is bound up not with a time existing independently as a container uniting a flux of moments, but with time insofar as it *is* in entities as thing, insofar as it relates one thing to all other things, and insofar as this relation partakes in the totality of presence. The doctrine of presence must therefore be studied in conjunction with the doctrine of the fourfold; the latter differentiates and guides the former into a totality of limits, while the former "fills" the latter with the totality of temporal content invisible to contemporary modes of metaphysical thought. With the image of lingering, the language of poetizing has spoken a word which compels the integration of two essential totality-perspectives provided by the language of thinking.

The problem of thing-determination is perhaps the most obvious single ontological problem which emerges from the confluence of thinking and poetizing. Lingering, the word which epitomizes that confluence, names both a partial answer to that problem and also a demand that the proper limits of the thing be determined in all relevant aspects of presence and the fourfold. Thinking has been directed toward this end by poetizing about the deity, its mode of existence as lingering, and the temporal effects on all other entities within the fourfold. Thinking must now determine what constitutes a thing so that this constitution responds to the dictates of being, as well as preserves the difference between things. As we shall see, the difficulties encountered in the attempt to distinguish between poetizing and thinking are mirrored in the difficulties of determining the limits to the nature of the thing. Heidegger is certainly aware of the problem, however, and some of his most ingenious and difficult thought has been aimed at its solution. One prominent example is the short work entitled *Gelassenheit*. The next chapter is an interpretation of this remarkable work in light of the problem of determining and differentiating entities as things, an ontological problem which emerges in its present form as the result of the distinctive confluence of poetizing and thinking.

8. Thinking and Releasement *(Gelassenheit)*

THE DOCTRINE of presence and its development through the notion of lingering is intended to assert the essential nature of being in our epoch. But unless thinking is to be reserved solely for the disclosure of being as such, the structure of thinking must also encompass the relation between being and beings or things. And as noted in the previous chapter, Heidegger certainly includes this relation as part of the proper province of thinking.

Determining the relation between being and beings is, of course, an exceedingly complex problem, both in terms of its intrinsic difficulty and in terms of the history of thought within which that problem occurs. If all metaphysical thinking has distorted being in the process of representing it, then metaphysical thinking has also distorted the being of beings. The consequence is that the being/beings distinction must be reconstructed from the ground up, as it were, to ensure that the results obtained are as far from the vista of representational thinking as possible. An attempt at such reconstruction, principally through an analysis of the connection between thinking and the thing, is the central purpose of Heidegger's opusculum *Gelassenheit*.

Gelassenheit is an especially difficult work, both because of its terminology which is couched in dialogue setting and because of the doctrine which is presented through that format.[1] But this chapter is devoted to the work for reasons other than its textual and thoughtful difficulties. My commentary has been arranged into a sequence of enumerated parts which captures the primary direction of the argument as well as allows the language of Heidegger's thought to be correlated to his poetic illuminations. Not all parts of this commentary will contain references to explicit illuminations; in these instances, my aim will be to develop the general outline of the argument according to the thoughtful content contained in that part. This conjunction of thought with the explicit language of poetic illuminations is mine and not Heidegger's. The purpose of this conjunction is to illustrate how one of Heidegger's most distinctively thoughtful works depends on these illuminations. At times, the effect of poetized language is directional—i.e., a word will hint at the next step which thought must explore in its own way. At times, however, poetized language (lingering is one of the primary instances) is not merely directional but constitutive. Heidegger incorporates the principal meaning of the poetized word or words directly into the course of the argument as presented in thought. Once the resulting doctrine of thought is developed and put into practice, the representational barriers will be overcome and replaced by a structure adequate, or more adequate, to the demands of being. *Gelassenheit* will, if properly understood, guarantee the origination and continuation of that thinking in which all entities may be experienced in their ontological fullness.

1. The work published as *Gelassenheit* is in two parts. The first part is a transcription of a public lecture also titled "Gelassenheit" and first given in 1955; the second part is a recorded conversation along a country path involving a scientist, a scholar, and a teacher—all without proper names—which is dramatically dated as occurring during the period 1944–45. This conversation is named "Zur Erörterung der Gelassenheit," or "Towards the Situating of Gelassenheit." The work as a whole was first published in 1959.

   The occasion for the public lecture "Gelassenheit" was the 175th birthday of the Swabian composer Conradin Kreutzer, and Heidegger plays on the name for a commemorative event *(Gedenkfeier)* to introduce the problem of thinking *(Denken)*. Modern man, Heidegger says, is "in flight from thinking." It is true that there is thinking in abundance, if thinking means research to implement planned projects of one sort or another, but Heidegger contends that such thinking deals only with "given conditions" for "determined purposes." Heidegger names this type of thinking "calculative" *(rechnende)*[2] and distinguishes it from "reflective" *(besinnliche)* thinking (G, p. 13). Both types of thinking are necessary—here as elsewhere the letter of Heidegger's argument is in no sense reactionary—but it is the second type, reflective thinking, which Heidegger has in mind when he claims that modern man is "in flight" from thinking.

   The distinction between reflective and calculative thinking is apparently intended to divide thinking into mutually exclusive domains (each, in its own way, essential). But how effective is such a distinction? There are many types of given conditions and an equally large number of determined purposes. For example, the practicing poet works with language as a given, and his determined purpose is to compose a poem, not a grocery list. Thus, at least on one level, the poet's work is a legitimate example of calculative thinking. One suspects that such objections miss Heidegger's point. What Heidegger here calls reflective thinking is that type of thinking elsewhere referred to simply as thinking *(Denken)*, to distinguish it from representational thinking *(Vorstellen)*. If so, then reflective thinking has as its purpose the cessation of purposes allied with the use of representational thinking as calculative means to practical and determined ends. There is no practical end to reflective thinking; rather, its purpose is to achieve an understanding of how being *is* in itself and how it can be appropriated to fulfill practical ends. Thus, before the poet can initiate the calculative techniques integral to his activity as poet, he must already have practiced what Heidegger has here named reflective thinking.

2. Evidence for the gradually increasing flight from reflective thinking is found in the homelessness of modern man—the automated diversions of radio, television, film, the illustrated tabloid, all have become "nearer" *(näher)* to man than "the fields around his farmstead, the heavens over the countryside, the sequence of hours of day and night." For Heidegger, one important effect of such technological innovations has been the loss of man's stability, his "rootedness" *(Bodenständigkeit—G*, p. 16).[3] But Heidegger does not yearn for an impossible return to the rootedness of *Schwarzwald* rusticity and eighteenth-century village life. He asks, rather, for the ground toward a "future rootedness" which would embrace the historical nature of man and thus man's technological works up to and through our own epoch, the atomic age. Heidegger provisionally names this ground "the releasement to things" *(die Gelassenheit zu den Dingen—G*, p. 23). Through such releasement, the products of technology will not control or destroy the human and mortal creators of those products, a catastrophic possibility which may well have to be faced. Not all calculative thinking results in the production of technological mechanisms, but Heidegger assumes that a sufficiently large percentage of the human activity now known as thinking (i.e., calculative thinking) either insti-

gates or is ultimately controlled by technology and the ends it imposes on society—hence, the immediate connection Heidegger establishes between a kind of thinking and a kind of reality distinct from that thinking but essentially related to it.

Heidegger does not develop here what this comportment toward things entails; but he insists that another notion must be considered as parallel in importance with *Gelassenheit*. The complete meaning of technology is unknown at this moment in history, but man must so conduct himself in relation to this unknown that his conduct guarantees what Heidegger names "the openness for the sake of the mystery" (*die Offenheit für das Geheimnis*—G, p. 24). Mystery names the connection between what is known about the essence of technology—not simply how to elaborate on present technological techniques—and how men act toward what is unknown. The problem of technology is mysterious now, but openness to this mystery will provide access to the problem of how to "release" things into their proper domain. Both notions, releasement to things and openness for the sake of the mystery, are accessible to further development only through "courageous" (*herzhaften*) thinking (G, p. 25).[4] And it is reflective thinking, that activity from which modern man is taking flight, which requires courage before it can be practiced in the age of the atom.

We should reflect on why a virtue such as courage is introduced at this point in the argument. Aristotle may be correct when he claims that all men by nature desire to know, but there is little doubt that such desire does not extend to ontological knowledge of the world. Only the few care to pursue this sort of intellectual quest, and such activity requires a low form of courage simply in virtue of the fact that thinkers tend to be scorned by the many as do-nothings. But courage in the face of mass apathy is only a faint residue of the courage Heidegger has in mind. The courage to pursue reflective thinking is necessary to face (a) those mortals who refuse to think about anything; (b) those mortals who think that technology will answer any problem that technology raises; (c) the very technological environment in which thinking of all forms must take place in our epoch; (d) the technological mode of existence of the thinker himself as he addresses the problem of technology in its most fundamental roots.

The need for courage in such a universal sense has been

hinted at in poetizing. Courage is required to ground that daring which, as spoken in Rilke's poetizing, assumes proportions of comprehensive and even ontological dimension. If all language attains its impetus from man to the world through daring, and if language is as fundamental as the being which it says and speaks, then all human activity must be related to this daring since all human activity is related to language. In this case, the daring involves the attempt to restore man's relations to all that is other than man so that the totality of world and thing is preserved according to the demands of being and not simply the demands of technology. To think such a restoration entails an essential interplay of moral, epistemological, and ontological concerns. One must approach *Gelassenheit* with the courage to rethink these presently delimited philosophical domains as they emerge from the primordial unity of being as such. In an age when survival in academic philosophy compels the professional seeker of wisdom to "specialize," the project at hand will be pursued only by those with at least a modicum of the courage which is itself part of that project.

3. The public lecture "Gelassenheit" announces the relevance of releasement to the problem of thinking and provides a technological context for its importance, but the bulk of Heidegger's analysis of releasement is presented in the second part of *Gelassenheit*, the conversation which follows the lecture. The three participants—a scientist, a scholar, and a teacher— are on a country path, far from human habitation. The discussion begins after the teacher has declared that the questionable character of man's nature suggests that this nature may be determined only after considering what is other than man. If thinking, as in the definition "rational" animal, is posited as the fundamental characteristic of man, then the limits of this essence can be established only by looking away from thinking. The scientist then wants to know "what releasement has to do with thinking" and the teacher replies "Nothing, if we grasp thinking according to its existing concept as a representing. But perhaps the essence of thinking which we now seek is fixed in [*eingelassen*] releasement" (G, p. 34). Releasement is thus both a condition for the possibility of thinking and a necessary factor in the very process of that thinking, especially in relation to things insofar as they are hidden as technological entities. The scholar

then points the way when he concludes that "what we name releasement, but hardly know, and above all in no way provide a place for, we should see in connection with the already discussed essence of thinking" (*G*, p. 36). Releasement can be achieved only in conjunction with thinking as thinking is currently represented.

We should note the intimate connection between content and form in *Gelassenheit*, both here and elsewhere. The setting of the conversation is not accidentally chosen, but (as in a Platonic dialogue) is a necessary feature in determining the tone of what is being said. The fact that the conversation occurs far from human habitation shows the need for a certain isolation from all that currently passes for significant human activity. The opportunity for a successful investigation into that which is properly human increases as the distance from the popular locus of human activity increases. But the distance is not merely the dramatic distance separating the conversants and their respective homes. The distance is also present in the need to introduce an otherness between traditional conceptions of man and an apprehension of his nature which will allow an understanding of his relation to technological entities.

We thus discover an important dramatic and thoughtful application of the poetized name *apartness* as found and illuminated in Heidegger's work on Trakl. Apartness implies that something is apart from something else, but this condition obtains without man recognizing its presence. In this instance, the traditional notions intended to determine the nature of man must be kept apart from a nature of man as yet indeterminate. The dramatic force of apartness pervades the general context of the action—the three conversants are apart from their homes, apart from each other in terms of their respective technical vocabularies, and apart from a proper understanding of man. Just as thought had to consider what was other than language to determine the essence *(Wesen)* of language, so now we must stay apart from man to determine the essence of man with respect to the thinking of things in their releasement.

4. The establishment of a new (or perhaps merely forgotten) notion of thinking is possible only if developed from the reigning historical view of the nature of thinking. Such thinking, as we have already seen in chapter 7, is "in the form of transcendental-

173

horizonal representation" (*Transzendental-horizontalen Vorstellens—G*, p. 36). The strategy at this point in the conversation is to show that and how another mode of thinking is necessary in order to make representational thinking possible. An example will serve to illustrate the point. Thus, in representational thinking, something "typical of a jug" *(das Krughafte des Kruges)* is given to an observer when "that thing in the appearance of a jug" *(jenes Ding im Aussehen des Kruges—G*, p. 36) stands against that observer. Why a jug? My conjecture is that the reference to a jug and its hidden status as a thing is intended to recall the technical ontological discussion of the jug as thing in the *Vorträge und Aufsätze* lecture "Das Ding." There Heidegger has provided an extremely persuasive account of the way in which an entity like a jug can be experienced and described as a thing. What, in general, is required to discern the thinghood of the jug has yet to be determined, but the inference is clear that the jug as entity is derived from the jug as thing. And, of course, the same derivation holds for all entities now constituted in and through representational thinking.

The "horizon" of representational thinking is that which "encircles" and "exceeds" the "exterior of objects" *(Aussehen der Gegenstände)* in a manner parallel to the way that "transcendence surpasses the perception of objects" *(das Wahrnehmen der Gegenstände)*. But both concepts, horizon and transcendence, are necessarily defined in relation to the representation of objects. And representational or calculative thinking is the predominant mode of thinking in our epoch. Consequently, the sense in which horizon and transcendence are ontologically possible independently of such represented objects is difficult to approach, much less visualize and describe. The way toward this possibility must be prepared. The teacher names the ground which allows objects to be represented through horizon and transcendence as "an openness which does not come about through that which we see into" (*G*, p. 37). The horizonal aspect of thinking is only one perspective of the openness which "surrounds" us, a perspective from which objects "appear" as objects through the immediacy of perception as the primary foundation of representational thinking.[5]

The jug is not what it appears to be, at least if we concern ourselves with the jug in its ontological completeness. Here

again we discern an apartness which establishes the difference
between the jug as an entity and the jug as a thing. If we
determine the nature of the jug solely in virtue of how we repre-
sent it, then the jug is little more than a receptacle for dispensing
liquid. Therefore, if it is possible to question whether the mode
of existence of the jug is something apart from its use, then it
must also be possible to question the medium through which
this use is calculated. The horizon from which the jug is repre-
sented as a jug as well as the perception which receives the jug's
appearance must be placed apart from the jug determined as
thing from a different and more comprehensive ontological per-
spective. This perspective must eventually be named, but at this
point its name should preserve a neutral state as far as incursions
into the being of the jug are concerned. The name *openness (Of-
fenes)* serves this purpose, hinting at a spatio-temporal con-
tinuum present but as yet indeterminate and only partially filled
by jugs determined as entities through representational thought.

5. The teacher initiates the project of circumscribing this openness
by remarking that such openness can be called region *(Gegend)*.
This region is not one among many other regions, their respec-
tive limits arbitrarily selected or calculated according to prag-
matic ends, but rather *the* region *(die Gegend*—the *die* is
italicized—*G*, p. 39).[6] The scholar remarks that the older form
of the word was *"gegnet,"* meaning "free expanse" *(freie Weite),*
and he suggests that this older name be employed in subsequent
discussion. The region, described by the scholar as "expanse
and lingering" *(die Weite und die Weile*—G, p. 40), is now defined
by the teacher as "the lingering expanse, which, collecting ev-
erything, opens itself so that in it the open is held and controlled
letting everything expand in its resting" (G, p. 40). The things
which appear in the region no longer "stand opposite" us as
objects do in the traditional mode of representation. Rather, the
things "rest in the return to lingering" (G, p. 41). The scientist
admits that he is now lost, that he cannot understand the expla-
nation of the region in terminology such as lingering and ex-
panse, return and rest. The teacher responds that the region
explained in this manner is not accessible to representation and
that perhaps they must "wait for its essence," a waiting which
"releases itself in the openness in the expanse of remoteness in
which nearness it finds lingering through which it remains" (G,

p. 42). The scientist then chances the inference that thinking would be "the coming-into-nearness of remoteness," a characterization which the scholar finds "daring."

The name for openness, the noun *Gegend*, is transformed by the scholar into the older verbal form *gegnet* to emphasize both the activity inherent in the region and the historical and temporal character of the notion (just as the conversation will conclude with a single Greek word from Heraclitus summing up what has been argued to that point). The suggestion is that the older form of the word in German (and in Greek) contains hints of the notion to be disclosed, not just in the meanings hidden in these names, but also in the sense that the names themselves are richly historical, past names no longer used in the present but still animated by presence. The saying concealed in these past names can now be brought into the open through present speaking.

The scientist's inability to grasp the argument through the limited conceptual medium of representation (that medium which is particularly appropriate to the scientist) compels the teacher to introduce the important notion of "waiting" within the region. The teacher distinguishes between "waiting" *(warten)* and "awaiting" *(erwarten—G,* p. 42).[7] Awaiting is always relative to representation and what is being represented—thus, when we await some entity, we know that the entity will appear as an object, and identical qua object with all other representations in our store of past and future knowledge. Awaiting is that state of prerepresentational expectancy in which what is expected can be formally specified (e.g., according to the Kantian program). In contrast, however, waiting implies the reunification of the space and time which Kant had distinguished in service to the demands of a thinking which, for Heidegger, merely extended the historical slant of metaphysics. The mobility of expanse and lingering proper to the region may be considered as Heidegger's response to the static space and time of Kantian epistemology. The limits of waiting cannot be made determinate in the same way that the intuition of percepts can for Kant, but waiting can be localized, as it were, by associating Heidegger's illuminations with the letter of his own thinking. The primary instance of relevant poetized language is the need for renunciation, with the context of renunciation more inclusive than that hinted at in Stefan George's work. Instead of renouncing control of the relation between word and thing, the waiting essential to releasing entities as things entails renouncing the entire set of cognitive and practical presuppositions conditioned by representational thinking.

But even though such renunciation is in one sense comprehensive, it is only the first phase in determining the nature of that which is waited for within the region. Man waits for things by, as it were, lingering with them. As we have seen, lingering is a property of the temporality of presence and has its roots in the poetized language about the lacking deity and its immediate effect on the holy and the divine. Lingering and waiting must now be correlated. Man is always in the region, but man does not wait for the divine presence or for any other thing in the same way that man awaits a potential object of knowledge. We are waiting in the midst of a perspective on totality—the region—through which any occurrence of the actual existence of divine presence must be realized. This presence has in fact been manifest in the past appearances of the deity. This is why lingering is such an important name; it gives some indication how a sense of divinity can still be in the continuum of presence without itself being present. Since any entity is incomplete as a thing until it is related to the divine, lingering is the poetized name for the temporality of any thing within the totality of presence. When fully determined, the thing is at rest with being as collected within presence and the fourfold, just as the saying of both poetizing and thinking is at rest in the silence which grounds language as such. The studied indeterminacy of the poetized names of *lingering* and *rest* marks the limit of Heidegger's own precision as far as determining the nature of the region in the language of thinking.

6. The teacher, the scholar, and the teacher again then transpose waiting into the interplay of the near and the remote: "Waiting in the open releases itself . . . / in the expanse of remoteness . . . / in whose nearness waiting finds the lingering in which it remains" (*G*, p. 42). The scientist admits that he now has some experience of the meaning of waiting. However, he feels that the experience resulted more from "the course of the conversation" than from the linguistic stipulation of what had been discussed. This is an important point, for almost immediately the question

arises whether the name *releasement* is adequate for the doctrine just subsumed under it. The teacher asks the scientist what he (the scientist) had designated by the word; the scientist replies that not he but the teacher has done the designating; and the scholar asks who, if any, of them first suggested the word. The teacher then says that presumably no one of them has instigated the word *releasement*, but that "in the region in which we are staying, everything is in the best order when no one of us has done it" (*G*, p. 47).

An important reason why the conversation includes a teacher, a scholar, and a scientist can now be more clearly discerned. All three individuals are exemplars of disciplines which, each in its own way, contribute to that knowledge which represents the growth of human experience. The fact that they are named only by their disciplines broadens the scope of the conversation by excluding the narrowness of specific ideological rifts within any one of these disciplines. Now, if the word which all agree is the appropriate word cannot be found in any one technical vocabulary, then the source for that word and its meaning can be located by shifting the perspective from language itself to what language is of, or in the terminology of *Unterwegs zur Sprache*, from speaking to saying as the manifestation of the fourfold. This is why the teacher calls releasement "the region of the word which alone answers itself" (*G*, p. 47). The region "alone answers itself" because only through the region is there language in the first place. In a sense, language itself says the word *releasement*. Heidegger makes this point by dramatically presenting all three participants in a state of bewilderment as to who first introduced the crucial word. The thoughtful development of language in *Unterwegs zur Sprache* is only obliquely present to the substance of *Gelassenheit*. But although Heidegger's concern in the latter work is different, that concern is still related to language as the essential medium for stating and partially constituting the doctrine of releasement. There was no "word for the word" in the sense that language does not provide terminology adequate to describe its own limits; analogously, the region "alone answers itself," since whatever words do arise which appear to be adequate to show the region must come from the region itself rather than through the speculation of mortal speakers about the region.[8]

Just as the poet, the spokesman of language as poetized, is in between gods and men, so man himself is waiting in a between which joins thinking and releasement (*G*, p. 51). Man is not completely appropriated to the region because his relation to being as such is unfulfilled in this epoch. Man is in the between because he must express what experience he does have of being through a mode of thought which only partially reveals entities as things. However, man is aware of the divine, that aspect of being which in this epoch is principally lacking, and can express that awareness insofar as the deity is approaching. Thus, man exists in the region which includes the possibility that man can experience this deity and all things in relation to the deity and to being as such. The notion of releasement establishes an ontological foundation for man's participation in the experience of what is lacking in this epoch and how this lack relates to all other entities. To determine any entity as a thing requires thinking responsive to the totality of presence and the fourfold, and to man's place between the various limits of that totality.

Releasement may then be described as a waiting in which one is "released into the open of the region" (*auf das Offene der Gegnet sich einlassen*—*G*, p. 48). This relation between the region and releasement occurs through a specifically human dimension to the extent that man is "originatively appropriated to the region." The notion of region becomes the pivot on which turns the connection between thinking and releasement: "Thinking is the releasement to the region because its essence (i.e., thinking) rests in the regional capacity [*Vergegnis*] of releasement" (*G*, p. 50). Is man sufficiently appropriated in the region grounding thinking and releasement? The scholar answers that "we are, and we are not" and that our "stay in this between is waiting [*das Warten*]" (*G*, p. 51). Man is and is not appropriated in the sense that he thinks representationally more than he thinks reflectively. But insofar as he is moved toward experiencing the entity as a thing, he is in a position to wait for the thing.

7. If man is in between thinking and releasement of entities as things, what effect does this intermediate condition have on that toward which man is released—the thing? The teacher notes that "things are obviously things through the regional capacity of the region" insofar as this capacity occurs, e.g., through the "lingering of the jug in the expanse of the region" (*Verweilen des*

Kruges in die Weite der Gegend—G, p. 52). The problem is to generalize the names for the relation between the region and the thing when the region lets the thing, any thing, linger within the region. The scholar suggests that it best be described as determination *(Bedingnis)*. To determine *(bedingen)* an entity as a thing *(Ding)* can be achieved only by experiencing the essence of thinking as waiting in the region.

Releasement situates man within the region and toward the approach of objects as things. But this relation is two-directional—from the region toward things as well as from the region toward man. Determination is that aspect of the region in which an entity can become a thing. The notion of determination is amplified in the form of a hint, a single sentence shared by all three participants in the conversation—the scientist, the teacher, and the scholar in that order: "we must therefore first learn to think the nature of determination/ while we learn to experience the essence of thinking/ consequently, to wait on the determination and the regional capacity" (G, p. 54). This unusual tripartite assertion is apparently circular in logical form, since thinking is described in terms of thinking. But the circularity is given new dimension if the factor of lingering is considered with respect to the dramatic form of the assertion. The relation of the region to the determination of things is expressed in a linguistic sequence which itself lingers among all three conversants. This duration hints that what constitutes thinghood involves all three protagonists as representatives of different attitudes toward the entity. The fragmentation of this assertion indicates that the logical circularity is temporal as well as conceptual, that thinking must think on itself now before it can become what it is not now, or is only partially—i.e., reflective thought. If the lack of the deity is confronted in all respects, then thinking as related to the complete interplay of all sectors of the fourfold will be fully determinate. But the fact that man is in flight from such thought forces Heidegger to characterize thinking in terms of thinking, in a circular but not self-destructive fashion.

8. The scientist remarks that someone overhearing this conversation could easily get the impression that releasement is a "will-less letting in of everything" resulting in "the denial of the will to live" (G, p. 58). But this impression would be a serious mis-

understanding. The daring and courage that underlie reflective thinking are hardly consonant with a denial of the will to live and the will to engage the technological world as it is and as it should be. The German verb *lassen* has, even in ordinary usage, a secondary sense of ordering and commanding. The only passivity involved in releasement is that which results from waiting for the nature of the entity to become a thing. But this very passivity also necessitates the active confrontation of the thinker with all his presupposed convictions about what the entity is and how it pertains to his existence.[9]

The scientist pursues the relation between releasement and the willing essential to releasement by naming this relation "the resolution [*Entschlossenheit*] to the essential nature of truth" (G, p. 59). Resolution in this sense is accomplished through a comportment which may be named *steadfastness (Inständigkeit)*, a name which signifies man's resolution to wait with the "simple patience of noble remembering."[10] Steadfastness guarantees the "spontaneity of thinking" as a "recalling" *(Andenken)* which approaches the burdens of nobility by "lingering in the origin of its essence." The spontaneous character of reflective thought is a function of the interplay of the fourfold in and through the totality of presence. The Kantian spontaneity becomes the Heideggerian interplay, both notions applied to thought and the products of thought. Lingering names how thinking as a continuing activity must recall what is past as that past is "noble," i.e., as that past plays into the present within presence.

The etymological connection between *Inständigkeit* and *Gegenstand*, steadfastness and object, should not go unnoticed. Steadfastness is required to experience the entity as a thing, not merely as an object, the present result of metaphysical reflection on the entity. Nevertheless, the pathway to the thing for that mode of thinking midway between representation and reflection is through the entity as an object. This is why the moral directive of *Inständigkeit* is derived from that standing which is essential before man can be in the presence of the entity as a thing. It should be noted that the language of thought, even the approximation of reflective thinking exemplified in the conversation, is not adequate to say what must be said about steadfastness. The scholar repeats a few lines which resemble, in form, the text of an eight-line poem (G, p. 60). The title of the poem is "Inständigkeit." The poet is unnamed; presumably it is Heidegger himself. The language spoken in the poem connects thinking with the nobility of steadfastness. The insertion of poetic language at an especially crucial junction in the thoughtful conversation is a recollection of the need to complement the saying of thinking with the speaking of poetizing, regardless whether the human source of that poetizing is known or remains nameless.

The scholar has made the general claim that "what has origin is noble" (*Edel ist, was Herkunft hat*—G, p. 61). But why noble? The answer must begin by noting that thinking is remembrance *(Andenken)* of the source of what is to be thought. The scientist and teacher combine to describe the source as "what comes before, of which we cannot properly think/ because the essence of thinking begins there" (G, p. 61). What has "come before" is, presumably, being *(Sein)* disclosed now as presence and as the fourfold, and the origin of this present manifestation comprises the limit of what we cannot properly think. The nobility of the man or men who experience this source is an essential attribute of the steadfastness which characterizes man within the releasement to the region. Assuming man could persevere in the experiences necessary to name the divine presence (and all things insofar as they relate to this presence), he would then be noble because the source of nobility is the primordial unity of man with the other parts or phases of being. The extent to which man is "lingering in his origin" *(in seiner Herkunft weilend)* is the extent to which he "would foresee his noble nature" (G, p. 64). Thus, the nobility of man's origin names not only man himself, but also being as such, insofar as man and all that is other than man once coexisted and still lingers in an apparently harmonious and noble totality. Nobility in this sense should be understood in a manner analogous to the thoughtful illuminations of pain, joy and sadness, that is as an ontological word rather than as a representational or psychological or, in this case, evaluational name. The nobility of the origin shows the nature of the totality as totality. The possibility of a retrogression into an ignoble condition exists only if some part or parts are not as they were when the totality was indeed whole. Since, as we have seen, differentiation of the totality implies a form of ontological and poetized pain, the impetus to experience the totality as whole may bestow nobility on the thinker who strives for and at least partially achieves the linguistic expression of that whole. It is the nobility proper to the totality of being as presence and as the fourfold.

9. The teacher observes that perhaps the experience of the conversation may be summed up as follows:—"that we come into the nearness of the region and thus at the same time remain remote from it, although this remaining is to be sure a return" (*G*, pp. 65–66). The region then becomes "the nearness of remoteness and the remoteness of nearness" (*G*, p. 66), a characteristic which should not be construed dialectically, but according to the essence of the region as heretofore advanced. Near and remote, with respect to the region, are misrepresented if understood in a quasi-Hegelian manner. The nearness of remoteness and the remoteness of nearness are relative to the structure of the region. The fact that their reciprocity is not dialectical implies that there is no single omega point toward which all things constituted by their participation in the near and the remote are directed.

It follows that the nearness of the holy and the remoteness of the deity does not imply an epochal succession of divine lacks and regenerations. And, in general, there is no inherent ontological force or drive to "sublate" a given thing into a more diversified or higher thing, a thing which could manifest more aspects of presence or sectors of the fourfold than some other thing. The thing must linger in the near and the remote, but the limits of the near and the remote are always relative to the limits of the thing. A jug has its own circumference of nearness and remoteness through which the jug-as-object can be determined as jug-as-thing. A deity has its own circumference as well. The point is that the near and the remote are not dialectical, that regardless how ramified the thinghood of the jug becomes, it can never become coincident with the thinghood of the deity in some higher unity.

10. The scholar recollects a single Greek word which may approximate the relation between the region and thinking. It is Heraclitus's fragment 122, the single word "*angchibasie,*" in German "*herangehen,*" in English "to go forward." The teacher comments that perhaps this single word could also be rendered "to move into nearness" (*In-die-Nähe-gehen*), and the scholar adds that this suggestion could name the entire course of the conversation

along the country path. All three representatives of their respective disciplines have come nearer to reflective thinking because of their joint linguistic intercourse, an integrated activity whereby each contributes toward the understanding of the other and to the totality of language from which all draw their stock of terminology.

After the Greek fragment is translated into vernacular German and then retranslated into technical language (insofar as the conversation has engendered technical language), the scholar notes that "one can scarcely begin with a single word" (G, p. 69). Why is this word, a single word, chosen? First, it is Greek, and not the Greek of Plato or Aristotle but Greek which is closer, or nearer, to the source of the historical origin of being as hinted at in the Heraclitean doctrine of flux. Second, it indicates that releasement to things is through the penumbra of nearness surrounding objects. For Heidegger, this movement into nearness originates with the holistic pre-Platonic Greek experience of being, a movement now difficult to recreate because of the progressive distortion of representational thinking. The reflective thinking embodied in the conversation has thus taken the step back by allowing the hints present in the Greek language to speak, thereby preserving the saying which was hidden in that speaking. The scholar is perfectly within his rights to question whether any meaning whatsoever can be reliably attributed to one ancient word. But the fact remains that the word means what it means, even in isolation and from our limited representational grasp of the Greek language. This meaning shows how thinking and language have converged in the Greek experience and how ancient language can direct contemporary thinking along the right path to the correct ontological apprehension of things.

The nearness man enters into (in the present) is the remoteness of the Greek world (in the past) for purposes of gathering (for the present and the future) those hidden dimensions of the object as thing present as presence. When the conversation draws to a close and the trio has returned near to human habitation, the teacher remarks that the nearness named by Heraclitus's word guided them "deep into the night" (G, p. 70). The image of night is significant on at least two different levels. First, it is not inappropriate to reflect on the dramatic date of the conversation—1944–45. This period is the night of the German nation insofar as the Second World War ends with disastrous consequences for the Nazi regime. The conversants, although representing disciplines which are international in membership, are nevertheless German, and the night of their nation is their night as well. The sombre tone of the conclusion of *Gelassenheit* marks the imminence of this night. There is also just a suggestion of a possible connection between technological advance as such and the misuse of that advance by those who have tragically misunderstood how man and being are appropriated. Thus, the second level of night is more comprehensive in scope. It is the darkness threatening our epoch, a darkness which permeates man's nearness to technological objects (as the conversants draw near to a human habitation well-stocked with such objects) and the remoteness from those same objects thought as things (presumably, things would not pose a dark threat to their maker). In this respect, Germany, Europe, and the entire world are all on the same level.

The teacher closes by noting that "the night remains the nearness of stars for the child in man" (*G*, p. 71). The mysterious and hypnotic coda of *Gelassenheit* is based on this image. The child is a man whose simplicity (as in the simplicity of a Hölderlin) permits him to experience the stars as part of the darkness of night. These stars and their light are the things which are present in entities, but things which are overshadowed both by their representational status as objects and by the surroundings which they themselves objectively illuminate. The light of stars and the darkness of night recall the illuminations of Hölderlin's poetized language. The appearance of twilight as the intermediary between day and night and the appearance of heavenly thunderstorms heralding the divine presence—both are implicitly present here when the conversants speak within the movement of day to night and from the night of national disaster and possible international technological mismanagement to the light of reflective thinking and its capacity to release objects into things. In general, the interplay of light and dark hints at the need to relate these appearances to the temporality which grounds them. The thinking which will allow the releasement of things must take these poetized hints and transform them into a vocabulary adequate to the demands of temporality as lingering insofar as this temporality is the principal factor in the determination of things. If the conversation as a whole is taken as partially poetized language, then the night and the stars spoken about at its conclusion say in an imagistic way the same thing as the fundamental problem of thinking—the need to relate properly the being of things and time.

Gelassenheit has many centers of gravity. The notion of reflective thinking is one of those centers, and a summary of the main points in this interpretation of *Gelassenheit* may take that notion as its point of departure. Reflective thinking is an activity, one which calls into question the totality of the thinker's environment, in both human and nonhuman respects. The literary format of *Gelassenheit* indicates this active aspect of thinking—first, a lecture delivered to a nonacademic audience, i.e., an audience of Everyman, then a dialogue, the most intensive form of intellectual investigation and discovery. The literary format itself contributes to the activity of thinking; in thinking out the meaning of the dramatic conversation, the reader grows in understanding how both the products and process of reflective thinking can be actualized.

The purpose of thinking is to revitalize the relation between the prospective thinker and things, things understood in the widest possible sense. This relation is realized within the limits of the region proper to the thing insofar as this region is itself part of the totality which grounds all things and all discourse about things. Within that region, thinking takes root and therefore grounds the thinker in the stability of the earth in conjunction with the other parts or sectors of the whole. Thinking approaches an entity, recognizes its perceptual exterior, then releases the entity into its proper ontological thinghood by experiencing that exterior as a directional guide to the interplay of the four sectors of the fourfold. Each thing becomes a thing in its own relation to the region; here the entity as thing rests and lingers in a temporality which constitutes the limits of space-time as presence and through the play of the near and the remote. The thinker must wait for the entity as thing to settle into its proper place before showing that thinghood through spoken language. The thinker is therefore active as well as passive, as the German word *Gelassenheit* denotes. His activity involves maintaining himself within the flux of presence and the totality of the fourfold and also within the counterflow of a kind of thinking which has historically concealed presence at the same time that is has revealed and represented the entity as an entity (but not as a thing). This activity requires courage, not the courage of the soldier in battle with and against his fellow mortals, but the solitary courage of one who recognizes the need to experience the things of the world to preserve them as they should be preserved. If the thinker can properly think entities as things, then perhaps this experience can be translated into language which will be susceptible to consideration by those in positions of authority over the practical affairs of a technological world. The nobility proper to being as totality will then be present in the mode of existence of the thinker insofar as he thinks being as such and dwells in accordance with its demands.

Heidegger's *Gelassenheit* is a singular mixture of ontology, epistemology, and ethics, all in language which is both thoughtful—borrowing seminal themes and terminology from the history of philosophy and channeling them through Heidegger's own thinking—and poetized—developing the thought content from hints in the poetizing of Rilke, Trakl, George, and Hölderlin. The work as a whole presents a unified position with respect to the differences which normally follow from the apparent indiscriminate merging of these three disparate philosophical domains. But the interpretation of this position offered here is, like the doctrine of releasement itself, "only in the mode of supposition" (*G*, p. 65). I have attempted to discuss releasement only in its most immediate connection with thinking and only in the most immediate connection in which thinking is linked with poetizing.

But the resulting interpretation is necessarily inadequate. By writing in dialogue form and with apparent mastery of that form, Heidegger has invited the same sort of close scrutiny that should be accorded the Platonic dialogue as exemplar of this form of thinking. In short, all the apparently literary or dramatic features must be integrated into the structure of thought that emerges. But this would be only the first step. The next phase, far more complicated, would be the transformation of that thought into an argumentative form of presentation accessible to all those doctrines in the history of metaphysical thought which *Gelassenheit* is intended to supplant. If this transformation is not accomplished or is simply ignored, there can be no real confrontation between the Heideggerian position and any one of the "metaphysical" positions still considered viable by many students of the history of metaphysics. If this confrontation does not occur, then Heideggerian scholarship will continue to become threatened by its own scholastic weight, a consequence in direct conflict with Heidegger's own injunction to think—not merely comment upon the thought of others, including himself. Thus, the tremendous difficulties inherent in Heidegger's thought must at some point be considered solved so that such a confrontation can occur. I offer this chapter as an example, at best partially successful, of the type of fused poetized-thoughtful commentary which is appropriate for Heidegger's later work. But obviously the commentary only starts on the path toward a proper understanding of what Heidegger means.

With this chapter, my interpretive summary of Heidegger and the language of poetry is complete. I wish to conclude this study with a critique of Heidegger's position insofar as this position leads to and culminates in the doctrine of releasement. There is an important sense in which Heidegger's approach to releasement is on the same level as his approach to the nature of language—both doctrines are exhortative as well as substantive. Heidegger begins by studying language in such a way as to instigate an experience with its essence; he ends by discussing the nature of the thing in order to instigate an experience with the essence of thinghood. But much ground has been traversed on the way between these two end points. And although the "final" doctrines may have been presented in a purely suppositional way, the confluence of poetizing and thinking is certainly, for Heidegger, a necessary condition for attaining any sort of certitude in these matters. Given this necessary condition, the critique I offer is based on the fundamental relation between being and time insofar as this relation is spoken in the language of poetizing and thinking. For Heidegger, some ontological theses (e.g., being as presence) are as ultimate as the necessary interplay of poetizing and thinking; as such, these theses are not questionable in the way releasement and the doctrine of language may be questionable. But these are precisely the theses I wish to examine in light of all that has gone before.

The critique is arranged under three main heads—historicism, individuation, and truth. These three fronts are associated with a body of metaphysical thought sufficiently diverse to assess Heidegger's position to the extent that his position has been formulated in this study. A confrontation of this sort is obviously perilous; we have already seen numerous instances in which Heidegger can be readily misunderstood because of the imposition of alien categories and distinctions on his thought. But my belief is that such a confrontation, if handled in the proper spirit and even if mistaken in point of detail, can only deepen our understanding and appreciation of both traditional metaphysics and Heidegger's own ontological position.

9. Three Perspectives on Being and Time: A Critique

Historicity

For the later Heidegger, being is presence *(Anwesen)*, and thinking must differentiate the nature of presence and express that differentiated nature in language. Any connection between the part, a given being, and the whole, being as such, requires a relation constituted by the temporality of presence. Language grounds thinking, but thinking does not exhaust the linguistic expression of being. For Heidegger, poetizing is the ontological and linguistic conterpart to thinking. The role of poetizing is characterized as "the taking of the measure [*Masses*]" which "is appropriated in poetizing" (*VA*, p. 196). Poetizing establishes standards in accordance with which being as presence can be appropriated and experienced as such. And since poetizing and thinking are modes of the saying of language, the measurement proper to poetizing is essentially related to the measurement proper to thinking.

Even if we allow Heidegger to take certain liberties with *measure* as a word, he must still preserve some aspects of its common denotation in order to preserve the sense of the word as a representational name. Therefore, the notion of measurement becomes central to the relation of poetizing and thinking to being and for that reason may serve as the locus for the conclusion of this study. A number of related problems emerging from the notion of measurement will be explored insofar as they pertain to the fundamental unity of being and time as appropriated in and through language.

Care is essential before this technical sense of measurement can be understood. Heidegger warns that "the essence of measure has as little to do with quanity as the essence of number" (*VA*, p. 199). Here, Heidegger is consistent with his principle (already applied to language, technology, and man) that the essence *(Wesen)* of something is necessarily related to what is other than that something within the context of being as such. Thus, to determine the essence

190

of measure, it must be possible to state the meaning of the name *measure* as spoken from poetized saying, that is, from being itself insofar as being is appropriated in the speaking of this type of language. Thinking must then construe what is appropriated and then express the content of this appropriation in its own way. But these problematic relations involve even more fundamental considerations than the correlation of thinking with being in terms of being as measured in poetizing. For in *Was Heisst Denken?*, Heidegger straightforwardly asserts that "we would lapse into a mistake, should we intend to affirm that the being of beings means now and for all time—the presence of that which is present" (*WD*, p. 143). This crucial text suggests that at some other time, or in some other epoch, the meaning of being could be something other than presence and its relation to that which is present. But if this difference were to be actualized, then the meaning of being would vary from epoch to epoch. If such variance is essential to being, then Heidegger's position becomes historicist. And if the doctrine of presence is based on a historicist principle, then in what sense can either poetizing or thinking be said to measure the being of things, since the standard against which those things are measured would itself vary with the movement of history? It appears that all discourse about standards or measurement becomes meaningless, given the perpetually changing flux of historical time. The problem of determining the meaning of measurement can be answered only after the more fundamental problem of determining the status of measurement within the temporal flux of history is resolved, to the extent that such resolution is now available.

The Historicity of Being

Historicism is defined by a certain conception of history, history is related to a certain conception of time, and time is the essence of presence. We must therefore determine whether and in what sense the Heideggerian position is historicist, not only to understand that position more adequately with respect to metaphysical notions (i.e., those notions which underlie all forms of historicism), but also to determine more clearly the relation between the temporality that grounds historicism and the temporality that grounds presence.

For Heidegger, the history of being is an epochal history. An epoch is not the demarcation of years or centuries, the convenient unit of measurement by which traditional accounts of history have been calculated. An epoch is defined by Heidegger as "the fundamental principle of sending [*Geschick*]"[1] in which being is given. There are several, perhaps even many such epochs, and all of them are strung together sequentially. In its progression, this sequence of epochs "overlaps, so that the original sending of being as presence is concealed more and more in different ways" (*SD*, p. 9). Is there a recognizable principle which binds these epochs together? Heidegger responds in the affirmative, but then adds that "in the sending of being, the sequence of epochs is neither accidental, nor is it calculated as necessary" (*SD*, p. 9). Although the character of the principle which binds these epochs can be construed as something stronger than accident but weaker than necessity, it nonetheless remains the case that "every epoch of philosophy has its own necessity" (*SD*, p. 62). The summation of these epochs is the history of metaphysical thought as seen from the contemporary standpoint. Furthermore, what is true of the epochal nature of philosophy is also true of the nature of poetizing. The essence of poetizing as spoken through Hölderlin's naming word is not a "timelessly valid concept" (*zeitlos gültigen Begriff*). It belongs to a "determined time" (*bestimmte Zeit—EH*, p. 47). If, for example, our time would be altered by the palpable arrival of the deity, then our epoch would be essentially different and the essence of poetizing would differ as well. Similar possibilities must be reserved for the epochal character of thinking. We may conclude that being certainly appears to be historicist, at least if judged by the fact that both thinking and poetizing are, or appear to be, historicist in character.

If, however, the history of being has a grounding principle which underlies all epochal variation in the appearances of being, then Heidegger can insist that each epoch of philosophy possesses its own necessity, without fear that this claim is threatened by a fatally relativistic form of historicism. Does Heidegger's position admit of such a principle? Let us consider the texts introduced above. Heidegger has asserted that the sequence of epochal manifestations of being progressively conceals "the original sending of being as presence" (*SD*, p. 9). Now, if "original" here is equivalent to something like "in the nature of," then it follows that being is always and necessarily constituted by presence. And if being is always presence of some sort, then being as presence is not equivalent in all respects to the history of being as a sequence of epochal manifestations of presence. Thus, at every given moment of any epoch, being is always presence. But it does not follow—and, in fact, it has not been historically the case—that the manifestation of being as presence must assume the same representational or even thoughtful form in the transition from epoch to epoch. When Heidegger said that it would be a mistake to assume that the being of beings means now and forever "the presence of that which is present," the key word becomes *means*. The point is not that being could be something completely other than presence, for such an admission opens up the possibility that the nature of being is (among many other antithetical candidates) the essentially timeless Platonic form, a possibility which Heidegger has explicitly rejected. The Platonic forms are and continue to be a necessary step in the history of being, but they cannot be considered equivalent to the nature of being as such. Therefore, this line of argument concludes that the *meaning* of being may not always be expressible as the presence of that which is present, even though being as such is always and necessarily temporality of some form.

In an analogous vein, when Heidegger asserts that every philosophical epoch has its own necessity, he does not mean that the necessity of one epoch will differ in toto from the necessity of another epoch. All epochs necessarily reveal (and conceal) the temporality of being. Epochs differ in the way in which each manifests being, but epochs do not differ with respect to the essential nature of what they reveal and conceal. In the epoch inaugurated by Heidegger's own efforts to practice thinking *(Denken)*, being is manifest as the presence of that which is present. Hence, Heidegger must say (since his own thinking is apparently no less epochal than that of Plato or Nietzsche or any other philosopher) how being is necessarily revealed in this epoch. And, in this epoch, temporality is the presence of that which is present, that temporality originally sent by being itself. Thus, to conclude, we have apparently unearthed an aspect of being, its essential temporality, which is, so to speak, transepochal. And the strength of this conclusion allows us to see Heidegger's position, regardless of whatever other objections might be raised against it, as impervious to a virulent form of historicism.

But this argument in Heidegger's defense is not entirely persuasive as it stands. The crucial step depends on an implicit distinction between essentially distinct types of temporality: the first type is that which grounds the sameness of being as such; the second type is that which determines the different epochal appearances of being as different from one another. But simply to assert, as Heidegger does, that being is necessarily temporal does not automatically elevate this perspective on being above the flux of historicity. The necessary temporality of being as such does not by itself imply that the temporality qua necessity differs in some recognizably essential way from the temporality of the various epochal manifestations of being. For such a difference to obtain, one must show how the necessity of being as temporality is constituted by a structure with the same transepochal base (thus precluding historicist objections) and which also allows the historical sequence of epochs in which being manifests itself as different forms of temporality. As far as I know or can determine from the available texts, Heidegger does not attempt such a demonstration. Of course, the fact that Heidegger has not articulated such a structure does not imply that this structure could not be articulated, whether indirectly from Heidegger's own writings or by someone sympathetic with his project in this context. The point is, however, that the introduction of a name like necessity compels Heidegger or the advocate of the Heideggerian position to detail the nature of this necessity. And if the necessity of being as temporality is itself grounded in temporality, then one may well wonder, given the apparent threat of circularity, whether the name *necessity* can be legitimately applied. Furthermore, if it should turn out that the necessity of being as temporality is itself grounded in some additional principle other than that provided by temporality, then the advocate of the Heideggerian position must rethink the entire foundation of ontology. This burdensome consequence follows because temporality and this hypothetical "other" would then become in some essential sense coequal and codeterminate. The claim that being is time would not be denied. But this claim must be supplemented by the recognition that being as such is also something other than time.

The principle required to protect Heidegger's position against historicism must apparently be sought for elsewhere than in the character of being as such. Perhaps a less ambiguous and more defensible nonhistorical base can be located within the sequence of epochs rather than in the universality of being as transepochally temporal.[2] Heidegger has affirmed that the sequence of epochs in which being appears can be calculated neither as accidental nor as necessary (*SD*, p. 9). Determining why Heidegger rejects both these

194

extreme alternatives is not difficult. If the sequence is accidental, then it would follow that the nature of being as such was closed off to all metaphysical thinking, since such thought was fixed more on the necessity grounding the epoch in which that thought occurred than on whatever manifestation of being was proper to that epoch. Furthermore, since thinking as *Denken* itself belongs to this epochal sequence, then thinking becomes no more capable of revealing being than has part or all of the previous history of metaphysics. Nevertheless, thinking (i.e., Heidegger's own thought) is not mute in this way, although Heidegger would be the first to grant that its results so far are only provisional. The doctrine of the appropriation of being has guaranteed that thinking will achieve some positive results in its attempt to reveal the nature of being. Therefore, the sequence of epochs cannot be merely accidentally connected, given the ontological possibilities in thinking as revealed by Heidegger himself.

If, on the other hand, the sequence is necessary, then Heidegger would be faced with problems of the classical Hegelian mold. Are the principles of necessity externally related to or participative in the various epochal manifestations of being? Does the necessity have a determinable end, a "final cause"? If the history of being is going somewhere, then where is it going, and why is it going there and not elsewhere? But these problems are appropriate to Heidegger's ontology only if that ontology duplicates, at some essential level, the structure of Hegel's Absolute. And surely such duplication is impossible, for it would reduce Heidegger's position in this respect to a mirror image of Hegel, whose thought is merely another of the prior epochal manifestations of being. Thus, either the sequence of epochs cannot be construed as necessary in any sense, or if it is necessary, then its necessity must be constituted entirely differently from that of Hegel, or indeed any other moment in the complete sequence of metaphysical speculation.

Heidegger attempts to steer a middle course between these two extremes. But his precise destination is still unknown, given that the determination of the principle or principles guiding the sequence of epochs is not made explicit. However, it seems clear that this destination must be located nearer to necessity than to accident. If such is the case, then being is not simply epochal or historical. A principle guides its epochal succession, cutting across the sequence of epochs and linking them to one another by something which, described with the unavoidable language of metaphysics, verges on necessity. And presumably the same or a similar principle guides the epochal succession of poetizing (presumably, because Heidegger does not say nearly as much about the historical aspects of poetizing as he does about the historical aspects of thinking).

It is obvious, of course, that this hypothetical suggestion raises more problems than it solves. A principle which is neither wholly accidental nor wholly necessary but which belongs more in the order of necessity than in accident must be described as concretely and completely as possible, not merely suggested by silence or by subtle hints. Stating the structure of this principle remains a problem to be solved. We may conclude by drawing an instructive parallel: the indeterminate mediation between necessity and accident with respect to the principle underlying the sequence of epochs is analogous to the tension between being as temporality and the various epochal manifestations of being. Thus, being as temporality is to necessity as the epochal manifestations of being are to accident. And the problem of determining the nature of the connection binding the epochal manifestations of being will also be analogous to the problem of determining the difference between being as temporality and being in its various epochal appearances.

The Historicity of Thinking and Poetizing

If it should happen that being is not historicist in some self-destructive sense, then it is possible that standards can be derived in accordance with which both thinking and poetizing can measure the being of things. But even if being as such is essentially historicist, it is conceivable that standards could be derived from a given epochal manifestation of being which preserve a meaningful sense of measurement when these standards are applied to the determination of things. There is, however, yet another relevant possibility. For it is also possible that either thinking or poetizing (or both) are historicist even if being as such is not. The fact that thinking and poetizing are appropriated to being does not, by itself, guarantee that the products of thinking and poetizing in this or any other epoch will escape a virulent form of historicism. We must therefore inquire into the problem of whether thinking and poetizing are as historicist as being itself appears to be.

It has been argued that Heidegger's notion of a unique and revisionist thinking is flawed by a peculiarly self-destructive reliance on the history of metaphysics. The argument contends that thinking cannot preserve its integrity as *Denken* at the same time that it follows in sequence an epochal series of metaphysical representations of being which must be preserved within the structure of thinking itself.[3] But I suggest that this objection is not entirely persuasive. In fact, to assume that thinking must be like any or every instance of metaphysics begs the question which the confrontation between thinking and poetizing intends to raise. Thus, if being as such is to be properly appropriated, then must the structure of thinking be complemented by another type of linguistic activity? Heidegger's answer is yes, and the burden of this study has been to show that and how this answer deserves serious consideration. Therefore, it is surely conceivable that thinking can be in one (or some) respects the same as metaphysical thought and in another respect different from that type of thought.

Of course, this argument does not ease the burden on the advocate of Heidegger's position to show how the contact between thinking and poetizing generates a defense against historicist criticism. Since both thinking and poetizing are modes of saying, it follows that saying appropriates the temporality of being as presence and that at some point what is spoken in saying as poetized is measured according to the same standard that governs saying as thinking. In order to indicate that standard, recall that Hölderlin's poetizing defines our epoch. But this poetizing does not define the epochal manifestation of being as temporality merely as an abstract form of presence. Hölderlin's poetizing names a certain entity, the deity, existing in a certain way, as lacking, from which the presence of all other beings is affected as far as the nature of their own respective modes of temporality is concerned. The content of this epochally definitive poetizing suggests that the contextual relations binding the deity to the divine, the divine to the holy, and the holy to all beings, culminate in the notion of a world, the fourfold, which is as fundamental ontologically as the presence of that which is present. Thus, to contrast the two elements, presence defines what being is, while the fourfold differentiates the various sectors within which presence is manifested. Is the fourfold then the nonhistoricist structure which we seek?

We have contended that, for Heidegger, being is always temporality. In our epoch, this temporality is the presence of that which is present. In future epochs, temporality may assume other forms. Now, if the fourfold is no more fundamental than presence, does it follow that in future epochs being may be differentiated in some manner essentially other than that defined by the fourfold? If temporality underlies being as presence, then to answer this question we must determine what underlies being as differentiated by the fourfold. The most suitable candidate is totality, in conjunction with a principle of specification. Thus, the earth, the heavens, the mortal, and the divine combine to form both a heuristic and a constitutive whole. The history of metaphysics may then be characterized as a series of variant specifications of these parts according to different hierarchical priorities—e.g., materialism, idealism, realism, systematic theology (as a kind of metaphysics). Therefore, since the history of metaphysics can be reduced to the implicit and explicit differentiations of the fourfold, the question becomes whether being can be differentiated in some way which cannot be recognized as a function of the fourfold. For if being cannot be so differentiated, then the fourfold is apparently itself nonhistoricist, since it transcends all the epochal variations in which being as temporality is thought and differentiated.

As far as I am aware, Heidegger does not discuss the possibility that historicism pertains to the fourfold. But it is surely worthwhile to speculate on this matter, using as a base our understanding of Heidegger's other principles. In order to stand impervious to historicism, the fourfold must contain at least one characteristic by virtue of which the fourfold as such is fundamentally different from any previous moment in the continuum of metaphysical thought. Can this characteristic be specified? First of all, we note that the drive for totality inherent in the fourfold does not distinguish it from the vast majority of metaphysical systems, since nearly all metaphysical systems attempt a comprehensive account of being. The problem must therefore be resolved, not in the quest for totality as such, but with respect to the ways in which being is made determinate. But even this respect appears incapable of providing the requisite characteristic. For regardless how being as totality is differentiated, by however many elements and whatever the content of these elements, we must assume that being as differentiated by the fourfold is the same at some essential level as being when it is differentiated by presence. For if being were not the same at this level, then it would be possible that a given property of being as constituted by the fourfold could not be predicated of being as constituted by presence. And surely this possibility must be rejected. But if, as we have suggested, being as presence is essentially historicist, then the unavoidable implication is that being as differentiated by the fourfold must also be historicist. In other words, it is possible that the fourfold may vanish as an essential perspective on the nature of being, just as the presence of that which is present may also vanish in subsequent epochs. Although both these totality-perspectives are presently necessary, they are so only with respect to past metaphysical history and to the needs of the epoch in which contemporary thinking and poetizing find themselves.[4]

To differentiate being by means of the fourfold may be both necessary and fertile, but the fourfold as such remains in the flux of an ontological historicism. And if the fourfold is subject to such historicism, then so is that thinking and poetizing which must say and speak in accordance with its stipulated sectors. As far as the measurement of beings as things is concerned, both thinking and poetizing are brought to the same impasse. Thus, if the Heideggerian position is reducible to a form of historicism, both of being as such and of the thinking and poetizing of being, then the possibility of preserving the notion of measurement appears remote at best. And if it is impossible to measure the being of things, then it is redundant to say that any two things are the same and impossible to say that any two things are different.

This conclusion is certainly harmful, if not fatal, to the persuasiveness of Heidegger's overall ontological program. Nonetheless, a two-phase rejoinder is still available to those who wish to continue along the Heideggerian way. First, the apparently essential historicism in Heidegger's thought must be seen in conjunction with the attempt to think being as such by rethinking the underlying principles which have grounded previous attempts to think being. Therefore, to reject the Heideggerian position because it entails a self-destructive historicism in effect begs the question, since this rejection is based on the unexamined conviction that historicism is impossible because it runs counter to some set of established metaphysical principles. But to question the stability and adequacy of these principles, whatever they may be, is precisely the matter at hand. Nevertheless, if it should happen that the proper structure of ontology is characterized by historicism, then that structure must still be open to description in language which does not fall prey to inconsistency or impenetrable obscurity. This task is, of course, considerable. If, for example, the possibility of an alternate historicist ontology is allowed, analogous to the fact of alternate metaphysical systems, then the description of a proper historicist ontology must not only be clear and self-consistent, but must also generate principles of rightness so that both it and any alternate historicist ontology can be evaluated in terms of these principles. Without such principles, the only guidelines available for determining the adequacy of a historicist ontology are those derivable from some metaphysical base, from which it will doubtless follow that the historicist ontology cannot even be consistently formualted, much less be ontologically incisive.

The second phase of this rejoinder is that even if the hypothetical grounding of historicism cannot be realized, it does not follow that adopting the Heideggerian position compels abandoning the description and analysis of being and its relation to beings. After all, the thinker must think the necessity of that epoch in which he, the thinker, necessarily exists. Thus, even if the thoughtful response to being is as epochal as being itself is epochal, the thinker must attempt to name the presence of being according to some standard of measurement. This standard may vary from epoch to epoch, but in *this* epoch it is *this* standard. As such, the standard possesses a kind of epochal necessity (just as our mortal existence is defined by epochal necessity). Thus, the problems unearthed but still unresolved in this section should not by themselves forestall further investigation into the possibility that thinking and poetizing can measure the temporality of things. However, even if we grant the real possibility of thinking within the boundaries of varying epochal necessity, other serious problems remain for Heidegger's position, as we shall see in the following two sections.

INDIVIDUATION

If, in some sense, poetizing can be said to measure when it appropriates being, then one of its most important functions will be the ontological individuation of that which poetizing speaks. Given one world and a plurality of things defined in relation to that one world, the determination of an entity as a thing should proceed so that any one thing is different from any other thing. Toward the conclusion of the essay "Das Ding," Heidegger affirms that all things *(Dinge)* are things "according to their own way" (*VA*, p. 181). What then is the

200

principle of differentiation which distinguishes (to use Heidegger's own examples) that thing which is an old bridge from that thing which is a jug? Both are things because they collect all four sectors of the fourfold, and each thing does so in its own way. But what principle measures each thing's "own way"?[5] In exploring this problem, we shall find considerations coming into play other than those discussed in the historicist section.

The differentiation of things depends on the correlative notions of identity and difference. Although this correlation has a venerable metaphysical heritage, it is apparently, for Heidegger, not one of those categories which distorts the proper nature of things. Therefore, we may look for some form of thing-differentiation in the relevant phases of Heidegger's ontology of things. Yet even if this principle is absent or is only partially developed, it would be premature to conclude that Heidegger's ontology is fundamentally flawed. The problems generated by the classical notions of identity and difference are relative to a set of metaphysical principles which, according to Heidegger, have progressively distorted being by concealing its necessary temporality. Although a comprehensive ontology must be equipped to discriminate between different things, the way in which difference coheres with this ontology might be other than the way difference coheres with various metaphysical systems. However, given that difference must now be understood according to some version of traditional metaphysical thinking, it is not inappropriate to question Heidegger's own doctrine of things on this issue. Heidegger himself has stated that things are different, and even if the way to formalizing difference as such is itself partially hidden (as the doctrine of releasement seems to imply), the context of that way must be explored as far as possible.

The principle of differentiation must be found in the appropriation *(Ereignis)* which determines all entities in their ontological relations to being. Appropriation constitutes the totality, but which part or parts of that totality determines difference as difference? Two prominent possibilities shall be considered here, the fourfold and presence. First, consider the fourfold. In chapter 7, it was argued that the distinctive feature of the contemporary epoch, the lack of the deity, made the nature of any prospective thing problematic. But although the lacking deity may affect the constitution of an entity as a thing, its pervasive influence in this sense cannot be the source of principle of differentiation between things. Either the deity is lacking, or the deity is not lacking. Each disjunction affects, at times definitively, the epoch in which it occurs. In either case, however, the deity exists in relation to the divine, and the divine is one sector of the fourfold and always one such sector. Thus, the divine is a necessary part of the entity's thinghood—regardless whether or not the deity fills that sector. As a result, the mode of existence of the deity—whether absent or present—is identical with respect to all nondivine entities as potential things. Considered from this admittedly partial perspective, we may conclude that the fourfold offers no distinction qua thinghood between the old bridge and the jug. Both bridge and jug are identical with respect to their relation to the divine.

In fact, we may generalize from this conclusion that none of the sectors of the fourfold, taken in isolation as the divine was just taken, can supply the required differentiating principle. But if all four sectors as parts are not adequate, can an aspect found *within* one of the four sectors serve as the principle in question? We have assumed, since Heidegger has not explicitly said otherwise, that no one of the four sectors is any more ontologically primordial than any of the others. But if no sector is itself more fundamental, then no part or aspect of any one sector can be more fundamental. For if one part or aspect of a given sector would, for example, contribute the principle of differentiation, then that sector would be more fundamental in the sense that it grounded the ontology of things with respect to their differentiation. If it is necessary to emphasize one (or several) of the sectors in order to preserve a particular metaphysical category, then it will be necessary to resort to the same kind of emphasis to preserve other metaphysical categories (whichever are suitable for Heidegger's ontology). The more categories preserved, the more shifts in emphasis required. If the preservation of metaphysical categories includes all or even the majority of such categories (this may or may not be Heidegger's intent), then Heidegger's ontology will eventually be difficult to distinguish from one or a mixed variation on some traditional metaphysical position. And this is surely a damaging conclusion, given Heidegger's stated position on the progressive concealment of being as found in traditional metaphysics.

Examples drawn from various sectors of the fourfold will illustrate this interpretation. Assume that the deity—not the divine—is of such a sort that his nature includes the principle of differentiation, i.e., that a thing is different from another thing by divine fiat. However, the deity is sometimes lacking. Therefore, in an epoch when the deity is lacking, the deity can no longer perform this differentiating function. As a result, things cannot be differentiated in such an epoch. Since this condition is proper to our epoch and since the duration of this epoch is unknown, it follows that things cannot be differentiated now or in the foreseeable future. Surely this conclusion is impossible, and an ontology which admits of such a possibility must be questionable at some basic level. Now, if the differentiating principle is based neither on the deity as such nor on the divine, but rather is material in some earthly, heavenly, or earth-heavens sense, then what distinguishes one thing from another is its connection to a principle of "natural" (i.e., nondivine and nonmortal) origin. But this would only transform Heidegger's ontology (at least with respect to differentiation) into an Aristotelianism of sorts, but without the diversity and scope of Aristotle's own metaphysics. More importantly, Heidegger's position would once more fall victim to the reductionist criticism. His fundamental ontology becomes indistinguishable from yet another of those historical moments which that ontology intends to correct.

Only the mortal sector of the fourfold remains, and man as mortal is perhaps the most likely candidate to satisfy our present requirement. Note that the two entities Heidegger analyzes as things—the old bridge and the jug—are artifacts. Man made them, and man uses them. Perhaps man is the principle of differentiation by reason of the modes in which he experiences entities. The difference between the bridge and the jug, qua thinghood, is based on whatever interests or concerns are localized in these entities by human agents. Both as entities and as things, the old bridge and the jug are different because of the different uses to which they may be put. The particular mode of experience does not matter; the crucial point is that it be human and mortal and therefore differentiating. The same span of experiences would include all natural entities, as well as artifacts. Thus, a tree as entity and as prospective thing is differentiated from water or sunlight because the tree can be used to make a bridge while the latter two cannot. Thus, whether the entity is natural or an artifact, it is differentiated as thing in and through human agency and purpose. But surely this possibility must also be rejected. If the entire history of metaphysics has progressively distorted the nature of being, part of the reason for this distortion has been the imposition of human concerns onto the nature of being as if it were ontologically proper for being to bear these concerns. Nietzsche's Will to Power is only the most palpable example from a tradition which has its roots in Plato. If man as mortal were the principle of differentiation, then (again with respect to the category of differentiation) the fourfold is once more reduced to another moment or series of moments in that essentially concealing history of metaphysical thought. Clearly this conclusion is incompatible with Heidegger's intent.

As interpreted here, the doctrine of the fourfold does not appear to generate a principle of differentiation. But the fourfold is only one of the modes in which Heidegger has discriminated being. The other principal mode is presence *(Anwesen)*, and we now attempt to determine whether presence has been sufficiently developed for this purpose. Recall that presence is "proper time," the "nearness of presence out of present, past and future—the nearness that unifies time's threefold opening extension" (SD, p. 17). And Heidegger explicitly connects presence with the notion of difference: "Not everything which is [*ist*] in some way or other exists as presence [*anwest*] in the same manner" (WD, p. 143).[6] Thus, it may be possible to derive a principle of differentiation from the doctrine of presence.

Consider the jug. As entity, the jug is finite. At one point it was not, it exists now, and there is every reason to believe that it will eventually break and thus cease to be the entity jug. But do the same temporal considerations hold for the entity jug as hold for the thing jug? If the temporality of the jug as thing is not identical with the temporality of the jug as entity, then the jug could continue to be a thing while ceasing to be an entity. This possibility raises the general problem of the relation between entity and thing. If Heidegger maintains the nonidentity between thing-temporality and entity-temporality, then he must show how thinghood can be preserved when the entitative status is nonexistent. To obviate this particular aspect of the problematic relation between entity and thing, let us assume that the principle of differentiation as presence (if there be such principle) applies only to existing entities. In other words, an existing entity may or may not be determined as a thing (presumably all entities are potential things), but a nonexistent entity is not amenable to thing-determination.

But this obviation does not reach the heart of the problem. If presence is a totality-perspective on being as temporality, then the determination of things requires that one thing bear relations to temporality in a manner differentiating it from another thing. If each thing is a thing in virtue of having all aspects of presence, then presence as such is identical in every thing and thus cannot serve to differentiate between things. All things would be simultaneous, as it were, in that the temporality of each thing would be constituted by all possible relations to each past-, present-, and future-aspect proper to presence as such.[7] If each thing has the totality of presence but has it uniquely, there is no common ground—other than being as a completely indeterminate substratum lacking even temporal reference—on which to base difference claims. Things different in all respects from one another cannot be compared in any sense whatsoever. There must be some common basis of identity which grounds different things so that the difference can be determined as difference. Now if, on the other hand, thing A has some part or aspect of presence and thing B has some other part or aspect of presence, then things A and B are differentiated by reason of presence. But since they are only partially related to the totality of presence, they cease to be things in the stipulated sense which Heidegger's principles require. We conclude, therefore, that if presence in all its dimensions constitutes each thing, then the proper ontology of things is achieved—but the achievement apparently precludes the category of differentiation; if things are differentiated by reason of partial relation to presence, then presence as being and as temporal totality cannot constitute a given thing. It seems then that if Heidegger preserves totality, he loses differentiation; if he attempts to establish differentiation, he loses totality.

Presence apparently shares the same fate as the fourfold as far as affording sufficient diversity for determining both the constitution and the differentiation of things. We have examined the fourfold and presence in isolation from one another and have not attempted to merge the two totality-perspectives. In a sense, this procedure is artificial and distorts the letter of Heidegger's teaching (although the distinction between the two is warranted, I believe, for purposes of clarifying Heidegger's position). In fact, the two perspectives are not opposed to, but complement each other. Heidegger explicitly connects presence with the fourfold (W, p. 244) and carries through their interrelation by describing the thing as temporally constituted in conjunction with the fourfold: "Every thing lingers toward the fourfold in its own respective lingering from the unity of world" (VA, p. 179).[8] The fourfold and presence are complementary perspectives on the proper ontology of things. Their conjunction must now be examined to determine whether differentiation can be found from this confluence of totality-perspectives.

For our purposes, the important point is that both are totality-perspectives on being and each perspective is dissimilar from the other. But if it is impossible to preserve totality when each perspective is faced with the problem of differentiation, then the conjunction or intersection of the two totality-perspectives will also be inadequate for this purpose. If an entity has presence in all its constituent phases and shows relations to all four sectors of the fourfold, then the entity becomes a thing. But if both totality-perspectives are necessary before the entity is a thing, then instantiating just one of the totality-perspectives is insufficient to constitute thinghood. Although the unity of the fourfold and the unity of presence are each constituted differently, qua unity neither the fourfold nor presence is ontologically privileged. To appeal to one of the two unities as the source of the principle of differentiation is to assume that there is a difference, qua unity, between the fourfold and presence. But to demonstrate that such a difference is tangible, Heidegger must take both the fourfold and presence onto a second level of being and show the difference in unities between the two totality-perspectives.

As far as I know, Heidegger has never attempted such a demonstration, nor is there even any indication that such a demonstration may be required. We may suggest parenthetically why this is the case. As noted, although both the fourfold and presence are perspectives on totality, they are very different from one another. Presence is temporality differentiated by the threefold dimensions of past, present, and future. The fourfold is the world differentiated by the fourfold sectors of the earth, the heavens, the mortal, and the divine. By itself, presence has no immediate relation to any nontemporal factors—e.g., the material quality of earth. Similarly, the fourfold as Heidegger has developed its structure does not directly imply a relation to any of the dimensions of temporality. To merge these two divergent but apparently compatible, indeed complementary, perspectives would involve showing how a given thing is determined by the constituent factors of both totality-perspectives. But at every possible intersection of the two perspectives, the problem of relating this thing to a universal totality will be compounded, given that the two perspectives are themselves different from one another.

206

One can appreciate the motivation behind Heidegger's claim that "thinghood [*Dingheit*] must be something unconditioned [*Unbedingtes*]" (FD, p. 7). If metaphysics has distorted the proper ontological nature of things, then it is necessary to search for the conditions that determine a thing in all that which is *not* the thing, that is, where the "not" includes whatever has been considered essential to the thing by metaphysical thought. But the domain of this negation is so inclusive that it must be made determinate. The fourfold and presence enter into this very extensive negation, the "unconditioned," but it does not appear that either totality taken singly or both taken as mutually complementary can determine things so that they are things and yet differentiated from other things.

This search for a principle of differentiation does not exhaust the alternatives selected from Heidegger's thinking, or other alternatives not discussed here. The arguments just sketched are interpretations based on my understanding of Heidegger's most recent attempts to ground the ontology of things. And it should go without saying that if my interpretations are misconceived, then Heidegger may be perfectly capable of establishing a principle of differentiation on the basis of the available ontological doctrines. But assume that my interpretations are not misconceived, and Heidegger's principles make differentiation problematic, perhaps even impossible. There are two directions open at this point. First, it might be mistaken to assume that Heidegger wants difference as an ontological category to function in the same way that difference functions as metaphysical category. But if he does intend to preserve some semblance of difference as traditionally understood, then it is difficult not to conclude that at some deep ontological level all things *(Dinge)* are the same. Heidegger could admit this conclusion and then assert that the notion of sameness is also other than the category of sameness in traditional metaphysics.[9] If so, then both relata of the identity-difference relation must be redefined in light of Heidegger's other basic ontological beliefs. I will not attempt to explore this possibility any further here.

The second direction is that the ontology of the fourfold and of presence is simply flawed. In attempting to rectify the distortion of an entire tradition, Heidegger has introduced two distinct types of totality-perspectives, each complementing the other. An entity must be experienced and determined as a thing by situating it within these totality-perspectives. Such determination will presumably rectify the distortion, but at the price of reducing entitative difference to ontological sameness without providing for the possibility of establishing ontological difference.

The preceding is but one example showing the type of problem which the Heideggerian ontology must face. To assert and reassert the openness of being and the region in which a being is to become determinate is insufficient; at some point beings must be made more determinate than the principles of the fourfold and of presence seem to provide for. And even if Heidegger's ontology does generate problems which are completely distinct from the problems of classical metaphysics, Heidegger must still address the relation between the problematic domain of his own ontology and the traditional problems of metaphysics. The letter of Heidegger's teachings certainly does not ignore the history of metaphysics; much of his published work is an attempt to think with and think through the great metaphysical masterpieces of the Western tradition. But if the letter of his teachings implies a fundamental doctrine which cannot argumentatively confront classical metaphysics, then Heidegger's own *Denken* is ultimately antihistorical in its apprehension and manifestation of the nature of being.

TRUTH

We have concluded, at least provisionally, that Heidegger's ontology faces a serious problem with respect to the differentiation of things. This problem was raised and discussed from a primarily extralinguistic perspective. But the fact that the appropriation of things includes language spoken about things will entail that the problems just introduced will arise again, even if the context is narrowed to strictly linguistic considerations.[10] Heidegger himself has asserted that the word as a name exercises a "measured command over things" (*US*, p. 225). Consequently, the isolation of language from its ontologically necessary extralinguistic relations is justified, at least for purposes of inquiry into the precise nature of this measurement.

The poetizing of Hölderlin (and others in a supplementary sense) has named the divine sector of the fourfold as lacking its grounding deity. Since all four sectors must interplay to constitute the thing, the lack of the deity is one of the definitive characteristics of thinghood in this epoch. It is poetized language which provides the evidence for this particular determination. But notice that if the saying shown in the poetized base is changed, then the constitution of the thing is altered accordingly. For example, if the poetry of Gerard Manley Hopkins is substituted for that of Hölderlin, then the existence of the deity ceases to be problematic and a veritable constellation of divine imagery is available to implement an intermediary divine sector between the existing deity and all that is other than the deity. Consider the first stanza from Hopkins's "The Wreck of the Deutschland":

> Thou mastering me
> God! giver of breath and bread;
> World's strand, sway of the sea:
> Lord of living and dead;
> Thou hast bound bones and veins in me, fastened me flesh,
> And after it almost unmade, what with dread,
> Thy doing: and dost thou touch me afresh?
> Over again I feel thy finger and find thee.

The language is vigorous, the imagery sharp and well defined, but more importantly, the existence of God is as real and vital as the absence of the deity in Hölderlin's poetizing. Which poetic language defines our epoch? On the basis of what standard does the poetizing of Hölderlin rather than the poetry of Hopkins measure our epoch (indeed, why employ poetizing for this purpose at all)?[11]

This confrontation elicits new aspects on problems already introduced. Hölderlin's poetizing says that the deity is lacking; Hopkins's poetry speaks the claim that the deity is not lacking. The statement of their respective positions on God is a contradiction. One of the conjuncts of that statement must then be false. But which, and why is it false? The Heideggerian agnostic will side with Hölderlin's view; the fervent theist will opt for Hopkins. The advocate of each side will reject the other as false. But before the conflict is taken any further, we should note that its ultimate basis is not so much the problematic existence of God, but rather the principle of contradiction and its influence on the way we think about being and beings. This principle is a principle of logic. For Heidegger, logic is based on a certain kind of thinking (*VA*, p. 137), and this thinking depends on an incomplete comprehension of being (*FD*, p. 136). Heidegger then suggests that "the essence of beings exists in the continuous abyss [*Abwesen*] of contradiction" (*NI*, p. 603). Thus, even if contradictory statements exist side by side, it presumably does not follow that one of the two statements is false. Such falsity would not necessarily follow because the being of entities named by either statement can be determined according to principles even more fundamental than that of contradiction. The nature of things must *begin* from the presuppositions implicit in the ontological character of contradiction, rather than rest upon the demarcations of being entailed by contradiction in its formal logical position of supremacy.[12]

Since contradictory statements may be asserted about any entity (of which class the deity is only one instance), Heidegger's contention applies to the relation between language and *all* extralinguistic entities. Now let us assume that Heidegger's thinking can sustain itself independently of contradiction as an ontological principle. Surely it remains inconceivable that, e.g., there *is* and *is not* a deity. It seems clear that the Heideggerian agnostic and the Hopkinsian theist will still be at odds about what is and is not real. From the standpoint of logic, if it is possible that neither conjunct of the Hölderlin-Hopkins confrontation is false, what meaning would the "true" component of that conjunction possess? At this point, however, the perspective must be shifted from logic to ontology. We recall that Heidegger has devoted considerable thoughtful energy analyzing the presuppositions of propositional truth in search of what might be called ontological truth. Only if an entity reveals itself in a certain way will it be possible to make true statements about that entity as a thing. The logic of propositional truth is based on a metaphysics which may or (as Heidegger contends) may not be adequate to the being of entities spoken about in "true" or "false" statements. But in any event, truth by disclosure is ontologically prior to logical truth.

For present purposes, we need not consider Heidegger's notion of truth by disclosure in any detail.[13] But let us assume that Heidegger's search for ontological ultimates in this sense will be successful, if not by Heidegger himself, then by someone who follows his lead. If so, then what is now known as formal logic will have to be restructured to accommodate the principles of this more fundamental ontology. But does it follow that in this restructuring the entire distinction between true and false (or right and wrong, proper and improper—the opposition is the important point, not the names that describe it) will in principle disappear? Will the Heideggerian ontology now hidden deep in the principle of contradiction, as well as in all other preconceptions of representational thinking, do without logic (of some form) altogether? Surely not, as Heidegger himself has admitted by explicitly introducing the problem of the rightness of thinking. If thinking can be right, then it can also be wrong. Also, and just as vital, since thinking must remain "near" to poetizing, the principles which govern right thinking must determine not only how right thinking differs from wrong thinking but also how right thinking differs from both right and wrong poetizing. For if there is right and wrong thinking, and if thinking and poetizing are equally fundamental modes of showing the being of things, there must also be right and wrong poetizing.[14]

The hypothetical confrontation between Hölderlin and Hopkins accentuates the need for a standard of measurement to resolve such differences. If rightness pertains to thinking and poetizing in the same sense in which logical rules pertain to valid and invalid argumentation, then such rightness will generate only formal rules for correct thinking and correct poetizing. But there is the additional problem of deciding which names rightly measure and determine the entity as a thing. And this problem is especially relevant to poetizing. Thus, if poetizing as a mode of saying names a relation between an entity and all four sectors of the fourfold, then presumably that entity is determined as a thing. But surely the resulting set of named relations is insufficient for thing-determination. For if there are no limits on such naming and if the poet has free rein to connect a given entity to any other entity, then *any* such naming determines the transition from entity to thing. It is characteristic of poetic imagery to render the entities spoken about more translucent, as it were, by naming a given entity through an indefinitely large number of possible metaphoric stances. In fact, theoretically (although perhaps not aesthetically) it is possible to relate any word with any entity and to maintain that the linguistic results are poetry. Therefore, the problem of recognizing those names which determine an entity to be a thing is more comprehensive and intricate than the problem of the individuation of things as presented in the previous section of this chapter. Presumably the number of potentially determinative poetized words is considerably larger than the number of potentially determinative aspects of the fourfold and presence. As a result, rightness for poetizing must include a standard whereby all words capable of determining thinghood are measured so that only the appropriate words are, in fact, determinative. And presumably this sense of rightness is different from that rightness necessary for right and wrong thinking. But perhaps not. It seems pertinent to distinguish between rightness as the measure of formal correctness and rightness as the measure of appropriate determining words for thinghood. A formally correct set of right propositions need not necessarily be ontologically proper. But since Heidegger leaves the nature of rightness in either sense open, such a distinction is perhaps premature. It is possible that the desired rightness will satisfy both requirements without the need to draw an initial distinction between formal correctness and properly constituted content.

Earlier I suggested that it was inconceivable, or at least apparently inconceivable, that a deity both be and not be. To make such a state of affairs conceivable, Heidegger must describe being and not-being as they relate to the measurement of a given being and as this being is apprehended by thought. The Hegelian gambit of a dialectical notion of contradiction must be ruled out, since this would implicitly equate Heidegger's notion of *Sein* with Hegel's notion of the Absolute. How then can this project even be initiated, much less completed, much less completed successfully? A suggested measure for "right" thinking is cast in terms of rigor, but as one might expect, rigor understood in a very distinctive sense. For Heidegger, "the most exact [*exakste*] thinking is never the most rigorous [*strengste*] thinking," since the most exact thinking is bound up merely with "the calculation of entities" (W, p. 104).[15] Formal logic would doubtless be the most obvious example of thinking which attains its results about the being of entities merely by "calculation." Heidegger insists, to the contrary, that "the element in which thinking must move itself in order to be rigorous is ambiguity [*Mehrdeutigkeit*]" (WD, p. 68). Ambiguity has traditionally been the bane of philosophical discourse, especially in recent times, when apparent lack of clarity is almost immediately equated with self-evident philosophical naivete and confusion. But ambiguity in this context should be understood initially in its literal sense of many meanings, that is, the Heideggerian "spontaneity" of thinking which "plays" into the interplay of presence and the four sectors of the fourfold. Can this notion of ambiguity be stabilized, as it were, with respect to the logical problem at hand?[16]

One formulation of the principle of contradiction, stated in terms of properties of entities rather than in terms of propositions about entities, appeals to time—a thing cannot be and not be at one and the same time and in the same respect. If thinking is essentially ambigu-

212

ous, then perhaps the temporality of presence is also essentially ambiguous. It would then be possible to range the temporality of a given entity as thing over all dimensions of presence so that the prerequisite "at one and the same time" would not apply, since the time of a given entity as thing would be *all* time as presence. The problem with this gambit is that even if the temporality of presence could be differentiated to fit the respective temporality of distinct things, the notion of negation would appear to lose the crucial force it purveys in contradiction as temporally formulated. The ancient battle between being and nonbeing recurs, only now in the restricted arena where both notions are bound by temporality and the history of attempts to represent that temporality. Thus, in his only major work which could be expected to address logical principles, *Identität und Differenz*, Heidegger barely touches on the formulation of the principle of identity as a logical axiom; rather, he reflects on figures such as Parmenides and Hegel, two philosophers who have played a crucial role in establishing the primacy of these correlative principles. Heidegger sees this primacy in an ontological rather than a formal logical dimension. Therefore, since he rejects the notion of eternally true logical principles, the historical temporality which grounds this primacy must be explicitly introduced into the discussion of the ontological significance of identity and difference. The same requirement must hold for contradiction.[17]

But surely the objections raised above will retain their force, regardless of the historical context in which Heidegger situates his own discussion of these principles. Ambiguous meanings may be essential to the development of thinking which is appropriate to the appropriation of being, but at some point the meaning of such thinking must be stabilized. Ambiguous meanings may be incorporated into propositions which are contradictory, regardless how the being of the entities or things named by these propositions is constituted. And if there is no foreseeable way to derive a standard of measurement to differentiate between ambiguous and unambiguous thinking, then the self-reflexive character of the principle of essential ambiguity becomes damaging to Heidegger's own pronouncements. Thus, does ambiguity apply to Heidegger's own illumination of Hölderlin's poetized speaking? If so, then the meaning of that poetizing might be such that the deity is not concealed in the way Heidegger thinks the deity is concealed, perhaps even that the deity is not concealed at all. Heidegger's own principles for rigorous thinking carry the possibility that the thinking he has directed on epochally definitive poetizing is partially or wholly misdirected. A standard of measurement is required which goes beyond Heidegger's undeveloped (and apparently inadequate) distinction between exact and rigorous thinking.

The explicit mention of the need for ambiguity may serve to initiate a general concluding remark on Heidegger's project, in particular the confluence of poetizing and thinking. If Heidegger is to transform ambiguity from a name which represents a philosophical vice to a word which shows one of the virtues of thinking, then this transformation will require examining the entire structure of the appropriation of language. This structure includes the totality of being, or being as such, discriminated in a number of ways—e.g., world-thing, the fourfold, the temporality of presence. If the notion of ambiguity is not to be ultimately vitiating (surely this is Heidegger's intent), it must be explained in terms of the motion or interplay between the totality and those discriminations which stabilize that motion or interplay. Ambiguity does not apply only to the contrast between exact and rigorous thinking. As we have seen, fundamental ambiguities persist in the two perspectives already discussed in this chapter. Thus, if Heidegger's historicity is not self-destructive, then the ambiguity between being as presence and being as something other than presence must be settled. If this ambiguity is resolved, then Heidegger still faces the character of the thing ambiguously constituted in such a way that it appears undifferentiated from other things. The products of rigorous thinking are as ambiguous as the process of rigorous thinking itself.

In general, the principal tension in all these ambiguities is between Heidegger's quest for a totality which restores what the Western tradition has progressively overlooked or forgotten and the intrinsic difficulty of mediating that totality with some form of discrimination. But until these ambiguities are settled, there is a crucial sense in which either Heidegger's position is and remains in principle obscure or in which the commentary on that position is without a compatible base of principles. The distinctions drawn in this chapter on all three fronts—time as historicity, the differentiation of entities as things, the relation between truth and being—and the arguments to illustrate and develop those distinctions are based on traditional metaphysical doctrines. If these doctrines are distorted, then it follows either that no critical analysis of an alternate position radically

214

different from those doctrines is possible or that whatever criticism is applicable must be generated and controlled by that very teaching which we have been attempting to understand and interpret. If the former, then only Heidegger can speak and all others must remain mute, even those who desire to follow him but who are all too aware of their rootedness in the continuing flow of the Western philosophical tradition. If the latter, then given our historical existence, the business of understanding Heidegger still can be initiated only from the distorted presuppositions on which Heidegger's ontology is itself based and which that ontology is attempting to rectify. In this chapter, I have attempted to sketch some of the more obvious problems which arise when the ontology of poetizing and thinking meets that "distorted" tradition. The reader dissatisfied with the criticisms raised is invited to examine Heidegger's writings and either reformulate the problems or answer the objections. Heidegger's ambiguity may turn out to be a virtue after all. There is one more alternative—a direct visionary insight into Heidegger's thinking on being and the ability to translate that vision into language. One suspects, however, that the prosaic residue of that vision will be as idiosyncratic and elusive as the original texts which inspired it. The appropriate Heideggerian commentary will then itself require as much commentary as the original texts commented upon, surely an unsavory prospect for even the most devoted student of Heidegger's teaching.

Is the later Heidegger a thinker, a poet, or some fusion of the two? If he is exclusively or even primarily a poet, then of course his work should not be confronted with the canons of formal logic and the distinctions of classical metaphysics. Heidegger's prodigious output will then demand a critic or, doubtless, critics who are sufficiently imbued with his terminology and various interests to hazard guesses about the meanings of his works. But since the poet qua poet (and Heidegger as an exemplar of such poetry) need not pursue truth or wisdom, or at least truth controlled by standards of "right" thinking, then Heidegger's work may perhaps be justly dismissed as beautifully mystical language rather than as language engaged in the pursuit of that truth which should compel assent from every right-thinking mortal lover of wisdom. If, however, Heidegger is not a poet but is one of the other two alternatives, a thinker or a thinker-poet, then standards of measurement governing what can and what cannot be thought or thoughtfully poetized must be imposed. The formal character of logical contradiction may be ontologically perverse, but until a suitable substitute is found, anyone who wants to be a thinker, even in Heidegger's apparently unique sense, cannot simply sidestep its strictures. Nor can the institution of a new ontology (or the remembrance of an ancient ontology couched in language comprehensible to modernity) be accepted as more persuasive than any of the great systems of Western metaphysics without an extremely meticulous and sympathetic comparative study of the fundamental categories of these systems. The Heideggerian ontology of thinking and poetizing must demonstrate where Plato, or Aristotle, or Kant, or Hegel went wrong, while the Heideggerian vision of the nature of being has found the proper path.

If such a series of epochal ontological encounters is to be realized, the language of poetry may serve both heuristic and constitutive ends. It may serve an heuristic end by presenting aspects of experience overlooked or misrepresented by the presuppositions or explicit pronouncements of a given metaphysical system (perhaps all such systems) and then by developing those aspects through penetrating and ultimately totality-oriented poetized imagery. It may serve a constitutive end by enjoining the thinker to fill the resulting gaps in his thought with precisely the words and their ambiguous connotations which poetizing has spoken. But the final result, whether in Heidegger's own work or in the work of those who profess to think by imitating his example, must be established in accordance with standards and evaluated by standards. And these standards must pay heed to, and perhaps even ultimately correspond with, those standards which have already governed the highest moments in the history of Western speculation.

My own conviction is that Heidegger's later work is the product of a thinker-poet, but one who would wish his work to be judged as primarily thoughtful (i.e., ontological and, by implication of Heidegger's own distinctive historicism, in some essential sense metaphysical). Heidegger is not a poet with scattered and unconnected thoughtful ruminations and insights. Nevertheless, it remains true that the extent to which Heidegger's later work can be understood by anyone other than Heidegger himself will be measured by the extent to which his students have a deep respect for the language of poetry and its insights into being, along with the desire to question the presuppositions of the entire history of metaphysics in light of those insights. If, as a result, the philosopher lays aside the fashionable conceptual puzzles of the day, he has the right to expect that following the Heideggerian way—if not Heidegger himself—will result in experiencing more profoundly and describing more accurately the nature of being and the ways in which being can be said of beings.

Notes

PREFACE

1. Pöggeler develops this view in his essay "Heidegger Today" in Edward G. Ballard and Charles E. Scott, eds., *Martin Heidegger: In Europe and America* (The Hague: Martinus Nijhoff, 1973), pp. 1–36.

2. A principle which, in my view, would apply to all studies comparing any aspect of Heidegger's thought with any notion or figure in the history of thought. Thus, the value of a work such as George F. Sefler's *Language and the World: A Methodological Synthesis within the Writings of Martin Heidegger and Ludwig Wittgenstein* is based on the extent to which Sefler understands both Heidegger and Wittgenstein. If Sefler fails to understand either Heidegger or Wittgenstein, then the results of such comparative study will not be persuasive. The same considerations hold for primarily historical works such as John N. Deely's *The Tradition Via Heidegger*. (See the Bibliography for complete information on these volumes.)

INTRODUCTION

1. All translations from Heidegger's works are my own. Additional texts will be footnoted in German when appropriate. See the list of abbreviations for the full title of the original work cited.

2. "Die vorliegenden *Erläuterungen* beanspruchen nicht Beiträge zur literaturhistorischen Forschung und zur Ästhetik zu sein. Sie entspringen einer Notwendigkeit des Denkens." See *EH*, p. 7 (italics in original). The fact that Heidegger found this warning necessary must have been due to the understandable tendency of literary critics to read his Hölderlin essays according to precisely those canons of interpretation here set aside.

3. For example, T. J. Casey, *Manshape That Shone: An Interpretation of Trakl* (Oxford: Basil Blackwell, 1968), pp. 23, 89.

4. This is obviously an important consideration, both in terms of interpreting Heidegger and in understanding his notion of thinking and its relation to formal logic. I shall consider this theme further in chapter 9.

5. To mention only two such derivations: Hans-Georg Gadamer, *Wahrheit und Methode* 2d ed. (Tubingen: J. C. B. Mohr, 1965), esp. pp. 240–50, 415–65 (with Gadamer's reference to Heidegger on p. 432); and Richard E. Palmer, *Hermeneutics* (Evanston: Northwestern University Press, 1969), esp. pp. 46–60, 124–217.

6. *US*, p. 37; cf. *H*, p. 29.

219

CHAPTER 1

1. This brief sketch is adequate for the context of the interpretation to be developed in this study, but obviously the sketch is not offered with a view toward analyzing sufficiently Heidegger's position on language in *Sein und Zeit*. As noted in the Introduction, my purpose is not to trace the evolution of Heidegger's thought but to describe a unified body of teaching which spans the relevant later works. For more specialized scholarship, see Jan Aler, "Heidegger's Conception of Language in *Being and Time*," in Joseph Kockelmans, ed., *On Heidegger and Language* (Evanston: Northwestern University Press, 1972), pp. 33–62. Also, Manfred Stassen, *Heideggers Philosophie der Sprache in "Sein und Zeit"; und ihre philos.-theol. Wurzeln* (Bonn: Bouvier, 1973). This work describes how the doctrine of language in *Sein und Zeit* is rooted in the thought of Aristotle, Augustine, and Luther.

2. Apparently the daring advance of *Sein und Zeit* also applies to the analysis of types of assertion in the relatively early (1935–36) *Die Frage nach dem Ding* (FD, 27). As we shall see later in this chapter and also throughout the rest of the study, the basis of this problem is the nature of representational thinking insofar as it conditions the formulation of all philosophical problems. The difference between thinking as representational, or *Vorstellen*, and thinking as *Denken* is discussed in chapters 7 and 8.

3. Laszlo Versenyi's account of Heidegger on language does not appreciate the comprehensiveness of Heidegger's project. Thus: "*Toward Language* does not introduce any new topics for our discussion. Word, language, speech are but new names for *logos, phusis, aletheia*, etc." This reductive claim reflects the overly simplistic attitude Versenyi brings to bear on Heidegger's later work. See Laszlo Versenyi, *Heidegger, Being, and Truth* (New Haven: Yale University Press, 1965), p. 132.

4. Cf. *H*. p. 286; *NI*, p. 308; *W*, p. 145; *US*, p. 166.

5. Cf. *W*, p. 149; *HH*, p. 27.

6. Cf. *H*, p. 297; *NII*, p. 337; *W*, p. 105; *VA*, p. 54; *EM*, p. 131.

7. This perspective on the relation between word and entity as thing also occurs in the early (written in 1935) *Einführung in die Metaphysik* (*EM*, p. 11).

8. Cf. *WD*, p. 84.

9. Heidegger does not indicate the source of *der Wink* as a technical term, but the word occurs in an important passage in Hölderlin's poem "Rousseau" (written in 1799, the same year as Hölderlin's "Wie Wenn am Feiertage"). The passage is as follows:

> Den Sehnenden war
> Der Wink genug, und Winke sind
> Von Alters her die Sprache der Götter.
>
> (To those yearning,
> The hint was enough, and hints are
> From the oldest times the language of the gods.)

For the crucial relation between gods *Götter)* and hints *(Winke)*, see *EH*, p. 46.

10. Erasmus Schöfer's *Die Sprache Heideggers* is a careful examination of Heidegger's use of language from the perspective of stylistics, but the work offers little philosophical commentary. For example, *das Geviert* and *das Ereignis* are mentioned (p. 279) but not discussed. Cf. Erasmus Schöfer, *Die Sprache Heideggers* (Pfullingen: Neske, 1962). Part of this book has been translated and appears as a separate study, "Heidegger's Language: Metalogical Forms of Thought and Grammatical Specialities," in Kockelmans's *On Heidegger and Language*, pp. 281–301.

11. The references are: William J. Richardson, *Heidegger Through Phenomenology to Thought* (The Hague: Martinus Nijhoff, 1967), p. 572; Stanley Rosen, *Nihilism: A Philosophical Essay* (New Haven: Yale University Press, 1969), p. 132; Etienne Gilson, Thomas Langan, and Armand A. Maurer, C. S. B., *Recent Philosophy: Hegel to the Present* (New York: Random House, 1966), p. 151. Additional speculation on the origin of the fourfold is in Dieter Sinn, "Heideggers Spätphilosophie," *Philosophische Rundschau* 14 (1967): pp. 81–182, esp. p. 130.

12. If one insists on locating a historical precedent for the fourness of the fourfold, I suggest that the four cosmogonic elements of the pre-Socratics have a certain plausibility (although Heidegger has seen fit to alter their content). However, it could be that Heidegger named the four sectors as he did simply in virtue of reflection on a seminal poet. See in this regard the illumination of Hölderlin in *EH*, p. 17, where aspects of all four sectors are mentioned in close conjunction (without the use of the word *Geviert* to name their unity). Cf. also *EH*, p. 163 for additional evidence for this hypothesis. Pöggeler concurs with this conjecture, but without locating a specific source in Heidegger's works on Hölderlin. Cf. Otto Pöggeler, *Der Denkweg Martin Heideggers* (Pfullingen: Neske, 1963), p. 248. Pöggeler's discussion of the fourfold is valuable (pp. 247–67).

CHAPTER 2

1. Heidegger contends that the proper correlation with the word rather than reason defines the nature of man. Cf. *W*, p. 348.

2. Cf. *PT*, p. 41, in which Heidegger expressly rejects the "mystical" interpretation of his position on language.

3. Cf. *HH*, p. 29; *US*, p. 177.

4. Cf. *HH*, p. 26; *W*, p. 271; *VA*, p. 255. Although the presentation of Heidegger's later thought frequently appears lyrical, at times even rhapsodic, the content is rigorously developed, as here in the careful distinction between speaking and saying and earlier in the distinction between word and name. The existing translations of Heidegger's works on language fre-

quently blur this rigorous use of technical terms. As a result, the reader of Heidegger in English is unaware that a word or set of words functions in a technical sense. The fact that Heidegger's technical vocabulary is less obtrusive than that of Kant or even Hegel makes it all the more imperative that the serious student read Heidegger's work in the original.

5. Cf. *EM*, p. 123; *SG*, pp. 72–73; *NII*, p. 484; *SD*, p. 75. Also, see Werner Marx, *Heidegger und die Tradition* (Stuttgart: W. Kohlhammer, 1961), p. 117.

6. Cf. *AED*, p. 21.

7. Cf. *H*, p. 300; *AED*, p. 21; *SD*, p. 70.

8. Cf. *W*, pp. 9, 354; *EH*, p. 189.

9. Cf. Rosen, *Nihilism*, pp. xix, 39–45, 121. Rosen repeats his criticism in Kockelmans, *On Heidegger and Language*, pp. 268–70. Also, Versenyi, *Heidegger, Being, and Truth*, p. 195. I have replied to these criticisms in David A. White, "A Refutation of Heidegger as Nihilist," *Personalist* 56 (Summer 1975): 276–88. Cf. Merleau-Ponty's helpful remark, that we should "admit as a fundamental fact of expression a surpassing of the signifying by the signified which it is the very virtue of the signifying to make possible." Consequently, "the idea of complete expression is nonsensical, and all language is indirect, i.e., silence." Maurice Merleau-Ponty, *Signs*, trans. Richard C. McCleary (Evanston: Northwestern University Press, 1964), pp. 43, 90. Anyone inclined to render a moral verdict on Heidegger's "nihilist" activity in the 1930s must first read Otto Pöggeler's *Philosophie und Politik bei Heidegger* (Freiburg/Munich: Verlag Karl Alber, 1972). And for Heidegger's personal statement on the matter, see the important interview published posthumously in *Der Spiegel*, May 31, 1976, pp. 193–219.

10. *Stillness* and *silence* are important technical terms and are frequently employed. Cf. the use of *silence* in SZ, pp. 161, 164, 165, 273, 277. Also, *NI*, pp. 471–72; *W*, p. 174; *WD*, p. 171. The poetized source may be Hölderlin's line, "Schweigen müssen wir oft; es fehlen heilige Namen" (We must often be silent; holy names are lacking) quoted in *EH*, p. 188. If this is the source, then Heidegger has extended the meaning of silence from its poetized connection with the lack of holy names to a technical term which ranges over all entities insofar as they can be spoken about in language.

11. Cf. *W*, p. 271.

12. Cf. *SZ*, p. 163; *EM*, pp. 99–100; *SH*, p. 185; *W*, p. 303; *VA*, p. 214; *US*, p. 262; *EH*, p. 39; *WD*, p. 89.

CHAPTER 3

1. For other references to this technical sense of *Ereignis*, cf. *SD*, pp. 20–21, 24, 38–39, 41, 46 (in which Heidegger dates the origination of the technical sense of *Ereignis* as 1936–38); *US*, p. 261; *EH*, p. 40. However, the

word was used in the plural or in the nontechnical sense of "event" in earlier works: Cf. *H*, pp. 342, 336, 531; *NI*, pp. 241, 254, 297, 435, 437; *NII*, pp. 33, 401, 459; *EH*, pp. 58, 107. For the possible poetized source of *Ereignis*, consider Hölderlin's line (from "Mnemosyne") "Lang ist/ Die Zeit, es ereignet sich aber/ Das Wahre" (Time is long, but that which is true is nonetheless appropriated) quoted by Heidegger in *H*, p. 249. For commentary, see Otto Pöggeler, "Sein als Ereignis," *Zeitschrift für Philosophische Forschung* 13 (1959): 597–632, pp. 621–22. It should be noted that the publishing house Vittorio Klostermann has recently announced (as of this writing) that they plan to publish a Heidegger *Gesamtausgabe* of fifty-seven volumes. One of these volumes is devoted to *Ereignis*, and this work will doubtless provide important material for a more adequate interpretation. What I offer here is based on *Ereignis* as developed in the relevant works published to date.

The translators of the Harper and Row series render *Ereignis* as "event of appropriation" (Joan Stambaugh in *Identity and Difference*) and "disclosure of appropriation" (Albert Hofstadter in *Poetry, Language, Thought*). My contention is that both these translations are potentially misleading. First, *Ereignis* is not an event at all—rather, it is the set of ontological conditions which ground the possibility of an event. The phrase "event of appropriation" suggests that there could be an event which is not related to appropriation. But since appropriation names being as such and since *any* event, regardless of content, must have being to become an event, it is ontologically impossible for an event to exist unless that event derives from appropriation. Second, *Ereignis* may or may not be disclosed in an ontologically proper sense. Concealment is always present as a necessary feature in the structure of *Ereignis*, and the phrase "disclosure of appropriation" tends to diminish the presence and importance of this concealment. My translation, "appropriation," is terse but has the virtue of avoiding incorrect connotations. Hofstadter's remarks on *Ereignis* are useful, despite his problematic translation of the word. See Martin Heidegger, *Poetry, Language, Thought*, trans. Albert Hofstadter (New York: Harper & Row, 1971), pp. xix–xxii.

2. This text, emended from Heidegger's original German edition, is taken from the bilingual Harper and Row series. The translator, Joan Stambaugh, notes (p. 38) that in conversation with her, Heidegger altered the original "*aber auch*" to the very different "*und daher.*" Cf. Martin Heidegger, *Identity and Difference*, trans. Joan Stambaugh (New York: Harper & Row, 1969), p. 102. All references to *Identität und Differenz* are taken from this edition.

3. Cf. *WD*, pp. 95–96.

4. The analysis of presence *(Anwesen)* as the play of space-time is here directed at its role in the ontological structure of language. In chapters 7 and 9, the temporality implied by this doctrine is discussed with respect to the nature of things named through language.

5. Cf. the earlier use of *einräumen* in *SZ*, p. 111.

6. For other references to the close connection between saying and the Greek language, cf: *SG*, p. 179; *H*, p. 310; *ID*, p. 137; *WP*, p. 12; *VA*, pp. 212, 228 (where Heidegger contends that even the Greeks did not think through the implications of their own word for saying); *US*, p. 237; *WD*, pp. 6, 102, 141, 171. See also the passage in *EM*, p. 43, where Heidegger juxtaposes German and Greek as the "most powerful" and "most spiritual" languages.

7. The fundamental words of the Greek language are historical in the ontological sense (*NI*, p. 231); it follows that an interpretation *(Auslegung)* of Greek language must pass through the metaphysical meaning of the name and into the ontological meaning of the word (cf. *NII*, p. 210; *EM*, p. 124).

8. The near–remote interplay appears frequently and in a variety of contexts in Heidegger. Cf. *SZ*, pp. 5, 102, 262; *H*, p. 24; *W*, p. 150; *VA*, pp. 108, 176, 180; *EH*, pp. 138, 146, 148. The poetized source of near-remote may be from this passage in Holderlin (quoted in Heidegger in *EH*, p. 185):

> Aber weil so nahe sie sind die gegenwärtigen Götter
> Muss ich seyn, als wären sie fern, und dunkel in Wolken
> Muss ihr Nahme mir seyn,
>
> (But because the present gods are so near,
> I must be as if they were remote, and dark in clouds
> Must be their names to me,)

The fact that Heidegger's technical terms *Wink, Schweigen, Ereignis, Nahe-Ferne,* and the substance of the fourfold are (a) all taken from Hölderlin, (b) all related to language, and (c) all directly connected with the gods or the divine is important to keep in mind. In chapter 6, the function of the divine is considered in greater detail.

9. The word *Zwischen*, used as a noun by Heidegger, has its own history of meanings in Heidegger's writings. Cf. *H*, p. 104 (in which it is equivalent with *Dasein*) and *FD*, p. 188 (in which it names the indeterminate relation between man and thing).

10. *Welt*, like *Zwischen*, has had its own history in Heidegger's writings. For a summary of the various meanings, see Vincent Vycinas, *Earth and Gods: An Introduction to the Philosophy of Martin Heidegger* (The Hague: Martinus Nijhoff, 1961), p. 118. Also cf: *SZ*, pp. 64–65, the essay "Vom Wesen des Grundes" (*W*, pp. 21–71); *W*, p. 180; *H*, p. 82. For references to *a* world, where the suggestion is that there might be other possibly divergent worlds, cf: *NI*, pp. 170, 364; *NII*, p. 449; *H*, p. 34; *S*, p. 21. For additional references to *Welt* in the technical sense elaborated in *Unterwegs zur Sprache*, cf: *HH*, p. 19; *VA*, pp. 151–53, 178; *K*, p. 43.

11. For discussion of *Gebärden* in the word's primary sense of "gesturing," see *WD*, p. 51.

12. Cf. the uses of *einfach* in a similar sense in *W*, p. 394; *WD*, p. 153.

13. Cf. *SZ*, p. 269; *WD*, p. 85.

14. Although the analysis of Heidegger on language developed here in part 1 is more extensive and systematic than any other discussion I am aware of, this treatment can hardly be said to exhaust the topic. The selection of themes was based on the problem of relating language in general to a certain type of language, i.e., poetic language. Heidegger's notion of language *(Sprache)* is sufficiently rich and diversified to merit a systematic study in its own right.

CHAPTER 4

1. This is an important point and will be taken up again in chapter 9.

2. Cf. Heidegger's distinction between *Poesie* and *Dichtung* in *H*, p. 61.

3. This necessity has been overlooked by some commentators. Thus, Stephen Erickson notes that "the use of poetic language complicates the task of interpreting Heidegger's philosophy immeasurably." This remark suggests that if Heidegger had not used poetic language his philosophy would be more readily understood. Such sentiments run counter to both the spirit and the letter of Heidegger's thought. Cf. Stephen Erickson, *Language and Being: An Analytic Phenomenology* (New Haven: Yale University Press, 1970), p. 100. For an interesting example of a similar attitude toward poetic language, cf. J. L. Austin's remark that language as it appears in poetry is used "in ways *parasitic* upon its normal use" J. L. Austin, *How to Do Things with Words* (New York: Oxford University Press, 1963), p. 22. The italics are Austin's.

4. Illumination here and throughout parts 2 and 3 is used in the technical sense discussed in the introduction.

5. As noted in the Introduction, my discussion of Heidegger's illuminations proceeds according to basic themes rather than according to the order of the lectures and essays which present these themes. Father Richardson's book contains a summary of the actual progression of these lectures and essays. For George, pp. 495–598; for Rilke, pp. 391–400, 527–29; for Trakl, pp. 577–82; for Hölderlin, pp. 423–33, 447–72, 588–94.

6. Cf. *KPM*, p. 146; *S*, p. 107 (on the metaphysical implications of the Platonic notion of *eros*).

7. Another possible poetized source is this passage from Hölderlin's "Mnemosyne" (quoted by Heidegger in *WD*, p. 52):

> Ein Zeichen sind wir, deutungslos,
> Schmerzlos sind wir, und haben fast
> Die Sprache in der Fremde Verloren.
>
> (We are a sign without meaning;
> We are painless, and have almost
> Lost language in that which is alien.)

We note again the connection between the technical term and language *(Sprache)* in Hölderlin's poetizing.

8. This etymology is typical of Heidegger's attempts to show language as saying as it is hidden in spoken Greek names. Classicists frequently find little or no evidence for such etymologies, but on Heidegger's principles their scepticism is a function of their own deep roots in the Western grammatical (and thus metaphysical) tradition. Cf. Heidegger's response to criticisms of his etymologies in *VA*, p. 173.

9. Cf. *WD*, p. 32; *VA*, pp. 90, 99, 108.

10. Cf. *SZ*, p. 345; *W*, p. 8; *NI*, p. 65.

CHAPTER 5

1. The notion of measurement will keynote a critical discussion of Heidegger's position in chapter 9.

2. For other texts on this problematic sense of measurement, see *SG*, p. 185; *NII*, p. 140.

3. Cf. *US*, p. 125; *K*, p. 39.

4. Cf. *VA*, p. 149. Thus, the earth-world dichotomy of the early *Holzwege* essay "Der Ursprung des Kunstwerkes" has now been reformulated. World is no longer opposed to earth; rather, earth (and the other sectors of the fourfold) are the constitutent parts of world. Therefore, when W. B. Macomber says that "the earth represents the density, enclosure, and darkness in the midst of which Dasein clears an opening and lays out the field in which decisions are possible," this designation refers to earth in the early *Holzwege* sense and not to the fourfold sense of earth in the later Hölderlin essays and in *Unterwegs zur Sprache*. See W. B. Macomber, *The Anatomy of Disillusion* (Evanston: Northwestern University Press, 1967), p. 64. For the relevant *Holzwege* references, see *H*, pp. 31, 36.

CHAPTER 6

1. Rilke's word "will" is the poetized saying of that phase of the metaphysical tradition which includes Leibniz, Schopenhauer, Schelling, and which culminates in Nietzsche's Will to Power. Heidegger takes the relation between being and willing very seriously and indicates its importance in various works. See, e.g., *NII*, p. 480; *W*, pp. 99, 382–94; *WD*, pp. 36, 39. As far as I know, there is little if any secondary commentary on this phase of Heidegger's thought.

2. See also, *EH*, p. 28; *W*, p. 366; *H*, p. 235. And the elliptic utterance "Wir kommen für das Götter zu spät und zu früh für das Seyn" in *AED*, p. 7.

3. Cf. *W*, p. 162.

4. Cf. *H*, pp. 235, 249; *VA*, p. 277.

5. For texts containing both "God" and "gods," see *KR*, p. 9; *W*, pp. 162, 169; *H*, p. 150.

6. For the relation between language and the deity, see *US*, p. 219; *EH*, pp. 40, 45.

7. See also, *W*, pp. 169, 182; *EH*, pp. 68, 73, 114. For additional commentary, see Karsten Harries, "Heidegger's Conception of the Holy," *Personalist* 47 (1966):169–84.

8. And, unfortunately, the distinction between the deity and the divine is not preserved in the Harper & Row translations, e.g., the important essay "Das Ding." There, *die Göttlichen* (as one sector of the fourfold) is translated as "the divinities," which obscures Heidegger's own stated distinction between *die Göttlichen* and the deity *(Gottheit)*. Heidegger says that "Die Göttlichen sind die winkenden Boten der Gottheit" from which it follows that the divine cannot be equivalent with the deity. Failure to draw the distinction between the divine presence and the deity which grounds that presence results in interpretive confusion. Consider this remark by James L. Perotti: "Heidegger assumes both that the divine has been authentically present to man in the past, and that the divine in our age is no longer present. On the basis of these assumptions, the problem of God becomes the problem of the absence of the divine in our time." But clearly the divine (as a sector of the fourfold) *is* present in our time—it is the *deity* which is absent. If the divine were not present now (indeed, at any given time), man could not discourse about the presence or absence of the deity at all. See James L. Perotti, *Heidegger on the Divine: The Thinker, the Poet, and God*, (Athens: Ohio University Press, 1974), p. 95.

9. See Heidegger's own admission in the conversation with the Japanese *(US*, p. 96) that "without this theological background I would never have arrived at the way of thinking [*Denkens*]." For other sources detailing Heidegger's conviction that both philosophy and thinking *(Denken)* are in some respects essentially theological, see the essay "Die Onto-Theo-Logische Verfassung der Metaphysik" *(ID*, 107–43). Also, *S*, pp. 61–147 passim; *K*, p. 46; *H*, p. 325.

CHAPTER 7

1. If all great philosophers are poets but do not know that they are poets (and vice versa), perhaps this is why Heidegger can maintain that "no thinker, as well as no poet, understands himself" *(WD*, p. 113). Hence, Heidegger's concern to situate modern thinking with the doctrine of hints and the unspoken saying implicit in such great philosophy. See *W*, p. 192; *US*, pp. 145–46; *WD*, p. 64.

2. See also: *H*, pp. 61, 303; *S*, p. 70; *NI*, p. 492; *W*, p. 145; *SD*, p. 58.

3. For other texts which maintain that *Denken* and *Dichten* (a) share

properties—*PT*, p. 44; *MHG*, p. 32; (b) are near to one another—*US*, p. 187; *EM*, pp. 11, 101; *WD*, p. 154; (c) are different—*WD*, p. 154; *NI*, pp. 471–72; *WP*, p. 30; *VA*, p. 193.

4. But the influence Husserl had on Heidegger's early development is freely admitted. Heidegger makes special mention of Husserl's *Logical Investigations* in *SD*, pp. 84–85.

5. Cf. *SG*, pp. 44, 140, 148.

6. See also *H*, pp. 80, 84, 266–67, 281; *ID*, pp. 129–30; *NII*, pp. 298, 378–79; *W*, pp. 79–80, 281; *SD*, p. 62.

7. For more on the "step back," see *ID*, p. 117; *SG*, p. 148; *W*, p. 199; *SD*, 87. The need to take the step back is presented in a number of subtle ways. Notice, for example, the sequence of topics discussed in *Vorträge und Aufsätze*. The four essays of part 1 deal with contemporary questions—e.g., technology, science, and the need to surpass metaphysics. Part 2 is composed of three essays on, respectively, the nature of thinking, the nature of things, and how to dwell with things. And part 3 is a set of three commentaries on fragments from Heraclitus and Paramenides. The sequence of topics is significant in that it suggests that (e.g.), to solve the problem of technology, modern man must step back behind (a) present problems as we understand them, (b) the metaphysics which underlies present problems, and even (c) the Greek saying which originated that metaphysics. If Heidegger's arrangement of topics is purposive in *Vorträge und Aufsätze*, one may suppose with some justification that purpose is also present in the sequence of essays in *Unterwegs zur Sprache*. The fact that the Harper & Row translation series of *Unterwegs zur Sprache* does not preserve the original sequence of essays is therefore at least unfortunate and perhaps something more.

8. We recall the illuminations of poetizing about human feelings (discussed in chapter 4), presumably intended in part to illustrate this openness. In *WD*, p. 12, Heidegger widens the notion of openness to include even the mysterious.

9. Cf. *W*, p. 80; *PT*, p. 41.

10. Heidegger is careful to note that the project of showing the being of things in appropriate language may or may not succeed—Cf. *SD*, p. 55; *US*, p. 185.

11. See the important passage on the relation between *Sprache* and *Denken* in *WD*, p. 143.

12. Heidegger thus rejects the notion of an "eternal truth": See *S*, p. 136; *NI*, p. 357; *KPM*, p. 216; and especially *SZ*, pp. 227–29.

13. The unity of past-present-future in temporality as presence is frequently mentioned in a variety of contexts. See *H*, p. 320; *VA*, pp. 47–48, 142, 176, 212, 220, 227, 242; *PT*, p. 47; *AED*, p. 19; *MHG*, p. 37; *WD*, pp. 19 (where Heidegger accuses the principal Greek philosophers of failing to express correctly the presence of the external world), 41, 77, 144. Also, of course, the discussion of *Zeitlichkeit* in *SZ*, pp. 323–72 passim. And consider

Sherover's remark concerning the late Heidegger: "The curious thing is that, for the most part, Heidegger has pursued, in subsequent work, neither the problem of the nature of Time nor the question of its 'and' with Being." But certainly this is not the case. Heidegger pursues both these problems when he illuminates poetizing and applies the results of these illuminations to problems which appear to have little relevance to temporality. There is as much thought in the illuminations as in the manifestly thoughtful works. See Charles H. Sherover, *Heidegger, Kant & Time* (Bloomington: Indiana University Press, 1971), p. 279.

14. The notion of lingering *(Weilen)* and its cognates appears already in *SZ*, pp. 61, 138, 172. See also, *H*, pp. 54, 327; *NII*, p. 406; *VA*, p. 73; *WD*, p. 144.

CHAPTER 8

1. The most helpful general commentary on *Gelassenheit* is John M. Anderson's introduction to the Harper and Row translation. See Martin Heidegger, *Discourse on Thinking*, trans. John M. Anderson and E. Hans Freund (New York: Harper & Row, 1966), pp. 11–39.

2. Cf. *SG*, pp. 42, 168; *VA*, p. 58; *W*, pp. 104–5.

3. Cf. the much different use of *Bodenständigkeit* in *SZ*, p. 168.

4. Cf. *AED*, p. 9.

5. For Heidegger, the connection between appearances and what appearances are of is fundamental, if not axiomatic. Thus, all investigation of the relation between thinking and appearances will always be grounded in metaphysics or ontology. See the discussion of appearances in chapter 6; also, the important essay "Platons Lehre von der Wahrheit" (*W*, pp. 109–44); *VA*, p. 140; *W*, p. 29.

6. Cf. the use of *Gegend in SZ*, pp. 103, 368; also *SG*, p. 111; *H*, p. 322; *KR*, p. 10; *US*, pp. 179, 255.

7. Cf. the use of *Erwarten* in *SZ*, pp. 261, 337; also *VA*, pp. 139, 151.

8. For additional references on the relation between the notion of *Gelassenheit* and language, see *VA*, p. 68; *US*, p. 261; *EH*, p. 65; *WD*, p. 90.

9. The aspect of passivity is susceptible to overemphasis by commentators. Thus, Richard Palmer remarks that in Heidegger's later writings "the stance of man seems almost a devotional passivity which will be completely open to the voice of being." Palmer, *Hermeneutics*, p. 49. See also the article by Peter Kreeft, "Zen in Heidegger's *Gelassenheit*," *International Philosophical Quarterly* 11 (1971): 521–45; the number "Heidegger and Eastern Thought," *Philosophy East and West* 20 (July, 1970); and the entries by non-Western authors in Hans-Martin Sass's bibliography, *Materialien zur Heidegger-Bibliographie 1917–1972*.

10. Cf. *H*, pp. 55, 322; *W*, pp. 106, 203; *VA*, p. 161; *EH*, p. 125.

CHAPTER 9

1. Cf. *SG*, p. 109; *VA*, pp. 32, 63–64.

2. See the discussion of the epochs of metaphysics in *SD*, pp. 61–64 and *VA*, p. 83, and also the important passage in *WD*, p. 45 in which Heidegger connects the appearance of being with, in some essential respect, its expression in the representational language of metaphysics. For a summary of Heidegger and the history of metaphysics, see the section "Heidegger and the Tradition" in Bernd Magnus, *Heidegger's Metahistory of Philosophy* (The Hague: Nijhoff, 1970); pp. 59–95. For an extended comparison of Aristotle and Heidegger, see David E. Starr, *Entity and Existence: An Ontological Investigation of Aristotle and Heidegger* (New York: Burt Franklin & Co., 1975). And for an account of the influence of both Aristotle and Hegel on Heidegger, see Werner Marx, *Heidegger und die Tradition* (Stuttgart: W. Kohlhammer, 1961).

3. Emil L. Fackenheim, "The Historicity and Transcendence of Philosophic Truth," in *Inter-American Congress of Philosophy*, 7th, Laval University, Quebec, 1967 (Quebec: Presses de l'Université Laval, 1967), pp. 77–92.

4. Is the structure of appropriation itself nonhistoricist? See the outline of "Zeit und Sein," esp. *SD*, p. 44. This outline is not Heidegger's own work, although we are informed that he reviewed and approved it. Hence, I only mention the possibility here. Without Heidegger's own explicit word, it would be premature to interpret appropriation in such an apparently un-Heideggerian way.

5. Cf. *FD*, pp. 6, 12; *SD*, p. 62; *W*, p. 385; *VA*, pp. 168 (in which Heidegger states that the thinghood of the thing is "hidden" from language), 178.

6. Cf. *SD*, p. 13.

7. Heidegger has anticipated this possible objection in *SD*, p. 14.

8. Cf. *VA*, pp. 172, 181.

9. Cf. Heidegger's distinction between sameness *(Selbe)* and likeness *(Gleiche)* in, e.g., *VA*, p. 193. See also the discussion of sameness in *ID*, pp. 85–95.

10. See the important passage summarizing the historical interplay of *Sprache, Sage,* and *Ereignis* in *US*, pp. 264–65.

11. Heidegger himself raises this problem, and then leaves it "questionable" *(fraglich)* in *WD*, p. 8. But Heidegger nonetheless insists that no other poet can "surpass" *(überholen)* Hölderlin as far as the thoughtful needs of our epoch are concerned. Cf. *H*, p. 295.

12. For other texts on the implicit metaphysics in logic, see *SZ*, pp. 165–66; *EM*, p. 94; *NI*, p. 603; *W*, p. 228, *VA*, pp. 119, 137; *H*, p. 287.

13. I also omit discussion of how the appearances of things (Cf. chapters 5 and 6) are related to the disclosure of entities as things. As we shall see, the

Heideggerian position will face problems which need not be complicated further by the business of measuring the proper appearances of entities. The core of the problem can be reached without introducing the aspect of appearances into the discussion.

14. Heidegger himself refers to proper and improper poetizing in *VA*, p. 203. See the relevant objections on this head by James Edie and Stanley Rosen in Kockelmans, *On Heidegger and Language*, pp. 141, 270. See also Albert Hofstadter's earlier criticism that Heidegger's failure to establish a standard of ontological rightness reduces Heidegger's position to "a contemporary phenomenological version of the old light metaphysics." Cf. Albert Hofstadter, *Truth and Art* (New York: Columbia University Press, 1965), p. 197.

15. For similar uses of rigor, see *EM*, p. 94; *W*, p. 147.

16. Heidegger insists that ambiguity is not equivalent to arbitrariness. See the important passage in *W*, p. 251 in which Heidegger asserts that the "rule" *(Regel)* which dictates how thinking is rigorous is still "hidden" *(verborgenen)*.

17. See Heidegger's essay "Grundsätze des Denkens" for additional discussion of the ontological implications of the principles of identity and contradiction. See *Jahrbuch für Psychologie und Psychotherapie* 6 (1958): 33–41. Also, *W*, pp. 306–7; *FD*, 136.

Bibliography

THIS BIBLIOGRAPHY is in three sections: first, the works by Heidegger referred to in this study; second, those books which were helpful in the formulation and development of this study; and third, relevant articles on Heidegger. For additional sources, consult the updated bibliography compiled by Hans-Martin Sass and published in 1975. It is the most comprehensive bibliography available.

WORKS BY MARTIN HEIDEGGER

Aus der Erfahrung des Denkens. 2d ed. Pfullingen: Neske, 1965.
Einführung in die Metaphysik. Tübingen: Max Niemeyer, 1953.
Erläuterungen zu Hölderlins Dichtung. 4th ed. Frankfurt on the Main: Vittorio Klostermann, 1971.
Die Frage nach dem Ding. Tübingen: Max Niemeyer, 1962.
Gelassenheit. Pfullingen: Neske, 1959.
Hebel der Hausfreund. Pfullingen: Neske, 1957.
Holzwege. Frankfurt on the Main: Vittorio Klostermann, 1950.
Identity and Difference. Bilingual edition. Translated by Joan Stambaugh. New York: Harper & Row, 1969.
Kant und das Problem der Metaphysik. Franfurt on the Main: Vittorio Klostermann, 1951.
Die Kunst und der Raum. St. Gallen: Erker, 1969.
Martin Heidegger zum 80, Geburtstag. Frankfurt on the Main: Vittorio Klostermann, 1969.
Nietzsche I, II. Pfullingen: Neske, 1961.
Phänomenologie und Theologie. Frankfurt on the Main: Vittorio Klostermann, 1970.
Zur Sache des Denkens. Tübingen: Max Niemeyer, 1969.
Der Satz vom Grund. Pfullingen: Neske, 1957.
Schellings Abhandlung über das Wesen der Menschlichen Freiheit (1809). Tübingen: Max Niemeyer, 1971.
Sein und Zeit. Tübingen: Max Niemeyer, 1963.
"Sprache and Heimat." In *Dauer Im Wandel*, edited by Hermann Rinn and May Rychner. Munich: D. W. Callwey, 1961.

Die Technik und die Kehre. 2d ed. Pfullingen: Neske, 1962.
Unterwegs zur Sprache. Pfullingen: Neske, 1959.
Vorträge und Aufsätze. Pfullingen: Neske, 1954.
Was Heisst Denken?. Tübingen: Max Niemeyer, 1961.
Was ist das—Die Philosophie?. Pfullingen: Neske, 1956.
Wegmarken. Frankfurt on the Main: Vittorio Klostermann, 1967.

SECONDARY SOURCES—BOOKS

Allemann, Beda. *Hölderlin und Heidegger.* 2d ed. Freiburg im Breisgau: Atlantis, 1954.
Austin, J. L. *How to Do Things with Words.* New York: Oxford University Press, 1965.
Ballard, Edward G., and Charles E. Scott, eds. *Martin Heidegger: In Europe and America.* The Hague: Martinus Nijhoff, 1974.
Borgmann, Albert. *The Philosophy of Language: Historical Foundations and Contemporary Issues.* The Hague: Martinus Nijhoff, 1974.
Buddeberg, Else. *Heidegger und die Dichtung.* Stuttgart: J. B. Metzlersche, 1953.
Casey, T. J. *Manshape That Shone: An Interpretation of Trakl.* Oxford: Basil Blackwell, 1964.
Couturier, Fernand. *Monde et Être chez Heidegger.* Montreal: Presses de l'Université de Montreal, 1971.
Danner, Helmut. *Das Göttliche und der Gott bei Heidegger.* Meisenheim am Glan: A. Hain, 1971.
Deely, John N. *The Tradition Via Heidegger.* The Hague: Martinus Nijhoff, 1971.
Duroche, L. L. *Aspects of Criticism: Literary Study in Present-Day Germany.* The Hague: Mouton, 1967.
Erickson, Stephen A. *Language and Being: An Analytic Phenomenology.* New Haven: Yale University Press, 1970.
Gadamer, Hans-Georg. *Hegel, Hölderlin, Heidegger.* Karlsruhe: Bodenia Verlag, 1971.
———. *Wahrheit und Methode.* 2d ed. Tubingen: J. C. B. Mohr, 1965.
Gilson, Etienne; Langan, Thomas; and Maurer, Armand A.; C. S. B. *Recent Philosophy: Hegel to the Present.* New York: Random House, 1966.
Gray, Jesse Glenn. *On Understanding Violence Philosophically, and Other Essays.* New York: Harper & Row, 1970.
Hamburger, Michael. *Reason and Energy: Studies in German Literature.* New York: Grove Press, 1957.
Hofstadter, Albert. *Truth and Art.* New York: Columbia University Press, 1965.
Kockelmans, Joseph J., ed. *On Heidegger and Language.* Evanston: Northwestern University Press, 1972.

234

Langan, Thomas. *The Meaning of Heidegger*. New York: Columbia University Press, 1959.

Macomber, W. B. *The Anatomy of Disillusion*. Evanston: Northwestern University Press, 1967.

Magnus, Bernd. *Heidegger's Metahistory of Philosophy*. The Hague: Nijhoff, 1970.

Marx, Werner. *Heidegger und die Tradition*. Stuttgart: W. Kohlhammer, 1961. English translation *Heidegger and the Tradition*. Translated by Theodore Kisiel and Murray Greene. Evanston: Northwestern University Press, 1971.

Mehta, J. L. *The Philosophy of Martin Heidegger*. New York: Harper, Torchbooks, 1971.

Merleau-Ponty, Maurice. *Signs*. Translated by Richard C. McCleary. Evanston: Northwestern University Press, 1964.

Palmer, Richard E. *Hermeneutics*. Evanston: Northwestern University Press, 1969.

Perotti, James L. *Heidegger on the Divine: The Thinker, The Poet, and God*. Athens: Ohio University Press, 1974.

Pöggeler, Otto. *Der Denkweg Martin Heideggers*. Pfullingen: Neske, 1963.

———. *Heidegger: Perspektiven zur Deutung seines Werks*. Cologne: Kiepenhauer & Witsch, 1970.

———. *Philosophie und Politik bei Heidegger*. Freiburg im Breisgau, 1972.

Richardson, William J. *Heidegger through Pehnomenology to Thought*. 2d ed. The Hague: Martinus Nijhoff, 1967.

Rosen, Stanley. *Nihilism: A Philosophical Essay*. New Haven: Yale University Press, 1969.

Sallis, John., ed. *Heidegger and the Path of Thinking*. Pittsburgh: Duquesne University Press, 1970.

Sass, Hans-Martin. *Materialien zur Heidegger-Bibliographie 1917–1972*. Meisenheim am Glan: Anton Hain, 1975.

Schöfer, Erasmus. *Die Sprache Heideggers*. Pfullingen: Neske, 1962.

Sefler, George F. *Language and the World: A Methodological Synthesis within the Writings of Martin Heidegger and Ludwig Wittgenstein*. New York: Humanities Press, 1974.

Seidel, George Joseph, O.S.B. *Martin Heidegger and the Pre-Socratics*. Lincoln: University of Nebraska Press, 1964.

Sherover, Charles M. *Heidegger, Kant & Time*. Bloomington: Indiana University Press, 1971.

Sladeczek, Franz-Maria. *Ist das Dasein Gottes beweisbar? Wie steht die Existentialphilosophie Martin Heideggers zu dieser Frage?* Wurzberg: K. Trilitisch, 1967.

Starr, David E. *Entity and Existence: An Ontological Investigation of Aristotle and Heidegger*. New York: Burt Franklin & Co., 1975.

Stassen, Manfred. *Heideggers Philosophie der Sprache in "Sein und Zeit": und ihre philos.-theol. Wurzeln*. Bonn: Bouvier, 1973.

Versenyi, Laszlo. *Heidegger, Being and Truth*. New Haven: Yale University Press, 1965.

Vycinas, Vincent. *Earth and Gods: An Introduction to the Philosophy of Martin Heidegger*. The Hague: Martinus Nijhoff, 1961.

Secondary Sources—Articles

Adamczewski, Zygmunt. "Martin Heidegger and Man's Way to Be." *Man and World* 1 (1968): 363–79.

Caputo, John D. "Being, Ground and Play in Heidegger." *Man and World* 3 (1970): 26–48.

———. "Heidegger's Original Ethics." *New Scholasticism* 45 (1971): 127–38.

———. "Meister Eckhart and the Later Heidegger: The Mystical Element in Heidegger's Thought." *Journal of the History of Philosophy* 12 (1974): 479–94; 13 (1975): 61–80.

Cress, Donald W. "Heidegger's Criticism of 'Entitative Metaphysics' in His Later Works." *International Philosophical Quarterly* 12 (1972): 69–86.

Demske, James M. "Heidegger's Quadrate and Revelation of Being." *Philosophy Today* 7 (1963): 245–57.

Fackenheim, Emil L. "The Historicity and Transcendence of Philosophic Truth." *Inter-American Congress of Philosophy*, 7th, Laval University, Quebec (1967): 77–92.

Fulton, James S. "The Event of Being." *Southwestern Journal of Philosophy* 6 (1975): 7–13.

Gerber, Rudolph J. "Heidegger: Thinking and Thanking Being." *Modern Schoolman* 44 (1967): 205–22.

Goff, Robert. "Saying and Being with Heidegger and Parmenides." *Man and World* 5 (1972): 62–78.

Gray, J. Glenn. "Splendor of the Simple." *Philosophy East and West* 20 (1970): 227–40.

Harries, Karsten. "Heidegger as a Political Thinker." *Review of Metaphysics* 29 (1976): 642–69.

———. "Heidegger's Conception of the Holy." *Personalist* 47 (1966): 169–84.

Heaton, J. M., ed. "Saying and Showing in Heidegger and Wittgenstein: A Symposium." *Journal of the British Society for Phenomenology* 3 (1972): 27–45.

Hoeller, Keith. "Heidegger Bibliography of English Translations." *Journal of the British Society for Phenomenology* 6 (1975): 206–8.

Hyland, Drew A. "Art and the Happening of Truth: Reflections on the End of Philosophy." *Journal of Aesthetics and Art Criticism* 30 (1971): 177–87.

Jonas, Hans. "Heidegger and Theology." In *The Phenomenon of Life*. New York: Harper & Row, 1966, p. 235–61.

Köchler, H. "Das Gottesproblem im Denken Heideggers." *Zeitschrift für Katholische Theologie* 95 (1973): 61–90.

Kreeft, Peter. "Zen in Heidegger's *Gelassenheit.*" *International Philosophical Quarterly* 11 (1971): 521–45.

Krell, David Farrell. "Nietzsche in Heidegger's *Kehre.*" *Southern Journal of Philosophy* 13 (1975): 197–204.

Lampert, Laurence. "On Heidegger and Historicism." *Philosophy and Phenomenological Research* 34 (1974): 586–90.

Langan, Thomas. "Heidegger and the Possibility of Authentic Christianity." *Proceedings of the American Catholic Philosophical Association* (1972): 101–12.

Magnus, Bernd. "Nihilism, Reason and 'the Good.' " *Review of Metaphysics* 25 (1971): 292–310.

Maly, Kenneth. "Toward *Ereignis.*" *Research in Phenomenology* 3 (1973): 63–93.

McCormick, Peter. "Heidegger on Hölderlin." *Philosophical Studies* (Ireland) 19 (1974?): 7–15.

———. "Interpreting the Later Heidegger." *Philosophical Studies* (Ireland) 22 (1970): 83–101.

Morrison, James C. "Heidegger's Criticism of Wittgenstein's Conception of Truth." *Man and World* 2 (1969): 551–73.

Nicholson, Graeme. "Heidegger on Thinking." *Journal of the History of Philosophy* 13 (1975): 491–503.

Oshima, S. "Barth's *Analogia Relationis* and Heidegger's Ontological Difference." *Journal of Religion* 53 (1973): 176–94.

Pöggeler,Otto. "Metaphysics and Topology of Being in Heidegger." *Man and World* 8 (1975): 3–27.

———. "Sein als Ereignis." *Zeitschrift fur Philosophische Forschung* 13 (1959): 597–632.

Rollin, R. E. "Heidegger's Philosophy of History in 'Being and Time.' " *Modern Schoolman* 49 (1972): 97–112.

Rorty, Richard. "Overcoming the Tradition: Heidegger and Dewey." *Review of Metaphysics* 30 (1976): 280–305.

Rotenstreich, Nathan. "The Ontological Structure of History." *American Philosophical Quarterly* 9 (1972): 49–58.

Schrag, Calvin O. "Heidegger on Repetition and Historical Understanding." *Philosophy East and West* 10 (1970): 287–95.

Sinn, Dieter. "Heideggers Spätphilosophie." *Philosophische Rundschau* 14 (1967): 81–182.

Vick, G. R. "Heidegger's Linguistic Rehabilitation of Parmenides' 'Being.' " *American Philosophical Quarterly* 8 (1971): 139–50.

Werkmeister, W. H. "Heidegger and the Poets." *Personalist* 52 (1971): 5–22.

White, David A. "A Refutation of Heidegger as Nihilist." *Personalist* 56 (1975): 276–88.

Williams, T. R. "Heidegger and the Theologians." *Heythrop Journal* 12 (1971): 258–80.

Index

Abgeschiedenheit. See Apartness

Absence *(Abwesen)*, 163; lack of God and, 166

Abwesen. See Absence

Accessibility *(Zuhandenheit)*, 165

Aesthetic value, 12

Aesthetics, ix

Ambiguity *(Mehrdeutigkeit)*, 11; as aspect of thinking, 212–15; 231 n

Anaximander, xiii

Andenken. See Remembering

Angelus Silesius, xii

Anwesen. See Presence

Apartness *(Abgeschiedenheit)*, 87–88, 173

Appearances, 229 n; and God, 95

Appropriation *(Ereignis)*, 52, 222–23 n, 230 n; and difference, 65, 201; of the holy, 127; and language, 68–71; and man, 159; and releasement, 179; and showing, 68; and thinking, 152; and time, 54, 159

Aristotle, 33, 144, 171, 184, 203, 216

Assertion *(Aussage)*, 19, 20; and meaning, 19

Augustine, St., 220 n

Aus der Erfahrung des Denkens, 165

Auslegung. See Exposition

Aussage. See Assertion

Availability *(Vorhandenheit)*, 165

Awaiting *(Erwarten)*: and waiting, 176; in *Sein und Zeit*, 229 n

Bedingnis. See Determination

Being *(Sein)*, xiii, 14, 32; concealment of, and fourfold, 32; and Hegel's Absolute, 212; and language, 20–21, and name, 31; poetizing of, 144; as presence, 158–67, 197–98; and saying, 53; and thing, 30; and thinking, 151–52; truth of, 150; as venture, 116–19; and word, 30

Belonging *(Gehören)*, 118

Between *(Zwischen)*, 64, 96

Bewegung. See Motion

Bezug. See Connection

Bläue. See Blueness

Blueness *(Bläue)*: in Trakl, 132–33

Bodenständigkeit. See Rootedness

Calculative thinking, 167

Cloud *(Wolke)*: in Hölderlin, 106–7

Collection *(Versammlung)*, 47; being as, 58; and space-time, 66; and apartness, 88

Concealment: and being, 71; in historical epochs, 193; and metaphysics, 71

Condition *(Zustand)*, 82

Connection *(Bezug)*, 96, 103; and relation, 96–97, 152

Contradiction: and God, 209–210; ontological character of, 216, 231 n; principle of, 11; and time, 212–13

Conversation *(Gespräch)*, 50; between thinking and poetizing, 76

Correspondence *(Entsprechen)*, 50, 133; between metaphysics and thinking, 150; and silence, 68

Dasein, 32, 33

Denken. See Thinking

Destiny, 135; as lingering, 135–37; and God, 123–24

Determination *(Bedingnis)*, 29; and fourfold, 34; and poetizing, 114; and region, 180; and thing, 29, 114

Dichten. See Poetizing

Difference *(Unterschied)*, 64–65

239

Dimension *(Dimension)*, 93
Ding. See Thing
Divine: distinguished from the deity, 126; and God, 125; and the holy, 125–32; as sector of the fourfold, 125–38; as source of differentiation, 201–2
Duroche, L. L., 12
Dwell *(Wohnen)*, 93, 97

Earth, 97–105; and heavens, 104–5; as sector of the fourfold, 97–105
Edel. See Noble
Einfachen. See Simplicity
Einfalt. See Innocence
Einführung in die Metaphysik, xii, 220 n
Entschlossenheit. See Resolution
Entsprechen. See Correspondence
Epoch and epochs, 93; and history, 191–96; and poetizing, 119, 155–57; sequences of, 194–96
Ereignis. See Appropriation
Erläuterung. See Illumination
Erläuterungen zu Hölderlins Dichtung, xii, 3
Erwarten. See Awaiting
Essence *(Wesen)*, 7, 190; experience of, 8
Eternity, 161
Exhortation *(Zuspruch)*: of name, 50
Exposition *(Auslegung)*, 10

Fackenheim, Emil, 230 n
Fate *(Geschickt)*, 75
Feeling, 80, 84, 89–92, 228 n
Fehl. See Lack
Feldweg Der, 36
Ferne. See Remote
Fourfold *(Geviert)*, 4, 9, 33, 221 n; and being, 32; and the deity, 126; determination of, 34; difference within, 104, 201–8; and dimen-sion, 93–94; historicity of, 198–99; and the holy, 157; and lingering, 165; and near-remote, 62–63; and plainness, 67; and presence, 197; and saying, 40; and simplicity, 67; and thing, 30, 34
Frage nach dem Ding, Die, 220 n

Gebärden. See Gestating
Gedächtnis. See Memory
Gegend. See Region
Gegeneinanderüber. See Reciprocity
Gegenstand. See Object
Gegenwart. See Present
Geheimnis. See Mystery
Gehören. See Belonging
"Gelassenheit." See Releasement
Gelassenheit, xii, xiv, 14, 168–89
Genet, Jean, 8
George, Stefan, 12, 79–81, 177, 225 n
Geschick. See Sending
Geschickt. See Fate
Gespräch. See Conversation
Gestating *(Gebärden)*, 65–66
Geviert. See Fourfold
Gleichzeitige. See Simultaneity
Gönnen. See Granting
God, 32, 37, 94–96, 111–12, 115, 120–38; death of, 123, 137; as deity, 121–25, 143; and the divine, 125–26, 227 n; existence of, 121–24; and the gods, 122, 229 n; as hidden, 166; hints of, 124; lack of, 155–57, 177, 209; naming of, 130–31; nearness to, 129; near-remote and, 135; and presence, 120; and theology, 122, 137–38
Goethe, Johann Wolfgang von, 12
Granting *(Gönnen)*, 65–66
Greeks: Heidegger's attitude to-ward, ix–x; language and the, 58–62, 87, 160, 184, 224 n; poetry

and philosophy connected for, ix
Greeting, 134–35

Hearing *(Hören)*, 38; perception and, 51–52
Heavens, 105–13; and earth, 104–5; fire of the, 112–13; as sector of the fourfold, 105–13
Hegel, Georg Wilhelm Friedrich, 32, 33, 115, 195, 212, 213, 216
Heidegger, Martin: and ethics, 9, 14; and the Japanese, 27, 28, 29; and mysticism, 36, 221 n; and nihilism, 48, 222 n; "I" and "II", 4; as thinker or poet, 215–16; and Western philosophy, 3
Heilige. See Holy
Heitere. See Serene
Heraclitus, 59, 176, 183–84, 228 n
Hint *(Wink)*, 27; of the gods, 124; as name, 28, 29, 34; poetized origin of, 220 n; space-time of, 31
Historicity, 190–91; and ambiguity, 214; of being, 191–96; of fourfold, 198–99; of thinking and poetizing, 196–200
Hölderlin, Friedrich, 10, 12, 54, 108–13; heavens in, 105, 115; lack of God, 129–32; memory in, 102; sadness and joy in, 83; science in, 97; and simplicity, 185; as speaker of Heidegger's technical terms, 224 n, 225 n
Hören. See Hearing
Holy *(Heilige)*, 112; and appropriation, 127; and the divine, 125–32; and greeting, 134; and near-remote, 131
Holzwege, 3, 116, 226 n
Homer, ix
Hopkins, Gerard Manley, 209; and Hölderlin, 209–11, 213
Husserl, Edmund, 7, 148, 228 n

Identität und Differenz, 213
Illuminations *(Erläuterung)*, xi, 10, 153, 219 n
Individuation: of things, 200–208
Innocence *(Einfalt)*, 111
Inständigkeit. See Steadfastness

Jesus: and the divine, 166
Jetzt. See Now
Joy, 83–84; poetizing cloud and, 106; and sadness, 88–90

Kant, Immanuel, 50, 144, 150, 216; space and time for, 176; and spontaneity, 181
Kockelmans, Joseph, x–xi
Kreutzer, Conradin, 169

Lack *(Fehl)*, 121
Langan, Thomas, 32, 33, 221 n
Language: appropriation of, 54–55, 68–71, 93; emotive-cognitive, 13–14, 15; essence of, 7–9, 21, 27, 35, 40, 49, 53, 159, 173; experience of, 8–9, 19, 27, 34, 35, 49; and grammar, 39; as "house of being," 20; meaning in, 52; and man, 35–37; ontology and, xii–xiii, xiv, 6–8, 20, 45; ordinary, ix, xii–xiii, 5–6, 26; prescriptive-descriptive, 14–15; and releasement, 178–79, 229 n; and space-time, 56–63; as "*Sprache*," 38, 225 n. 230 n; and thinking, 152
Leibniz, Gottfried Wilhelm von, 150, 226 n
Lingering *(Weilen)*, 107; as destiny, 135–37, 163; and man, 182; and metaphysics, 167; and the present, 162–63, 167; and region, 179–80; in *Sein und Zeit*, 229 n; and thing, 205
Literary criticism, 10

Locus *(Ort)*, 164–65

Logic: and metaphysics, 11, 159, 210, 230 n; and pain, 87; and representation, 159; and thinking, 209, 212

Logos: and saying, 58, 220 n

Luther, Martin, 220 n

Man: and being, 54, 159; and God, 122, and language, 35–37; as lingering, 182; and releasement, 179; as source of differentiation, 203; and speaking, 36–37

Meaning, 52; and space-time, 58–59

Measurement: essence of, 190; and God, 94–96; and poetizing, 95; and thinking, 153–54

Memory *(Gedächtnis)*, 102

Metaphysics: history of, 34, 71, 187, 192, 198, 203–4, 207, 216; and logic, 11, 159, 210, 230 n

Mortal: as sector of the fourfold, 78–90

Motion *(Bewegung)*, 37, 38, 47; of being, 156; and pain, 86; and time, 57

Mystery *(Geheimnis)*, 70; and openness, 171

Nahe. See Near

Name *(Name)*, 9, 24; exhortation of, 50; for God, 130; and the holy, 146–47; and near, 69; and presence, 69; and showing, 69; and thing, 31; and the unspoken, 43; and word, 24–26

Nature: as venture, 116–19

Nazis: and *Gelassenheit*, 185

Near *(Nahe)*, 60, 224 n; to God, 129; and the holy, 131; man and, 77, 184; pain and, 85; and region, 183; and releasement, 170; repre-

sentation and, 62, 152; "way" to, 62. *See also* Remote

Nietzsche, Friedrich, xiii, 22, 54, 128, 193, 204, 226 n

Nihilism, 48, 222 n

Noble *(Edel)*, 181–82

Now *(Jetzt)*, 61

Object *(Gegenstand)*, 149, 164–65; and perception, 174–75; and steadfastness, 181

Offene. See Open

Ontic knowledge, 60–61

Ontological knowledge, 60–61

Ontology: language and, xii, 26–27

Open *(Offene)*, 109; and mystery, 171; and region, 179; and releasement, 175

Ort. See Locus

Ordinary language, ix, xii–xiii, 5–6, 26, 64

Pain *(Schmerz)*, 4, 83–88; and speaking, 85; and stone, 99–101

Parmenides, 54, 213, 228 n

Past *(Vergangene)*: and "what has been," 161

Perception: and hearing, 51; and language, 31, and object, 149, 174–75; and space-time, 66

Philosophy: and the Greeks, 60; history of, 22, 144; language of, 22; and poetry, ix, xi, 143; and thinking, 3

Plainness *(Unscheinbaren)*, 66

Plato, ix, xi, 14, 29, 110, 144, 150, 173, 184, 193, 204, 216; *Euthyphro*, 126; *Meno*, 7; *Symposium*, 8

Pöggeler, Otto, xi, xiii, 3, 4, 221 n, 222 n, 223 n

Poetizing *(Dichten)*, ix, xi; of cloud, 106–7; distinguished from poetry, 76; historicity of, 196–200, and

the holy, 128, 146–47; and measurement, 190; nearness to thinking, 154, 211; proper and improper, 211, 231 n; and thinking, 76, 143–67
Poetry: and philosophy, ix; "purity" of, 9
Possible world, 25–26
Postscript to *Was ist Metaphysik?*, 146
Presence *(Anwesen)*, 57; as being, 158–67; of God, 120; in history, 192–96; and language, 159; and naming, 69; and remembering, 104; as source of differentiation, 204–5; and temporal ecstases, 158, 228 n; and word, 159–60
Present *(Gegenwart)*, 160; and object, 162
Preserving *(Währen)*, 163
Pre-Socratics, 39, 58

Reciprocity *(Gegeneinanderüber)*, 37; and near, 62
Reference, 35, 45; and pain, 86
Reflective thinking, 169, 186
Region *(Gegend)*, 162, 175–86; and determination, 180; and lingering, 179–80; and man, 179; near-remote and, 175–76; and the open, 179; in *Sein und Zeit*, 229 n
Relation *(Verhältnis)*: and connection, 96–97, 152; and God, 131; as name, 25; between poetizing and language, 144; and saying, 41; as word, 23–24
Releasement *(Gelassenheit)*, 172–87; and language, 178–79, 229 n; and man, 179; and morality, 172; and thinking, 186–87; and willing, 180–81
Remembering *(Andenken)*, 102
Remote *(Ferne)*, 60; and the deity, 125. *See also* Near

Renunciation *(Verzicht)*, 79–81
Representation *(Vorstellen)*, 15, 24; as name, 37, 45, 69; near-remote and, 62–63; and poetizing, 76; and releasement, 172–74; and speaking, 44; "step back" from, 150–51; and thinking, 37, 149–50, 170
Resolution *(Entschlossenheit)*, 181
Rest *(Ruhe)*, 47
Richardson, William J., xi, 4, 32, 33, 221 n, 225 n
Rilke, Rainer Maria, 3, 12, 115–20, 121, 172, 225 n; 226 n
Romans: and saying, 60
Rootedness *(Bodenständigkeit)*, 170; in *Sein und Zeit*, 229 n
Rosen, Stanley, 32, 221 n, 222 n
Ruhe. See Rest

Sadness, 81–83; and joy, 88–90
Sage. See Saying
Sagen. See Saying
Saint-Exupery, Antoine de, 102
Sameness: and likeness, 230 n; and things, 207
Saying *(Sagen)*, 22; and the holy, 146–47; as logos, 58; and the Romans, 60; as *"Sage,"* 38, 46, 53; space-time of, 39; and speaking, 42; and the unsaid, 40
Satz vom Grund, Der, xii
Schelling, Frierich, 226 n
Schmerz. See Pain
Schopenhauer, Arthur, 226 n
Schweigen. See Silence
Science *(Wissenschaft)*, 97–99
Sea *(See)*, 102–4
Sein. See Being
Sein und Zeit, 5, 19, 20, 22, 57, 60, 61, 158, 165, 220 n
Sending *(Geschick)*, 192
Serene *(Heitere)*, 106
Showing *(Zeigen)*, 37; naming as, 69;

243

and nearness, 62; and the poet, 127; saying as, 55

Silence *(Schweigen)*, 4; and light, 108; poetized origin of, 222 n; and Rilke, 118; and saying, 43, 68; and speaking, 46–49; and stone, 100–101

Simplicity *(Einfachen)*, 67, 224 n; and joy, 98; and renunciation, 79

Simultaneity *(Gleichzeitige)*, 57

Socrates, ix

Sophocles, xii

Space-time, 27–32; and language, 56–63; and near-remote, 60–63; and perception, 66; and saying, 39

Speaking *(Sprechen)*, 9; of God, 124; as "pure," 16; and saying, 42; and silence, 46–49

Sprache. See Language

Sprechen. See Speaking

Sputnik: word for, 23

Steadfastness *(Inständigkeit)*, 14; and object, 181

Stein. See Stone

"Step back," 150–51

Stone *(Stein)*, 99; and fourfold, 101

Strawson, P. F., 63

Technology, 48; and releasement, 170–86

Theology, 137–38, 227 n; and God, 122, 137–38

Thing *(Ding)*, 9, 23–24; and determination, 29; as fourfold, 31, 34; and God, 121; individuation of, 200–208; and lingering, 205; releasement toward, 170–186; and world, 63–67

Thinking *(Denken)*, ix, xi, 3, 148–54; and appropriation, 191; calculative and reflective, 169; confrontation with Rilke, 117; courage required for, 171; as epochal, 195;

historicity of, 196–200; literary criticism and, 10; and nearness to poetizing, 154, 211; and poetizing, 143–67, 227–28 n; and releasement, 186–87; remembering and, 103; rigorous and exact, 212

Time: and being, xiv; and name, 28, 39; and simultaneity, 57–58; types of, 193–94. *See also* Presence

Trakl, Georg, 12, 99–101, 105, 107, 111, 132–33, 173, 225 n

Truth: and assertion, 19; by disclosure, 210; and thinking, 144

Twilight: in Hölderlin, 107–9

Ungesagtes. See Unsaid

Ungesprochenes. See Unspoken

Unsaid *(Unsagtes)*, 40; and God, 95–96; and mystery, 70–71

Unscheinbaren. See Plainness

Unspoken *(Ungesprochenes)*, 63; and mystery, 70–71; and saying, 45; and silence, 48–49

Unterschied. See Difference

Unterwegs zur Sprache, xii, 3, 6, 20, 27, 28, 53, 145, 178, 224 n, 228 n

Venture *(Wagen)*, 116–19; and poets, 117

Vergangene. See Past

Verhältnis. See Relation

Versammlung. See Collection

Verzicht. See Renunciation

Vorhandenheit. See Availability

Vorstellen. See Representation

Vorträge und Aufsätze, 174, 228 n

Währen. See Preserving

Wagen. See Venture

Waiting *(Warten)*, 176–81; and near-remote, 177

Warten. See Waiting

Was Heisst Denken?, 148, 154, 191

"Way," 6, 217; and near, 62

Weilen. See Lingering

Wesen. See Essence

Whitehead, Alfred North, 16

Willing, 117; and releasement, 180–81

Wink. See Hint

Wissenschaft. See Science

Wittgenstein, Ludwig, xiii, 219 n

Wohnen. See Dwell

Wolke. See Cloud

Word *(Wort)*, 9, 22–24; and name, 24–26, 30, 75; poetizing of, 24; of saying, 36; and term, 22, 153; and thing, 30, 208

Wordsworth, William, 81

World *(Welt)*, 63; metaphysical conceptions of, 65; and thing, 63–67

Wort. See Word

Zärtlichkeit. See Tenderness

Zeigen. See Showing

Zuhandenheit. See Accessibility

Zuspruch. See Exhortation

Zustand. See Condition

Zwischen. See Between

Heidegger and the Language of Poetry

By David A. White

Since Heidegger's death in 1976 there has been heightened interest in his work, particularly in his later writings. This study focuses on one essential theme of these writings. Although some secondary literature on the later Heidegger considers his discussion of poetic language, *Heidegger and the Language of Poetry* is the first study to arrange these discussions systematically and to relate their poetic content to problems of traditional philosophical concern. It presents a systematic account of the later Heidegger's view of the function of poetic language and a commentary on Heideggerian illuminations drawn from Rilke, Trakl, George, and Hölderlin. Although this commentary originates from poetic sources, the author raises questions which deal with fundamental philosophical problems in such a way that Heidegger's inquiries into poetic language are situated in a properly ontological setting.

The introduction states the important principles of interpretation which have been applied to Heidegger's works; chapters 1 through 3 build the structure on which Heidegger has based his description of language as an ontological phenomenon; chapters